Advance Praise for *Unfiltered*

RUN don't walk to buy Jessica Abo's new book *Unfiltered: How to Be as Happy as You Look on Social Media*. This book is for everyone on social media including teens and tweens. If there is ONE book you need to read this fall, this is the one! #FabULyss, thoughtful, smart, and real, this book is a reminder of what is really important in life and will keep you focused on building the life that makes YOU happiest (not what your competitor or neighbor wants you to believe).

—LYSS STERN, CEO OF DIVAMOMS.COM, BESTSELLING AUTHOR,
AND MOM OF THREE

The best advice you can get is from someone who has been there and done that! Jessica's honest style and unplugged advice from real-life experiences will help you get past the messy middle and rise the ranks with grace and grit.

—SHELLEY ZALIS, CEO OF THE FEMALE QUOTIENT

Unfiltered is just what we need to navigate through this over-tech world we live in. Whether you're about to start your first job, you're a CEO, or anything in between, this book is a must-read! Jessica gives you everything you need to take back control of your life and have fun doing it. I just love it!

—RANDI SUBARSKY, EXECUTIVE PRODUCER OF *THE NEVER SETTLE SHOW*

From online dating to office bullying, Jessica Abo will help you get through it all. *Unfiltered* is a love letter to entrepreneurs who get caught in the I'm-not-good-enough trap. Get out of your rut and start #winning at life with this book!

—DR. JESS CARBINO, SOCIOLOGIST AND RELATIONSHIP EXPERT AT BUMBLE

Jessica Abo is the definition of what it means to be a changemaker. A rising leader in our country, Jessica thrives on building community wherever she goes and inspires others to do the same. If you want to make a positive impact on the world, start with reading *Unfiltered*. This book is relevant for everyone—no matter where you are in life!

—BERI MERIC, COFOUNDER AND CEO OF IVY

The fabulous Jessica Abo provides a brilliant breakdown of the "pursuit of happiness" in today's ultra-competitive, tech-driven world. *Unfiltered* is your go-to guide for pick-me-ups, real talk, and proof that you and your biggest dreams are worth every fight.

—LINDSEY POLLAK, *NEW YORK TIMES* BESTSELLING AUTHOR OF *BECOMING THE BOSS*

The rise of social media has led people to create their own narrative. In her new book, *Unfiltered: How to Be as Happy as You Look on Social Media*, Jessica does an amazing job at offering solutions to help bridge the gap between the happiness you portray and the happiness you want to have. Not only does Jessica dive deep into the need people have to curate this perfect universe, she also shares tool after tool to help you make your "social life" consistent with your real one.

— MIKE INDURSKY, CEO OF AUDACIOUS BEAUTY, FORMER PRESIDENT OF BLISS

Unfiltered

How To Be As Happy As You Look On Social Media

Entrepreneur
PRESS

Jessica Abo

Entrepreneur Press, Publisher
Cover Design: Andrew Welyczko
Production and Composition: Eliot House Productions

This publication is designed to provide accurate and authoritative information
in regard to the subject matter covered. It is sold with the understanding that
the publisher is not engaged in rendering legal, accounting or other professional
services. If legal advice or other expert assistance is required, the services of a
competent professional person should be sought.

Library of Congress Cataloging-in-Publication Data
Names: Abo, Jessica, author.
Title: Unfiltered: how to be as happy as you look on social media / by Jessica
Abo.
Description: Irvine, California : Entrepreneur Media, Inc., [2018]
Identifiers: LCCN 2018021720| ISBN 978-1-59918-633-7 (alk. paper) |
ISBN 1-59918-633-0 (alk. paper)
Subjects: LCSH: Social media—Psychological aspects. | Self-actualization
(Psychology) | Happiness.
Classification: LCC HM742 .A26 2018 | DDC 302.23—dc23
LC record available at https://lccn.loc.gov/2018021720

Printed in the United States of America

22 21 20 19 18   10 9 8 7 6 5 4 3 2 1

To my grandparents, who paved the way for me.
I miss you every day.

Contents

Unfiltered

Chapter 2

Name It to Tame It: Identify Your Pain Points 15

Chapter 3

Happiness Hacks: Tips for Getting Out of a Rut 29

Part Two

Staying Positive

Chapter 4

Feeling Lost Isn't Always a Bad Thing.............. 49

Chapter 5

We All Make Mistakes 67

Chapter 6

Sometimes Being Rejected from Something Good Is Directing You to Something Better............... 79

Unfiltered

Part Three
Taking Back Your Happiness

Chapter 7
How to Outsmart Your Bully 91

Chapter 8
Know Your Rights in the Workplace 105

Part Four
Building What Makes You Happiest

Chapter 9
Starting Your Side Hustle 127

Unfiltered

Part Five

Happiness Is Not a Pie

Unfiltered

Chapter 14

Mastering the Skill of Letting Go. 217

Part Six

Finding Your Happy Place

Chapter 15

Turn Your Pain into Purpose 227

Chapter 16

Find Your Passion. 239

Chapter 17

Amplify Your Activism. 247

Unfiltered

Kelly Rutherford
Mom, Actress, Activist, Philanthropist
@kellyrutherford

As I write this foreword, I'm on a plane. I just packed up my New York City apartment and am thrilled to be spending time with my kids before I move and start filming a new show called The Perfectionists. The title of my new show and this book, *Unfiltered*, have one thing in common—they remind us of the overwhelming pressure so many people face to showcase a picture-perfect life.

I know that burden all too well. As a kid, my family moved around a lot. I was often an outsider at school, observing different cliques, trying to figure out where I belonged. I spent my 20s, figuring out who I was and how I was different from my parents. I also started the journey of accepting myself, and my body. It's a journey I'm still on to this day.

My 30s were really about work, love, and becoming a mother, the greatest gift of all.

Unfiltered

My 40s have shown me to be thankful for my health and well-being, and to be grateful for everything I have. As I approach 50, I can tell you, I've loved; I've lost; I've learned; and, I've grown. I've been blessed with a career many actors dream of, but I have to tell you, some days were hard.

If you follow me on my social media, you know I don't shy away from posting on those hard days and try to use my platforms to lift up other people. I do it because you may be a having a #FML day while everyone else seems to be having a #YOLO day and I want you to know you're not alone. Life is a beautiful, imperfect mess—and that's OK. My only wish is that more people would embrace their real lives.

That real life—the one beyond the filters we use on our pictures before we post them—that's the good stuff. Your life is your own authentic experience, and you should be proud of your story—no matter what everyone else is posting today. That's why I love this book and Jessica's message.

I first met Jessica when she interviewed me in New York City for NY1 News about my handbag line. We ran into each other at New York Fashion Week and then again on the set of Gossip Girl when she played a TV reporter on the show. I really got to know Jessica when she asked me to host a black-tie event she was organizing for people who need a bone marrow transplant. As you will learn in this book, Jessica was so passionate about her Marrow Match Gala that she visited me while I was filming Gossip Girl, so I could get swabbed and join the international bone marrow registry.

The Jessica I met many years ago is the same one you're about to meet here—she embraces life in all its messy, complicated glory because she tries to live her life in an authentic way. In these pages, Jessica gets into the nitty-gritty of how you can get out of your rut. If you're frustrated with your career path or lack of community activism, she will help you find a new path. Her funny stories, personal reflections and spot-on tips are the perfect match for anyone who is newly single, on the romantic circuit or trying to move past their last relationship. Simply put—this book reminds us all that it's okay to not be OK and is designed to help you stop wishing your life away. After reading *Unfiltered* you will have new tools to help you and be inspired to create more love and joy in the world. I wish you the best of luck on your journey.

Sending you all so much love and enjoy this wonderful book!

—Kelly

IRL (In Real Life)

While I was writing this book, whenever anyone asked me what I did for a living, I skipped past my journalism career and simply said, "I'm writing a book called *Unfiltered: How to Be as Happy as You Look on Social Media.*" I loved seeing people nodding and laughing because they *got it*. I had always wanted to write about something that people could relate to—and create something that would help them help themselves. And I loved answering the questions that typically followed:

- "What made you come up with this title?"
- "Why did you want to write about this?"

The truth is, this project has been on my plate for a long time: an entire decade! But it didn't start out as anything *close* to what it is today. Quite frankly, this book has had a life of its own and has evolved as much as I have over the past ten years.

Here is the timeline of that evolution:

2008–2014: Despite my career as a storyteller, I didn't have enough confidence to write a book on my own, so I asked a friend with an incredible story if I could write a book about *his* life. He didn't want to be that vulnerable either, but he said he would let me share his story if I put my life story into the book, too. We worked on the book on and off for six years. I flew to do interviews for his chapters in the book, and my parents even changed their vacation plans to help make one of our work sessions possible. After all that effort, he started a new job and realized he no longer wanted details about his personal life out there for the world to read. He pulled out of the project, and I didn't touch the hundreds of pages I had written for a year.

2014–2015: When I finally decided to do something with all that work, my dear friend Jennifer S. Wilkov was my North Star. She pops up throughout this book, so you can learn a ton from her, too. I deleted everything I had about my friend's life and tried to make sense of the stories I had written about mine. Jennifer pushed me to figure out my "why" (the reason I was writing the book) and identify my audience. She also taught me the valuable lesson of writing for the reader. I took all her advice and worked on my book for another year.

In the meantime, I happened to attend a conference hosted by Entrepreneur Media in New York City. It was there that I learned Entrepreneur publishes books in addition to *Entrepreneur* magazine. I had just started my YouTube channel and thought it would be amazing if I could write a book for aspiring entrepreneurs. As you will learn, starting my YouTube channel was a grueling process, which included burning cash—and both ends of the candle. In looking back at the videos I recorded in the year leading up to my channel launch and the first year of the channel itself, every video had the same theme: *This is what I'm going through*

Unfiltered

right now, and this is how I hope it helps you. The same theme started to emerge as my writing project moved forward. I was lucky to have incredible mentees who were willing to read my work and give me feedback that year.

2016: At the same time I was working on reshaping the book, I met the love of my life and we got engaged. While my life had always been pretty public because I often shared TV news updates and charity happenings, this experience was something I wanted to protect. So when Brett proposed, we chose not to post anything on social media. For months, people asked me why I didn't share the news publicly. My answer every time was, "I know what it's like to be single because I was single for so long, and I don't want people who are still dating to go on Facebook and feel like my good news is being thrown in their faces." Bottom line: I didn't want to ruin someone's day if they were having a hard time with being single. I was happy. I felt blessed. Only Brett and I needed to know that information and share it with people who were close to us. I didn't need the world to know I had a ring on my finger (or even see the ring).

Many friends appreciated my sensitivity, while others told me seeing other people's good news gave them hope. I could appreciate both perspectives. Around that time, I was working on new chapters to show Jennifer (my North Star) and decided to send her a new introduction. In a nutshell, it included the fancy bio people read about me before I go onstage to deliver a keynote and another bio I wrote for the book that *really* told the story of who I was and how I got to where I am today.

The idea of showing the world who you really are has always been important to me. I included the real stuff going on in my life in my speeches and YouTube videos. When I became a contributor at Entrepreneur.com in 2016, I suddenly had a bigger platform to share similar stories on a larger scale—stories of how people turned their obstacles into opportunities. A year later, the Entrepreneur Network team introduced me to the books division, and I submitted my proposal for yet another version of my book idea.

2017: Brett and I got married in July, and we learned I was pregnant in August. We were also planning a cross-country move at the time, so needless to say, we had a lot going on. I submitted my book proposal to Entrepreneur Press in September, right before we packed up my New York City apartment and said goodbye to my bicoastal life. On our flight to Los Angeles, I kept telling Brett I no longer liked the title of my proposal, which was (at the time) *Chief Empowerment Officer: How to Be the CEO of Your Life*. I'm not sure if it was my gut or my pregnancy hormones steering me in a new direction, but when I signed my book deal with Entrepreneur, all I could think about was what to call the thing!

I felt the empowerment title wasn't striking the right tone. I wanted something along the lines of *Life Is F**king Hard: How to Be as Happy as Your Social Media Feed Looks*, but I couldn't imagine my parents proudly showing my book around my hometown with the f-bomb on the cover.

I spent October and November flying all over the East Coast, wrapping up my speaking tour, emceeing events, and going from meeting to meeting to try to see as many people as I could before I flew back to Los Angeles for good. I wanted to share that I was 20 weeks pregnant with everyone I saw, but Brett and I were waiting for stressful test results to come back, so I kept quiet. Meanwhile, everywhere I went, people saw a smiley and bubbly version of me.

During that trip, at nearly every breakfast, lunch, and dinner date I had with friends, someone always had a struggle to share. I wanted to share my own story, too, but I just couldn't bring myself to do it without knowing our test results. Those conversations only convinced me more that this book should be called *Life Is F**king Hard*.

While I was in New York, I had several meetings at Entrepreneur Media to discuss the videos I was doing for Entrepreneur.com and explained I wanted to include them in this book. From the beginning, I knew I wanted this book to be interactive and incorporate my love of creating content while highlighting other people's stories on these pages. That's why, if you're reading this book on your ereader, computer, or mobile device, you can click on links and watch the interviews in real time. If you're reading the paper version, you'll always be directed on where to go to watch the video components.

In meeting with the editorial team, I asked if there were any words that I should avoid and learned people tend to stay away from articles and videos with the word "CEO" and go for stories that use "entrepreneur" or "founder" instead. That was eye-opening for me because my entire brand was Chief Empowerment Officer, and being the CEO of your life was the central concept of my book.

So we went back to the drawing board for the title. I compiled my thoughts in a long email for Entrepreneur's editorial director, Jennifer Dorsey, and Vanessa Campos, the director of marketing and sales. I shared how my T-shirt line had a shirt that said #Unfiltered because I loved the idea that we didn't need filters on our phones to make ourselves look better, and I loved the idea of people being themselves. I explained my thoughts around the title and what I wanted this book to achieve, and *Unfiltered: How to Be as Happy as Your Social Media Feed Looks* was the winner. We later tweaked the title a bit for marketing reasons, but that's how this book came to be. And, honestly, it perfectly captures the message I hope you get when you read it: that you can take some steps to live a more authentic—and not necessarily picture-perfect—life.

WHAT TO EXPECT

So what should you know before diving into these chapters? For starters, I broke down this book into different sections because you may need something different from the other people reading this book with you in your book club. While this book isn't meant to be all things to all people (no book can do that), it is meant to meet you where you are in life. For example:

Unfiltered

+ You may be reading this book with your teenage kids and be excited about the business topics while they're interested in the sections that deal with rejection or finding a mentor.
+ You may be happily married but hate going to work. Or you may love going to work and wishing, one day, to be happily married.
+ You may be on a break from dating so you can invest all your energy into your new business or have more "me" time.
+ You may be dealing with a bully or a toxic boss and not sure what to do.
+ You may be facing friendship challenges and trying to figure out whom you can count on.
+ You may be in a ton of pain and navigating how you're going to cope.
+ Or you may be feeling motivated to amplify your activism or recovering from donor fatigue.

Whatever you're going through, you may find you want to highlight every word on some pages and skip others completely.

Or you may be none of the above and just wanted something to read on the plane. I get that, too. No matter where you are in life, my hope is that you find something here that resonates. I wrote this book because we're all a work in progress and we need different things at different times. To that end, I've included various touchpoints throughout this book—because no one wants to read block after block of dense text only to find that they missed a really great point that is meaningful to them.

As you read this book, you'll find that some chapters have tips. Those are there to provide easily accessible advice if and when you need it. The sidebars feature inspiring people or cool resources that you may enjoy or find useful. There are many exercises you can do throughout this book, from fill-in-the-blank questions to quizzes. It's up to you to do them—or not. No one is judging you. If they help, that's awesome! If they're not your thing, consider at least reading through them so you can give some thought to the questions.

You will also see sections labeled #MYSTORY throughout the book. If you like to feel you're not the only one going through something, then I hope you have fun reading about some of my ups and downs. If you'd rather just focus on the exercises, skip the #MYSTORY sections. If you choose to read my anecdotes, some of my struggles may seem small in comparison to yours. Some may make you feel better about your own situation. I don't want you going through these chapters comparing your life to mine. Chances are you're already doing that with people in your own circle, especially on social media.

Since success doesn't happen in a certain order, I've structured these chapters so that you can jump around. If you just got rejected, you may want to start with Chapters 5 and 6. If you are miserable in your job and know it's time to turn your side hustle into a career, go to Chapter 9. If you are fed up with the dating scene and need a laugh, I'd suggest reading about the bad dates others and I have suffered through in Chapter 13. Think of this book as a "choose your own adventure."

What I ultimately hope you get from reading *Unfiltered* is confirmation that your life is *yours* and that you can take steps to live beyond the veneer we present to others—both on social media and IRL. This book is not about empowering those people who make you feel "less than." It's about taking your power back and investing your effort, energy, and happiness into the time you have on this planet. That's why I hope you check out the videos whenever you see the cue "WATCH IT!" Those interviews may inspire you to take action.

DISCLAIMER

While all of these stories are true, some names have been changed to protect people's privacy. I'm not a medical or health professional. I'm not a licensed social worker or therapist. I will not be able to relate to everything you're going through because I'm not you, and I'm not living your life. I'm not a genie, nor do I have a crystal ball, so I can't promise you will finish this book with the ability to solve all your problems. I haven't started a company like Uber or Netflix, so I won't be using fancy business jargon that even I don't understand.

I *will* share my ideas and opinions on a variety of topics. I'm going to be honest about what I have experienced and share what helped me through each messy phase to help you get through yours faster. I've also included stories from experts and extraordinary people I've interviewed, who share how they managed to keep it together when nothing seemed to go according to plan. You can read their advice and, in some cases (as I mentioned earlier), watch videos from my YouTube channel and Entrepreneur.com. Lastly, I'm not being paid by anyone or any product I have mentioned or endorsed in this book, unless otherwise noted.

Given how much time people spend on social media, I want to make sure you're equipped with the tools you need to live a life you love online and off. I wrote this book to help you be happy with where you are and what you have—especially when it seems everyone has it *so* much better than you do. I hope these pages remind you that you're OK wherever you are in life. Finally, my wish for you is that you enjoy reading this book as much as I have loved writing it.

Part One

Know Your Self(ie)

Chapter 1

When Psychology Meets Technology

After a long day at work, all you want to do is catch up on your shows and have a glass of wine. You take out a glass, open Instagram, and see your friend's pictures from her "most amazing day" bodysurfing in Hawaii. Closing the app, you pull up LinkedIn to finally start your dreaded job search. Your shows will have to wait—and so will the moscato. #FML

Unfiltered

Maybe this has happened to you. You wake up in a perfectly good mood and grab your phone. You're curious to see what's happening around the world or what's happening in *your* world. Maybe you're just anxious to see how many "likes" your last post got since you went to sleep. Then, all of a sudden, you see it:

+ Your friends were at a party, but no one invited you.
+ Your colleague got your promotion.
+ Your ex got engaged.
+ Your younger brother just bought a house, and you're stuck in a studio.
+ Your sister's kid started walking and yours is barely rolling over.

Whatever it is, it hits you right in the gut. Something has now downsized your day into a reason to be unhappy.

If this has never happened to you, that's impressive. Either you're enjoying the lane you're in or you're just not on any form of social media. However, for most people, this feeling of "compare and despair" is all too familiar.

Then there's this scenario: You're having the worst day. Maybe you've hit a major bump with your significant other and someone on your team dropped the ball on a major deadline. Maybe that person was you. But instead of writing, "Having the worst day" on your feed, you snap a picture of your avocado toast/new handbag/car, pick a fancy filter, and post, "I love my life. #killingit".

You do this so no one needs to know how much your life really sucks. Then, to help you forget about your crappy day, you spend the rest of it checking your phone to see how many people reacted to or commented on your post—even though most of the people in your network are people you barely talk to, care about, or even know. You're now glued to your feed as though you were waiting for election results to tally. Before you know it, it's midnight, and you still have to do your laundry.

Finally, there's this scenario, which I hear all the time: You just had lunch with a friend who spent the entire meal telling you about everything going wrong in their life, from work to love and everything in between. You listened, maybe even gave some advice, and went your separate ways. Then, two hours later, that friend posts something that makes it look like everything in their life is AH-MAZING. And suddenly, you start to question why *you* can't afford those shoes/go to that awesome gym/live in that fabulous apartment. You suddenly feel like your life is less amazing. But you know the truth! You just listened to it over fish tacos—for two hours. So how on earth does your brain distort fiction from fact?

It's crazy how we are smart, capable human beings, and yet social media can send us into a tizzy. For real. It's bananas. Think it's bad if you're an adult? I feel worse for today's kids! I learned from the experts I interviewed for this book that our prefrontal cortex, our brain's controller, doesn't fully develop until age 25 or 26. So if you think you feel shitty because you weren't invited to someone's wedding or 40th birthday party, it's even harder for a kid to process being left out when everyone else shows up at school on Monday morning wearing the latest bar/bat mitzvah/sweet 16 swag.

So how do you care *less* about what everyone else is doing and *more* about what's good in your life? You may think the easy answer is to not go online or avoid downloading any apps that will depress or distract you, but that doesn't always work. Some schools, companies, and even wedding ceremonies are going tech-free, which is awesome. Some of the designers behind our devices are working on more features to help us monitor our own usage. But that doesn't explain why we, the people who go to school, hold down jobs, run our homes, and raise families, get so thrown off base when we see someone else's filtered life online. So what can we do about that?

We start with science.

THE LINK BETWEEN OUR BRAINS AND SOCIAL MEDIA

Social media has become the 21st-century escape from our everyday lives, whether it's to cure boredom when standing in the checkout line or seek a sense of belonging when no one is talking to us at a party and we want to give the impression that we're cool and connected. How many times have you been home alone and, without realizing it, reached for your phone and scrolled for what seemed like seconds, but really turned into an hour?

On the other hand, by plugging into our social networks, we can make meaningful connections. We can find long-lost friends, reconnect with relatives, discover community groups, or find jobs and love. We can even track down an ex or a high school crush. Our feeds enable us

Did You Know?

According to the Harvard Business Review's (March 19, 2018) article "America's Loneliest Workers, According to Research" (https://hbr.org/2018/03/americas-loneliest-workers-according-to-research) by Shawn Achor, Gabriella Rosen Kellerman, Andrew Reece, and Alexi Robichaux, "Research shows that loneliness has the same effect as 15 cigarettes a day in terms of health-care outcomes and health-care costs." The article also highlighted that lonely employees often don't perform as well and are more likely to quit. In his books and research, Shawn Achor shares how simple gestures such as peer-based praise and eating lunch with a co-worker can provide positive social support and improve a company's culture.

In *The New York Times* article "U.K. Appoints a Minister for Loneliness" (January 17, 2018), Ceylan Yeginsu cites a 2017 report by the Jo Cox Commission on Loneliness, which found "more than nine million people in the country often or always feel lonely." In addition to being fascinated by the fact that the U.K. appointed an official to tackle this issue, I was saddened to read government research found "about 200,000 older people in Britain had not had a conversation with a friend or relative in more than a month."

to remember people's birthdays and learn new things from the articles our friends post. We can "listen in" on people's conversations and debates without having to participate. With one click, we can promote our businesses or donate to a cause. We can drum up support for school walkouts, marches, and rallies from our kitchen table and reach people all over the world.

Our social networks are great for content sharing, too. Whether it's details for a local charity drive or suggesting tourist attractions for a friend heading to Greece, we can share a lot of useful information. Studies have shown people who are battling an illness benefit from the support they receive through social media, too. If you've ever had a friend send you the perfect inspirational quote, funny meme, or viral video when you're having a bad day, you know how quickly that can raise your spirits or LOL (laugh out loud). So no, social media isn't the enemy. Loneliness is.

OH, NO—IT'S FOMO!

While it's evident we need meaningful connections in our lives, many people who log onto social media seeking a sense of community and belonging only find superficial support. No matter how much weight we put on the number of followers, subscribers, or likes we get, that doesn't mean all those people would come to our birthday party or be there for us in the middle of the night. One way to achieve happiness is to invest your time in the people who would drop anything to FaceTime with you or actually show up at your front door when the shit hits the fan.

We know we don't *have* to check our phones every five minutes and that life will go on if we don't post something. So it's obvious social media isn't causing our pain points, but more times than not, being online doesn't help them, either. "I can't go on social media anymore," is something I hear every week from men and women of all ages. When people tell me they're deleting an app from their phone, it usually lasts a day before the need to check what they're missing kicks into high gear. Thank you, FOMO (Fear Of Missing Out).

In a study called "Out of sight is not out of mind: The impact of restricting wireless mobile device use on anxiety levels among low, moderate, and high users" (www5.csudh.edu/psych/Out_of_sight_is_not_out_of_mind-Cheever,Rosen,Carrier,Chavez_2014.pdf), Nancy Cheever and her colleagues found when you take away someone's phone, they reported feeling anxious and that anxiety continued until they got their phone back. One of the people behind that study is Larry Rosen, professor emeritus and past chair of the psychology department at California State University, Dominguez Hills. Rosen has been studying the "psychology of technology" for more than 30 years. In our interview for this book, he told me about research he and his colleagues conducted in 2016. They studied more than 200 students to see how they used their phones. The students used an app called Instant, which tallied how many times they unlocked their phone each day and tracked how long the device remained unlocked.

"The study revealed students unlocked their phones 56 times a day for [a total of] 220 minutes. That means the students checked their phones about every 15 minutes for just shy of 4 minutes," Rosen explains. "In 2017, we conducted the same study with a new, equivalent group of students and found the students unlocked their phones about 50 times, but they stayed on their phones longer. This time they spent a total of 262 minutes on their devices, which is 5.25 minutes per glance. The reason the students said they were spending more time on their phones when they unlocked them was because of social media."

What he found the most fascinating was *why* people log onto social media in the first place. Half the time, participants said it was because they received an alert, so they unlocked their phone to see someone's post, read a new comment, or check a text. "The other half of the time, there wasn't an update or alert, which means they had a slow accumulation of chemicals such as cortisol or adrenaline that signaled anxiety," Rosen says. "Your brain starts filling in with chemicals saying, 'Someone may have posted; you should check in,' and when that reaches a critical level, people act on it and go back to their phones." The fear of missing out causes so many health issues that Rosen wrote an entire book about it: *iDisorder: Understanding Our Obsession With Technology and Overcoming Its Hold on Us* (St. Martin's Press, 2012). He defines this

Unfiltered

disorder as the negative psychological impact of the use of technology, which can manifest as stress, anxiety, obsessive-compulsive disorder, and depression, among other mental health issues. Simply put, FOMO has taken over our social media habits.

So how did this happen? When did the very technology created to make our lives more efficient become the source of so much stress and distraction?

It happened gradually over time and is only accelerating. According to Rosen, before the internet, the way technology influenced our lives came in the form of physical products like radio, telephones, and TV. But to fully understand the rate at which technology penetrates our world today, Rosen points out that it took radio 38 years to reach 50 million users. Want to guess how long it took for Pokémon Go to do the same thing?

If you guessed one *week*, you are right!

FOUR WAYS TO BACK YOURSELF OUT OF THE NEED TO CHECK IN

If you think you're too attached to your digital device—if your phone goes where you go, whether it's to breakfast, the bathroom, the boardroom, or bed—and you want to rewire your brain, Rosen suggests trying the following:

1. Move all your social icons from your first page into a folder so you have to make an effort to find them.
2. Check your apps on a schedule, not on a whim. Let everyone know you're doing it so they don't get pissed off when you take too long to "like" one of their posts.
3. Pay attention to which apps are open in the background because we tend to check them unconsciously. If you're not scheduled to check an app, make sure that tab is closed or the app is in its folder.
4. Turn off *all* your alerts. You don't need to know every time someone posts something to your feed. It can wait.

It may seem silly to follow these steps because it may feel like your social media is controlling you and not the other way around. However,

Rosen says measures like these are often necessary because social comparison is a very real thing that's hurting a lot of people.

WHY DO WE EVEN CARE ABOUT OTHER PEOPLE SO MUCH?

If someone close to you is living the perfect life, it's understandable how that could bring you down a notch. But many people find themselves getting upset when they see posts from someone they rarely talk to!

Why?

Rosen says this can be best explained by the social comparison theory. He says, "The social comparison theory says as social animals we compare our status with the status of other animals. We tend to forget that people only post the ideal version of themselves and only positive things—not every second of their lives. Rarely do we see negative posts. Even when we see people close to us online, we take what we see as real life."

Rosen says even when we have lunch with someone, and that person spills what's going on at home, and it's not all good, we *still* believe they have a better life than we do when they post something amazing an hour later. That's just nuts! Human beings have managed to build everything from smartphones to space shuttles. How is it possible that someone could tell you to your face that business isn't going well or their relationship is on the rocks, and yet you still take their social media post at face value?

It's a practice that Aviva Goldstein (www.avivagoldstein.com) says is called "selectively positive," and our strong reaction to this behavior is tied to our emotions.

HOW WE ABSORB SELECTIVELY POSITIVE INFORMATION

Goldstein is an educator and family counselor who focuses on positive psychology. Her projects range from curriculum and app development to individual and large-scale interventions. She says people present "selectively positive" versions of themselves online not to be intentionally inauthentic, but because that's the cultural norm of how we present

Unfiltered

ourselves to the world around us.

"When you bump into a friend on the street and they ask how you're doing, the typical response is a positive one, like 'Great, doing well, all good,'" she says. "If it's a particularly close friend, we might be inclined to peel back a few layers and say, 'Well, you're catching me on a rough day. I have this awful cold I can't get rid of, the kids all had lice, and work has been tough lately . . .' But that's not the narrative we usually start out with. On social media, we have the same inclinations to present a positive narrative as we would with the friend on the street. The challenge is that one passing conversation in the supermarket with an old neighbor is not the same as being bombarded by hundreds or thousands of images, all day every day, that tell a very superficial story about how everyone's day is going."

Goldstein adds that on the other end of the spectrum are those friends and acquaintances who do, indeed, share the bumpier moments of their lives, but it's part of a cyclical impulse to share *everything*. "We probably all know people online who tell us what time they woke up, what they ate for breakfast, where they are sitting in traffic, and what's for dinner," she says. "And very often, those announcements are joined by selfies of their just-woke-up face and their taco night. The goal is to find a way to allow the instinct to present a 'best foot forward' approach while still being authentic."

It all makes sense, but social media can still get the best of us—even those of us who know much of what we see is all smoke and mirrors. "While we are aware of the intentional curation being presented online, many still engage in social comparison (consciously or not) because it's really hard to process rationally, intellectually, or cognitively when we are reacting emotionally," Goldstein says. "Even if we know that we're only seeing part of the story, it's still hard to resist the envy, jealousy, or self-doubt when we literally see, with our own eyes, other people's successes."

Goldstein says the quick and dirty solution is to block friends whose posts contribute to your own self-doubt. "But it's a temporary solution and doesn't get to the root of the problem. The bigger challenge, and the one that will yield long-term resolution of depth and breadth, is getting to a place where you are so OK with where you are in life that other people's experiences don't drive you to question your own worth. Reading this book is a huge step in that direction," she adds.

Goldstein also says our constant need to compare ourselves to others within our social networks is more harmful than helpful not only because we are consuming unrealistic versions of other people's lives, which inevitably leads us to question our own experiences, but also because it has serious health implications.

IS YOUR CONNECTION TO YOUR TECHNOLOGY MAKING YOU SICK?

Scientists aren't yet willing to declare that social media is addictive, but Goldstein says we do know that typical online behavior closely resembles the behavior seen with other addictions. "There are addictive properties of social media. For example, the dopamine neurotransmitter, which is a chemical in the brain that controls and regulates memory, mood, behavior, and emotion, is released when refreshing a page, seeing a like, or other response. The part of the brain that lights up when a heroin addict gets their fix is the same part of the brain that lights up when receiving positive feedback on social media," she says.

While many turn to social media as a way to curb boredom, it actually limits our opportunities to engage with people around us, enjoy the great outdoors, and be more present wherever we are. But as we already know, in addition to influencing our psyche, research shows the amount of time we spend online also affects our physiology. So when your eyes hurt, your thumb is sore, or your back aches, Goldstein says you may want to cut down your screen time—and go to the doctor.

WHY DO WE KEEP GOING BACK FOR MORE?

On top of feeling anxious that we're missing out on something important (think of your phone beeping or buzzing with alerts every few minutes), Goldstein says many people are attached to their devices because they crave the validation social media provides.

Unfiltered

"Social validation is crucial in adolescent development and remains important for many adults," she says. "Seeking social validation is actually a great ingredient in becoming functional members of society. It's how we learn normative behaviors, how to engage socially, and the nuance of drawing distinctions between different behaviors that are appropriate for different contexts. How we behave when we're eating pizza with friends is not how most of us would behave at a funeral. Social media provides easy access to validation with likes, emojis, etc. While this isn't all bad, it's not necessarily authentic validation and can distort reality. We can think that we are engaged in real friendship, when in reality we have only shared the superficial. You might consider someone a close friend, when in reality they've never seen you in pain, or hysterically laughing, or freaking out about anything. So we can easily misconstrue our understanding and definitions of friendships and supportive community."

Another issue with being too dependent on one's online social circle is the "online disinhibition effect," which Goldstein describes as people being comfortable posting something hurtful or offensive that they would not say to someone's face, since they don't have to see the emotional pain they're inflicting. "This behavior often leads to cyberbullying, which frequently spills over into real life," she says. (On the flip side, we also miss out on seeing the smile we can bring to someone's face when we only engage screen to screen instead of face to face.)

To help you curtail your screen time and reconnect with the real world around you, Goldstein offers the following tips:

+ Commit to speaking on the phone twice a day.
+ Make a point of noticing the eye color of someone you spend time with; ensure that you establish eye contact when you are together.
+ Create a no-phone zone: either a time (dinner, before bed, etc.) or a place (kitchen, table, bed, or bathroom) and stick to it.

Goldstein says these habits are important because they propel us out of our routines and remind us to establish human connections with others and ourselves. She adds that the next time you log on, strive for a more meaningful experience by trying out these suggestions:

+ Commit to engaging online with three people every day by commenting or messaging. "Likes" don't count.
+ Commit to one positive, complimentary comment on someone's post every day.
+ Commit to publicly sharing certain challenges and setbacks.

Goldstein says these steps will not only make you a less passive consumer of other people's narratives, but they will also turn you into an active participant in a shared social connection and encourage others—even subconsciously—to connect in real ways with real people.

Now that you have some tips you can use to help you have a more positive experience online, let's dive into some of the other areas of your life that may need some attention.

Chapter 2

Name It to Tame It:
Identify Your Pain Points

It's late on a Friday night and you're stuck in the office cleaning up your boss' mistake on a project for the fifth week in a row. You look at your phone on the way to the printer and see your brother's post: "On my way to Miami for the weekend. Who's around to meet up?" You comment: "Have the best time, Frank! Love you! ☺" And you wonder if you'd be a horrible person if you unfriended your sibling. #TGIF

Unfiltered

When you're busy doing meaningful work and spending time with loved ones, you genuinely don't have time to feel *woe is me* when you see someone else's status. When you're at peace with your life, you also don't get *as* irritated when other people tell you what you should want, as in, "You're 25, don't you think it's time you found a girlfriend?" or "You've been together for three years. Shouldn't you be engaged by now?" When you're busy being grateful for what you have, it's tougher for all the noise to get you down. But let's be clear: You're absolutely allowed to look at someone else's success and be annoyed your promotion is taking so long, frustrated your house still has not sold, or envious your sister just posted a picture of a sonogram when your wife is about to go through another round of IVF. Basically, you have every right to be a human being with real feelings; you are not a walking hard drive that's been programmed to be immune to the world around you.

Acknowledging your feelings and understanding where they're coming from is healthy. Evaluating what you can do with those feelings to improve your situation is what inspired this book. But it's easy to follow someone's social media persona down a black hole. Since all that does is waste time, I want to start with getting to the bottom of what's really eating at you. To do that, I want you to identify your pain points. After all, you're not really going to unfriend your brother because he's going away for the weekend (again). You know deep down that you don't begrudge him or his vacation—you just loathe your job. However, knowing you're in the wrong place is only half the equation. Figuring out what you really want to do with your life, finding a new opportunity that's in alignment with your career goals, and getting that job is the other half.

What we're going to do in this chapter is put your career, relationships, and contributions to society under a microscope to discover the root of your rut. My hope is that there will be some obvious things that you can change, as well as some challenges you may have been ignoring or not even realized were there.

CAREER

There are a lot of factors that go into picking a job and staying there. Sometimes we take an opportunity solely out of necessity. Other times, we may be lucky enough to accept an offer we actually wanted. My friend Tracey Felter, who works in human resources, once said, "It's normal not to love everything about your job every day. That's why it's called a job, not a vacation." While that's true, if you dread going to work every day, you need to ask yourself: *Why?* Is it because of where you work or what you're doing? Or both? Let's take some time to uncover what's causing your rut when it comes to your career path. Think about it and fill out the Career Choice Worksheet (Figure 2.1 on page 18).

TIP

If writing and/or journaling don't work for you, you can always create audio or video journals, use the voice memo function on your phone to record your thoughts, or use a list-making app.

If the questions in the Career Choice Worksheet are really what you need to be spending time on, go to Chapters 4, 5, 6, 7, and 8 to learn more about how to take back your happiness.

RELATIONSHIPS

Maybe you're not really jealous your brother is on a plane to Miami for a weekend getaway. You're just freaking out that he left town when he knows you and your significant other just broke up (for good this time). You wonder who you're going to call now. And suddenly you start to panic, think you've made a mistake, and keep your phone close by in case your ex decides to text you. Anyone who has been through a breakup will tell you it's not easy. If you're the one who initiated it, you may feel bad you've hurt someone. If you're the person who just had their heart broken, you may be in shock or in pain.

Relationships, whether they're romantic or platonic, can bring so much happiness into our lives, but the wrong relationships can cause damage, too. Sometimes we outgrow a relationship, and other times we may find ourselves having been deceived. If you feel your relationships are the root of your rut, let's look at which relationship is the culprit. If you know which relationships are making you unhappy, list them in your Relationship Worksheet in Figure 2.2 on page 19.

Unfiltered

FIGURE 2.1: **Career Choice Worksheet**

Ask yourself:

+ Am I not sure what I want to do?

+ Am I at a loss for how to use today's technology to help me find a new job?

+ Did I just miss out on a job or promotion?

+ Did I just get laid off or fired?

+ Am I upset about a mistake I made at school or at work?

+ Did my dream school just defer or reject me?

+ Am I realizing I'm pursuing the wrong major or industry?

+ Am I facing a setback that is keeping me from reaching my goals?

+ Am I stuck in an environment or job I've outgrown?

+ Do I have a toxic boss or colleagues?

+ Do I feel uncomfortable or unsafe in my workplace?

Now, fill in the blanks.

I wish I had the courage to _____

_____

(Quit? Speak up? Get help? Etc.)

In order for me to do this, I need to _____

_____

(Find a mentor, go to HR, update my LinkedIn profile, etc.)

Right now, what I feel is holding me back is _____

_____

(Fear of retaliation, losing my job, disappointing my family, etc.)

I would feel better about making a change if _____

_____

(I felt safe and protected, I had another job, etc.)

Unfiltered

FIGURE 2.2: **Relationship Worksheet**

Ask yourself:

+ Am I in a healthy group of friends who support my goals?

+ Am I having a hard time making friends in a new environment (school, job, or community)?

+ Am I having a hard time managing family/friends and a job?

+ Am I having a hard time managing family/friends, a job, and a romantic relationship?

+ Am I the only person in my group of friends who hates going to work?

+ Am I the only person in my group who is in a relationship?

+ Am I the only person in my group who is single?

+ Am I new to dating?

+ Am I stuck on an ex?

+ Am I currently in the wrong relationship?

+ Am I too busy to date because of school, work, or other obligations?

+ Am I dating like a machine but repeating unhealthy patterns?

Now, fill in the blanks.

I am happiest when I am _____
(alone, with my group of friends, with my family, in a romantic relationship)

The relationship I value the most is the relationship I have with _____

When I am around this person/these people, I feel _____

It is important to me that when I am in a group of friends, I feel _____

It is important to me when I am in a romantic relationship that I can share
my _____ with someone who is worthy.

It is important to me when I am in a romantic relationship that I feel _____
_____

When I think about being around family or friends or in a romantic relationship, I am embarrassed to admit that I _____

If you are attracting the same kind of partners, take a second to look at yourself. Where are you? What do you want? It is OK to want to be single for a while. It is OK to want to be in a serious relationship. It is OK to want to focus on schoolwork or your career. Whatever you want is fine. You are the expert on all things *you*.

YOUR LEGACY

Maybe your brother is off to Miami for the weekend not only to escape the winter but also to help out a friend in need. We all have the power to make someone's life better, whether it's a close friend or a stranger. The way we choose to pay it forward can be on a very micro level or a macro one. If you feel your life is lacking meaning or you can't read or watch the news because today's headlines make you feel helpless, not hopeful, I want you to know you have something to offer. If you are going through a hard time in your personal life, you may find strength in getting involved in your community. With the help of the Causes Worksheet (Figure 2.3 on page 21), try to pinpoint what causes are important to you and what may be holding you back from taking action.

We all have so much noise in our lives that it can sometimes be hard to hear our own thoughts. I want you to go through this exercise to pause in your busy life and see what your pain points are. This was very helpful for me when I hit my own rock bottom, and it took me time to learn that negative emotions can be the most powerful catalyst to make a change.

FILE A COMPLAINT

You've identified your pain points, but you may still feel you want someone to understand, and validate, that what you're going through is hard. So let's agree that everyone is facing their own battle.

+ If you are stuck in a rut—that is hard.
+ If you are in debt—that is hard.
+ If you have money—that is hard.
+ If you know what you want to be doing but aren't there yet—that is hard.

Unfiltered

FIGURE 2.3: **Causes Worksheet**

Ask yourself:

+ Am I trying to figure out what my passion is?

+ Do I know what I'm passionate about but don't know how to take the first step?

+ Am I passionate about a certain cause but facing challenges and not seeing any change take shape?

+ Am I burned out from volunteering?

+ Am I having a hard time getting others to care about my mission and vision?

+ Am I involved in an organization with toxic leadership?

+ Am I afraid of being in the spotlight?

+ Am I convinced I don't have anything to offer a cause?

+ Am I unsure of what it means to join a board?

+ Am I unsure of how to plan an event?

Now, fill in the blank.

Given my experience with _____ ,

_____

the one issue that keeps me up at night/breaks my heart is _____

Given the state of the world, one issue that keeps me up at night/breaks my heart is _____

The reason I haven't done anything more proactive until now is _____

_____

I would do more at this point, but _____

If I _____ ,

I would _____

Unfiltered

+ If you love your job—that is hard.
+ If you are starting a new chapter—that is hard.
+ If you have no friends—that is hard.
+ If you have a lot of friends—that is hard.
+ If you are being bullied—that is hard.
+ If you just got rejected from something or someone—that is hard.
+ If you are dating—that is hard.
+ If you are in a relationship—that is hard.
+ If you are waiting to get engaged—that is hard.
+ If you are engaged—that is hard.
+ If you are married—that is hard.
+ If you are getting separated—that is hard.
+ If you are separated—that is hard.
+ If you are getting divorced—that is hard.
+ If you are divorced—that is hard.
+ If you are moving—that is hard.
+ If you are trying to get pregnant—that is hard.
+ If you are pregnant—that is hard.
+ If you just lost the baby—that is hard.
+ If you are raising a child—that is hard.
+ If your child is hurting—that is hard.
+ If your child is a superstar—that is hard.
+ If your office is your home—that is hard.
+ If you have to leave your kids to go to the office—that is hard.
+ If you lost your job—that is hard.
+ If you just got diagnosed with an illness—that is hard.
+ If you are fighting a disease—that is hard.
+ If you are a caretaker—that is hard.
+ If you lost a loved one—that is hard.

I give you a lot of credit for dealing with everything on your plate and making the decision to read this book and do something for yourself. If you feel like you still have so much you want to scream about, I want you to get it all out before we go any farther. Seriously. Get it *all* out. Your crush likes someone else? Yikes. Just got fired? That hurts. In a

Unfiltered

fight with your body? Start writing. The complaint department is open and you have the right to bitch. Chances are, your friends and family have heard all this before. They may have even been helpful along the way, but you may still need to detox once and for all. If you feel like screaming, "WHY ME?" on a daily basis—or, just as bad, "WHY NOT ME?"—put it down here. Really. This is your last chance. Then we are going to get to work. (If you do not need to file a complaint at this time, skip this section and feel free to refer back to it when things do go south and you need to explore what's going wrong in your universe.) Use the worksheet in Figure 2.4 to register your complaint.

FIGURE 2.4: **Complaint Department**

Life is unfair because:

1. I am mad at _____ because:
   _____

2. I am jealous of _____ because:
   _____

3. I am sick and tired of feeling: _____
   _____

4. I am frustrated that I cannot: _____
   _____

5. I am not over: _____
   _____

6. I am not sure what to do about: _____
   _____

7. I am angry with myself because: _____
   _____

8. I am sick to my stomach thinking about: _____
   _____

9. If I could have one thing a year from now, it would be: _____
   _____

Unfiltered

Now that you have identified your pain points and filed a complaint, let's talk about how to get out of a rut.

#MYSTORY: Yes, This IS Your Life

I wish someone had sat me down when I turned 29 and warned me that 30, 31, 32, and 33 would have enough celebrations and heartache to deserve their own miniseries. I also wish that same sage would have explained that however hard those years seemed to be, 34 would be an entire series on its own.

A wave of panic hit me at 34 that I was not expecting. You may have been struck with the same feeling as you approached graduation, lost a job, or moved to a new city. I suddenly felt like I was always playing a game called "Holy Shit, Is This My Life?" On some days, the question was positive: "Wow! Holy shit! IS THIS MY LIFE?" and I'd want to pinch myself because I couldn't believe I was meeting with the head of a TV network, on a stage giving a speech to 1,000 people, or shooting a news scene for a TV show or movie.

Then there were the *other* days: when I didn't get the promotion or the guy I totally thought I hit it off with on a five-hour date completely ghosted me, not to mention the tough holidays, reunions, birthday parties, bachelorette weekends, bridal showers, wedding showers, and weddings. You know how those go: You stand in the room surrounded by family and friends, knowing you aren't where you thought you'd be, you think, "Is this my life?" and you want to cry.

That was me at Thanksgiving two months before my 35th birthday. As I scanned the room, I realized that aside from one other person, I was the only one who wasn't married. My cousin announced it was time for everyone to sit down for dinner. I listened and smiled as she shared how grateful she was to have us all around her table and thought about everything I had accomplished since the previous Thanksgiving. Some of the highlights playing on the reel in my mind were getting through an oral cancer scare and the eight procedures that made talking and smiling really tough, a speaking tour that took me all over the country and to the United Nations, launching my YouTube channel, starting a production company, and being featured on a national talk show and other national outlets. I had so much to be proud of, yet I still felt the need to fight back tears. After dinner, I went back to Pennsylvania with my parents and cried for three days. It was then I knew I had to file my own complaint and find a new path.

RUNNING ON NEGATIVE FUEL

It's easy to get consumed with what's wrong in our lives. For example, if you just filled out your complaint and start off tomorrow reading it before you leave home, chances are you're going to stay in that negative mindset the entire day. That isn't good! The purpose of knowing what's bothering you isn't to get bogged down in negativity—it's to address it and move forward. However, let's face it—that's easier said than done because the negative-thought train is ready to take off at any time. It is so much easier to fuel sadness and wallow in self-doubt and pity than it is to stay positive. Sure, people will say platitudes like, "Everything happens for a reason." But believing that things are going to work out—or, better yet, that everything *is* working out—takes major effort. No one tells you staying positive is a mental exercise that should be classified as a marathon with its own medal. But I applaud you if you're going through a tough time and are doing your best to keep it all together.

Have you ever noticed how quickly one negative thought can turn into a million? You start with, "I can't believe I didn't get the job," or, "I can't believe my date stood me up," and the next thing you know, you're on the express train to Negative City with no stops in sight. Suddenly, in your head, you're single forever. Or you're trying to figure out how to change the feel of your childhood bedroom now that you're moving back in with your parents since you are never going to get a job. Or get married. Or be able to afford your rent. Or own your own house.

Sometimes, these thoughts are so crazy they can make us laugh. Other times, they're the reason the muscles in our face feel like they forgot how to smile. The good news is this feeling doesn't have to last forever. When I returned to New York, I had dinner with a girlfriend. I asked how her holiday was, and she said it was OK. When she asked how mine was, I told her the truth. She confided that she had had a breakdown, too. I told her I was determined to approach my life, and turning 35, differently, and that's exactly what I did.

SOMETIMES YOU'RE WHERE YOU'RE MEANT TO BE

On the other end of sadness and struggle, there is an opportunity for growth and strength—and love, too. What helped me stop the "Oh my goodness, I don't have anything to show for the past decade of my life because I'm not married with kids" train was visiting a friend in Connecticut. On my way to see Rob, I wasn't sure if it was a date or simply two friends reconnecting. To be honest, I'm still not sure. It did, however, show me what my life could have looked like had I chosen to get married sooner.

As I walked around Rob's beautiful home in Greenwich, it hit me: Had this been my life before this moment, I wouldn't have fully enjoyed it. There was something about getting a tour of each room and looking at his amazing artwork that made me realize had I done the past 12 years differently, there would have been a colossal piece of me that felt like someone had clipped my wings. Someone once told me that when you're dating, you always date people who reflect something within you. I couldn't understand why I was attracting guy after guy who wasn't ready to settle down even though they said they were ready. I understood then, standing in Rob's backyard looking at his koi pond, that there was a piece of me that wasn't ready either, and until that moment, I was ashamed to admit that to anyone—especially myself.

From that point on, instead of dating through the lens of "I have to get married and have kids and balance my kids with my awesome career so I'm a good wife and good mom and successful businessperson," I started dating just to date. I looked at everyone I met through the lens of, "Are you a good partner for me *and* are you ready?"

If I learned anything being single as long as I was, it's that you can meet the hottest, smartest, coolest, most amazing person, but if he/she/

ze isn't ready, you will pretty much be at a standstill until that person is willing to take a step forward. You have to decide if this person's timing is right for you.

At that point in my life, my biggest complaint was number four on the complaint worksheet. *I am sick and tired of feeling: like I need to stand on a mountain and shout, "When will it be my turn?"*

In my case, I felt this way about my love life and my career. I was filing a complaint with myself that I hadn't checked the marriage box or made it to a major TV network. But once I visited Rob, I realized my "complaint" wasn't really something negative after all. In that moment, I realized I was ready for a serious relationship (even one that could require I move out of New York City), but that was the first time I really felt *that* ready. As time went on, I realized I didn't love working in a newsroom anymore either. I found running my own company to be much more fulfilling, but I had a hard time letting the TV dream go because I had dedicated my life to it for so long.

Look at your complaint(s) and ask yourself, "Do I even want these things anymore?" Sometimes, filing a complaint steers our thinking in a different direction and helps us identify a strength or the "why" behind our situation. Often, our complaints are things we have forced ourselves into believing we need or aren't really ready for. Your complaint may reveal that you're exactly where you're meant to be.

REFLECTIONS

Below are some reflections you can use to help you digest what we've covered in this chapter:

+ Are you in a rut because of your career, love life, or level of activism? Remember, when you feel yourself getting into a rut or find yourself already there, filing a complaint will help you get to the heart of what is going on.
+ Can you talk to someone about what you're feeling and what you need? Are you aware of what is holding you back? Remember, the purpose of this exercise is not to keep you stuck in your rut, but rather to help you work your way out of it.

Unfiltered

+ Are you someone who likes to ride the negative thought train? It's easy to get caught on it, so commit to staying positive and focus on what makes you happy.

If you don't know how to implement these things, don't worry. In the next chapter, I'm going to share happiness hacks, which are tools you can use to push out those negative feelings and keep them at bay.

Chapter 3

Happiness Hacks:
Tips for Getting Out of a Rut

Your friend sends you a DM asking if you're still volunteering at her 5K Run/Walk this weekend. She doesn't know you've called out sick the past three days because you've been in a funk and are using your personal days. You tell her you think you have the flu, so she doesn't ask too many questions. #sickofmylife

Unfiltered

Being stuck in a rut is uncomfortable. You may have noticed changes in your sleeping habits, eating habits, emotional state, and tolerance level for the people around you. You may feel disconnected, question everything about your life, and doubt every decision you've ever made. You may feel mad, sad, frustrated, anxious, bitter, mean, or more introverted than usual. The good news is these negative feelings can help you make positive changes. We all know we aren't wired to be happy all the time, but many people I've coached are so scared they'll never get out of their rut that they turn to quick fixes that don't fix anything. In this chapter, I want you to get a handle on the scope of what's chipping away at your happiness (those complaints you filed in Chapter 2) so you can target your thinking toward taking the steps you need to improve your situation.

GET REAL WITH YOUR RUT

I know you may be eager for an answer key for happiness, but it's important to dig out of your rut slowly as opposed to quickly mapping out a grand plan that has cracks in the foundation. Whether you're in a rut because of your home life, work situation, relationships, or role within society, the key to hitting "refresh" (like we do when our computer screen is stuck) is to use these times we feel down in the dumps as cues for us to do a personal audit. Here are some ways you can do that:

+ *Accept where you are, even if it's painful.* Close your eyes, think about this shitty feeling, and in your head, wrap your arms around it like you're giving it a hug. I know that sounds weird, but doing this may help you be more present and connected to what you're feeling. Are you angry? Sad? Jealous? Frustrated? Disappointed? Hurt? You first have to understand where you are to figure out how to work through it.
+ *If you feel alone, embrace the empty.* There is something within emptiness that enables us to discover something new. Try not to throw a new person or a million projects into this void to distract yourself. Instead, attempt to learn something while you're here so you can turn that mess into a message.

+ *Explore being more mindful.* I have learned how to course correct when I am having a bad day by developing the tools I need to help me through any situation. It's not always easy to do, but I feel better at any given moment knowing I can change how I am feeling by putting these tools to work. I couldn't show up to a marathon and run 26.2 miles without proper training. When I ran one in real life, I prepared for months. Similarly, I have trained my mind to help me process information without resorting to old patterns and behaviors. I have looked into why I do what I do and figured out what serves me well and what

Tips to Help You Meditate

Dina Kaplan is the founder of The Path, a meditation startup based in New York City. She recommends using your stopwatch to meditate. "It's so easy to use, every phone has one, and then you can choose each day what type of meditation you'd like to do and exactly how long you want to meditate for," she says. "I only wish I had frequent-flier points for all the hours I've meditated with the stopwatch on my phone!" She also recommends you check out these apps:

+ Kevin Rose's Oak for the self-experimenter

+ Insight Timer for expertly guided meditations and a Tibetan bowl chime to mark the end of your meditation

+ Calm to help you fall asleep (Dina thinks the lavender field story is so relaxing!)

+ Imagine Clarity with Matthieu Ricard for meditations guided by one of the top meditation teachers alive today, a French Buddhist monk known as "the happiest man in the world" sets me back. If you are in a similar place, you have to find your own way out. What helped me was finding my center. If it's hard for you to quiet your mind, try doing a guided meditation (there are so many on YouTube). Click through videos until you find a theme (love, abundance, resilience, etc.) and a voice you like. If you don't connect with the music or person, try a new app or video.

WATCH IT!
To watch my interview with Dina, you can go here: entm.ag/dinakaplan.

+ *Rejuvenate your personal space.* Try moving your furniture around, changing the color scheme in your apartment (even if it's just your bathroom), or buying a cool poster or print to brighten up the place. Print pictures of people, places, or pets and put them on display. Small changes can reset the tone in your home or office. When I was in my rut before my 35th birthday, I realized my studio apartment looked like a cool office space. I asked my mom to help me change my entire color scheme and vibe to help make my place warmer. I turned what was once black, white, and red into white, gold, and teal. Suddenly, my apartment looked and felt like a spa. I didn't go crazy on the makeover thanks to my partners in crime: HomeGoods, Bed Bath & Beyond, Century 21, and Overstock.com. Changing my environment was one small step in helping me feel a little better about turning 35 and where I was in my life. My cousin Eric suggested I buy a money tree to attract the energy of wealth and prosperity in my new apartment. I found those at IKEA, too. If you need some financial feng shui, maybe a tree will help you as well!

+ *Shake up your daily routine.* Try going to a different coffee shop, gym class, or hangout spot after work. Breaking out of your normal flow forces you to say hello to new people, learn something new about yourself, and experience what your neighborhood, commute, and community have to offer. Plus, you never know who you could meet by restructuring your day.

How a New App Can Help When You're Not OK

When Hannah Lucas was 15 years old, she was diagnosed with postural tachycardia syndrome (POTS), a condition that caused her to faint daily. "I fainted everywhere—the bathroom at school, almost every class, in the hallway," she says. "I was *that* kid, and it was really difficult to deal with." Hannah says her fears quickly spiraled into anxiety and deep depression. "Being scared was a permanent state of mind. When I was in school, another student constantly bullied me and even threatened he would take advantage of me the next time I passed out." During one of Hannah's lowest moments, she says, she was alone in her room and thought about committing suicide. "In that moment, I thought to myself, 'What if there was a button I could press and someone would immediately know I was not OK?'" she says.

Hannah's 11-year-old brother, Charlie, jumped at the chance to help his sister. The two started searching for apps that helped distressed teens, but they couldn't find anything. Charlie, who is a tech lover, spent several months developing their own app. Today, their notOK app is helping people all over the world.

"The way it works is a teenager or adult can open the app, tap the red button and a text message will be sent to up to five preselected contacts that reads: 'Hey, I'm not OK. Please call me, text me, or come find me,' along with a link to their current GPS location," Charlie says. The siblings say they hope anyone suffering from loneliness, anxiety, depression, stress, suicidal thoughts, or anything else can get immediate help with just the tap of a button. The app is available for $1.99 in iOS and Android versions. To learn more, visit www.notokapp.com.

+ *Channel your inner Elsa.* When my sister was pregnant with my niece, I went to Washington, DC to keep her company while my brother-in-law traveled for work. All I wanted to do was see *Frozen*. My favorite line then, and still to this day (after hundreds of screenings with my (three nieces) is from when Elsa is singing "Let It Go": "It's funny how some distance makes everything seem small." It's true. When we are in a rut, every problem feels huge and every setback feels extra crushing. That's why distance helps us put things into perspective. To help you rise from your rut, you have to let things go. You may be someone who likes to hold a grudge. This will not do you any favors.

  You also have to let some people go and stop saying yes to everything. What does that mean? No more meeting with every person who wants to meet with you. If someone wants to introduce you to a family friend who is looking for a job, internship, roommate, boyfriend/girlfriend, new friend, whatever, see if you can deal with them over email or on the phone instead. You are not being rude. You need to reinvest as much of your time as possible back into *you*. There will be plenty of time to meet with people and help them once you are feeling a little less like Humpty Dumpty. It's more draining than you realize when you're trying to get out of a rut and you're spending energy you don't have on random people. Someone I was trying to help once said, "My mom told me to call you, but I don't know why." WTF? So be sure to save your effort for your to-do list and help people, when time permits, in a more efficient way.

+ *Step out of your day.* If you need some distance from your life, focus on your relationships, whether they're with the people you love or your pet. On good days and bad days, when I was dating and building my business, my niece always made me light up. Whether in person or via FaceTime, seeing her brought me so much joy. So make sure you surround yourself with people you love, and who love you, because interpersonal relationships are so powerful (and because toddlers couldn't care less if you missed a deadline). This is also a good time to reconnect with nature or your favorite workout routine. SoulCycle, yoga, and Orangetheory Fitness were my go-to places to clear my head.

* *Pay it forward.* If you're craving connectivity, look into getting involved in a cause you can contribute to. While your time needs to be spent on healing whatever is causing your hurt, rediscovering what makes you *you*, donating your time to an organization that means something to you, and spending time with people who will appreciate you, is a wonderful use of your time and talent. Nonprofits need so many team players to put on events, fundraise, and support the people they are helping. Your gifts can help others, and using them can help you, too. Not only will you know you're making a difference, but you also will have an opportunity to interact with new people. Who knows? Maybe someone you meet will become a mentor, new friend, or business contact. If you want ideas on where to volunteer, go to Chapters 15, 16, and 17.

* *See the world.* Whether you get in your car and drive an hour outside your city, get on a train and explore a neighborhood you've been meaning to check out, or book a flight to somewhere new, traveling has amazing healing benefits. I truly believe that "wherever you go, there you are," so don't expect once you arrive that you'll feel like a completely different person. But do get ready to breathe some fresh air, eat great food, learn something new, and take some time to regroup.

* *Accentuate the positive.* If you're not feeling positive vibes within you, you have to bring more positivity to you. The first thing you need to do is mentally create some distance from you and your negative feelings. Find quotes that you connect with and write them down. Hang them up in your apartment, put them on a small piece of paper, and stick them in your wallet. Put these quotes anywhere you will see them or have access to them when you need them. Feel free to ask family members, friends, and colleagues to share their favorite quotes with you, too. This is a time social media can be very helpful. Follow positive people with inspiring content so more positivity pops up in your feed.

Instagram Accounts I Love to Follow

Need inspiration? Check out some of these great Instagram accounts:

Belletrist (@belletrist): Emma Roberts and Karah Preiss created a lifestyle community for intellectually curious women who love to read. Their online book club supports authors and independent bookstores.

Amy Poehler's Smart Girls (@amypoehlersmartgirls): Amy Poehler and Meredith Walker launched Smart Girls to help women be their truest selves. They post empowering quotes and video interviews.

Hello Sunshine (@hellosunshine): Reese Witherspoon's company is dedicated to celebrating female storytelling and changing the narrative for women. It features positive quotes, interesting facts and statistics, and Reese's monthly book picks.

Man Enough (@wearemanenough): Justin Baldoni created a powerful disruptive social movement to help men redefine masculinity. It's female-friendly, too.

Ty Hunter (@tytryone): Ty Hunter is a fashion director, stylist, and designer who says it like it is and makes you feel like he's talking directly to you through his content.

Travis Barton (@travbarton): Travis Barton is an international life and business coach, speaker, author, and adventurer who always posts amazing nuggets of wisdom you'll want to screenshot.

Rachel DeAlto (@racheldealto): Rachel DeAlto is a relationship expert, TV host, media personality, and coach who shares

Instagram Accounts I Love to Follow, continued

behind-the-scenes pictures of her life as well as profound, hilarious, and spot-on thoughts about love.

James Goldcrown (@jgoldcrown): James Goldcrown is an amazing artist known for his #lovewall mural and #bleedinghearts. Just looking at his work will make you smile.

Mari Andrew (@bymariandrew): Mari Andrew is a writer and author who illustrates pretty much every thought you've ever had.

Lyss Stern (@diva_moms): Lyss Stern is the founder of Divalysscious Moms (http://divamoms.com/) and the author of *Motherhood Is a B#tch: 10 Steps to Regaining Your Sanity, Sexiness, and Inner Diva* (Skyhorse Publishing, 2017). You can learn more about Lyss and her book in my interview with her here: entm.ag/lyss.

The Moms (@themomsnetwork): Denise Albert and Melissa Gerstein share motivational advice on parenting and business, event information, and fun photos from their multiplatform lifestyle brand for parents or anyone who spends time with children.

Alison Brettschneider (@25park): Alison Brettschneider is a no-nonsense anti-bullying advocate, social justice warrior, wife, mom, and philanthropist.

Headbands of Hope (@headbandsofhope): Founder Jess Ekstrom shares upbeat quotes and heartwarming updates about her company, which donates a headband to a child battling cancer for each headband sold.

Parvati Shallow (@pshallow): Parvati Shallow is a yoga teacher and professional growth strategist whose posts will help you slow down for a second and reflect on where you are.

Start to live out those positive ideas you put on paper in your everyday life and pay attention to how you feel when you do. One of the affirmations I put on my wall when I was going through this exercise in my own life was, "What you take for granted someone else is praying for." Another motto that made it onto my wall was, "I will let go of the people and things that no longer serve a purpose in my life." That meant I would no longer make plans with people I felt guilted into seeing, attend every networking event for the sake of building my business, or go on every blind date in hopes of finding The One. It also meant I would start purging the clothes, papers, and "things" I had crammed into my studio apartment and saved for far too long. The third motto I put on my wall was, "Be a fountain, not a drain," to ensure the people I kept around me weren't energy zappers. For inspiration, check out Lessons to Live By on page 39.

Getting a Lift Out of Your Rut

As I mentioned in the introduction, I am not a medical professional, so I want to be very clear that hitting a bump in the road and needing some guidance is different from being in a suicidal crisis or emotional distress. Help is out there, whether you start with telling someone you trust or reaching out to one of the resources below. Please know you are not alone. I also want to add that just because someone has a lot of "friends" or followers on social media, it doesn't mean they feel comfortable calling any one of those people in an emergency. Don't be afraid to ask someone if they're OK if you think something is off. In fact, sometimes it's the people with the most "friends" and the people who seem to have it all who really need those around them to check in. So don't just reach out to a friend who solicits your help and support, check on your strong friends, too. Please know you are not alone and seek out help immediately, whether it's telling someone you trust or reaching out to one of these resources:

+ *The National Suicide Prevention Lifeline.* You can call (800) 273-8255 24 hours a day, 7 days a week (https://suicideprevention-lifeline.org).

Lessons to Live By

As I was working on this chapter, I asked family and friends what their favorite quotes, mantras, affirmations, and life lessons are—especially since phrases like these show up often in our social media feeds. Here are some of my favorites they shared with me.

+ "Every day is a new day." —Alyssa Abo

+ "I have everything I need." —Shaun Sperling

+ "I am a bottomless well of patience." —Andrew M. Akers

+ "Don't look back, you're not going that way."
  —Jaynie Shainfeld

+ "In the grand scheme of things, it's really not a biggie."
  —Marcy Frank Fink

+ "Remember why you're here." —Laura Geller

+ "Run *your* race." —Amanda Farinacci Gonzalez

+ "Just be a nice person." —Wally Levitt

+ "Fuck your fears."—Stephanie Belsky

+ "I am safe in the world." —Marcy Clark

+ "Enjoy your journey." —Wendy Fisher

+ "Progress not perfection." —Rachel Milder Lubchansky

+ "You never know who you're going to meet." —Ay Oh

+ "If you don't love yourself, no one else will!"
  —Lisa Meyerowitz

+ "Onward and upward." —Beth Gabay

Lessons to Live By, continued

+ "In joy, there is a moment of healing." —Jennifer Mynear

+ "Fear nothing—accomplish everything!" —Mark Hewlett

+ "Values are caught not taught." —Brett Shainfeld

+ "You can't buy class." —Aliette Abo

+ "Be kind to everyone. You never know what's going on behind closed doors." —Marc Abo

+ "If you look at a mosaic on the ceiling and there are 1,000 perfect tiles, don't let your eye focus on the one cracked tile." —Mervyn Shainfeld

+ "Good, better, best. Never let it rest. Until your good is better and your better best." Glynis Shainfeld quoting an old proverb

+ "You're always one decision away from a totally different life." —Brandon Shainfeld

+ "Always believe something wonderful is about to happen." —Deborah Shainfeld

+ *Crisis Text Line.* You can text "HOME" to 741741 from anywhere in the United States to text with a trained crisis counselor. The service is free and confidential (https://www.crisistextline.org/).

+ *The Trevor Project.* Designed specifically for LGBTQ youth in crisis. Call (866) 488-7386 or text "Trevor" to (202) 304-1200. The hotline is available 24/7; texting and online chat have more limited hours (www.thetrevorproject.org).

Shifting your thinking can have a positive impact on how you go about your day and what energy you give off. Talking about energy management seems wacky to some people and essential for others. I hope the next story from my life gives you some food for thought if you've ever wondered what this "energy" concept is all about.

#MYSTORY: Is It My Chi? Or Just Me?

I was running late to a networking dinner for people in the media and PR and wasn't sure I even wanted to go. On a whim, I decided to stop by, and when I got there, I sat next to a woman named Lara Riggio (www.LaraRiggio. com), who seemed nice. She told me she did energy work and shared a little about her personal story and how she met her husband.

At first, I thought Lara's work was a little out there, even though I'm an open person. As she went into more detail about her clients, I told her I thought I might have a blocked chakra or something, because I didn't feel the way most people assumed I did when it came to dating:

+ I did not hate men.

+ I had not given up on dating.

+ I was making time to date.

+ I was not too career oriented (as though you can't have a career and a boyfriend).

She asked me a series of questions and said, "It's funny. Usually when I meet single women, I get a sense they *say* they're open, but they're really not. Or they have other issues they haven't worked through yet, so we have to tackle those first. But I really don't get that sense from you."

As someone who is obsessed with knowing the "why" behind everything, I had to know why I felt like it was me against the world. Was I giving off a vibe I didn't realize? I really wasn't sure anymore.

Lara emailed me about coming in for a session so I could better understand what she does. During my appointment, I learned Lara helps people discover and remove energy blocks in their bodies and their lives. People who work with Lara often want to overcome a specific physical pain or emotional upset, such as back pain, neck pain, insomnia, fear of the unknown, heartbreak, loss, a toxic relationship, weight loss, or the desire to make money, find love, get unstuck, or reach their pure potential. When someone comes to her because they are feeling sad, angry, anxious, fearful, jealous, heartbroken, or depressed, Lara helps them figure out where those feelings are coming from. Were they triggered by a childhood issue? An unresolved relationship? Today's terrible news headlines?

TIP

All of this energy talk may not be your "thing" and I understand that. Before you roll your eyes and dismiss these ideas completely, consider skimming through them. They may inspire you to think differently about whatever you're trying to change or teach you something new.

I walked away from my session with some new ways to approach my own pain points, and much of what we discussed directly relates to getting out of your rut. I asked Lara to weigh in on this chapter, so we can help you turn *your* pain points into possibilities, which she calls "turning upset into access." Below, Lara shares her tips on understanding the power of your own energy and how you can use it to overcome what's negative in your life.

Understanding Your Energy

If you are unhappy with the way you look or feel, or are feeling stuck in some area of your life, Lara says you are not at your best energy effect. "The crazy thing is that you are most likely unaware of most of the stressors that are causing you to be out of balance, unsatisfied, and less effective than you can be," she says. Lara says many of us have been taught by society to "keep calm and carry on"; however, our bodies are affected by stress, whether it be physical, emotional, or chemical. "If there are too many of these stressors being placed on you at one time, your body tells you it's overloaded, and you can experience fatigue, weight gain, pain, discomfort, insomnia, anxiety, depression, frustration, or unhappiness," she says.

Unfiltered

Lara also says this is a sign that your lifestyle, your relationships, and/or your mindset are not supporting you or your goals. "You are actually working against your best interest. You are living a life that is out of sync with your desires, and your body and emotions will definitely let you know you are not on a pathway toward happiness, if something is taking too long, and if you are not working at your best effect," she says.

According to Lara, at every moment our bodies are reacting to our environments, and our reactions are determining the way we feel as well as how people respond to us.

When you feel good, you act differently than when you feel bad, right? When you don't feel good, it shows, and you just aren't capable of being, doing, or attracting your best. The world mirrors how you feel. And people's reactions and judgments about you determine whether they want to date you, do business with you, or look for another job if you are their boss and they don't feel appreciated. This is not your fault; you're probably not even aware of what you are doing. Your body and brain remember the emotions, words, smells, and sounds associated with stressful events from your past. Sometimes that helps you react better in the future, but sometimes it prevents you from doing your best. Here are some examples:

+ When you got burned as a kid, you learned fast that stoves are hot and are **NOT** to be touched. That's a good lesson.
+ But if you saw your mom unhappy in her marriage, you may have learned that men aren't to be trusted, causing you to be drawn toward unavailable men.
+ If your dad gave you candy or ice cream when you were upset, you may have learned that sugar gives you emotional comfort. When eating is how you soothe yourself, it's easy to pack on the pounds!
+ If your family fled their country to create a better life somewhere new, the stress of that change may have affected your grand-parents and parents, causing them to teach you some limiting beliefs or emotional patterns that no longer serve you or the family in this day and age.

Unfiltered

These past beliefs may be keeping you from having the life you desire. Lara says rather than looking at any physical or emotional upset as a disaster, you can look at it as an opportunity to be more effective by managing your energy differently. "Making simple changes in your thinking and in your lifestyle can help you feel better and be more effective with less energy," she says. "Let's get your emotions, actions, and energy in sync with what you desire because you can live a life you love; you just have to focus your energy on having it!"

How to Refocus Your Energy

Rather than seeing your feelings as bad, Lara suggests you think of them as your body's way of telling you that you need to make a change. "The first step in transforming your energy and your reaction to stress is by noticing upsets vs. just denying your feelings and stuffing them down," Lara says.

"When you are upset, often your body goes into a fight, flight, or freeze stress state called a sympathetic nervous system response. It is a primal reaction designed to keep you safe by preparing your body to run, fight, or hide in the face of danger. In your modern life, most of your stressors are not immediately life-threatening, but your body still has a similar response. Your stress responses take energy and resources from your immune and digestive system to fuel your potential escape or fight, releasing stress hormones and making it difficult to relax, sleep, restore, and repair."

The second step is to learn how to calm yourself down. "The same way you can train your body to run a marathon, you can train it to calm down," Lara says. "Insomnia has become a big problem for people in modern-day society because people do not know how to relax. Stress can also create tension in your muscles when that stress energy is not released via exercise, which can cause pain or just make it difficult to relax your body." Lara says stress can impair our ability to think and problem solve. "When you are stressed, blood rushes from your brain to your limbs to power your fight or flight, so your cognitive abilities are affected. Your ability to solve problems and find creative solutions can be impaired from stress."

Unfiltered

Lara created a Seven-Day Energy Reset Challenge to help you relieve stress; sleep better; feel more effective at work; have a healthier relationship with money, your weight, and your family; and be able to move some familial blocks that don't serve you. To watch the videos and participate in the challenge, go here: www.LaraRiggio.com. Lara believes that over the next ten years these exercises, which may seem odd at first, will be as commonplace as yoga and meditation.

REFLECTIONS

In this chapter, we looked at how to embrace where you are and learned how to use our energy to move forward. This chapter may have made you somewhat uncomfortable, or you may feel ready to take on the world with your newfound understanding of yourself. I don't want you to forget how far you've come in a short amount of time, so let's take a quick snapshot of how you're feeling:

* What did you learn about yourself in this chapter?
* What is one step you are going to take to help you get out of your rut?
* What did you learn from Lara?
* What is a mantra, affirmation, or positive action you will try to implement in your daily routine?

In addition to holding on to your new tools to help you stay positive during challenging times, in the next chapter we're going to break down how to keep it together when you feel lost, get rejected, or are trying to recover from a mistake.

Part Two

Staying Positive

Chapter 4

Feeling Lost Isn't Always a Bad Thing

You walk into work wondering why you ever chose this profession. Your parents ask how things are going, and you say, "Never better." You post a picture of your stunning office view so no one knows you're miserable. #lovemyjob

Unfiltered

There is a quote I often share in my speeches that goes: *Sometimes you find yourself in the middle of nowhere, and sometimes in the middle of nowhere, you find yourself.* —Author Unknown

I love this quote because often on the other end of uncertainty is clarity. The reason corporations and most of my private clients reach out to me in the first place is because they want a personal GPS (like my friend Jennifer S. Wilkov, who I mentioned in the introduction is my North Star). We all need those people in our lives sometimes who not only confirm that yes, we made a wrong turn or our company is on the wrong path, but also help us turn around and "recalculate." Just like when we're driving, sometimes in life we can't see there is a better, more direct route.

In this chapter, we will look at why mentors matter, how to find a mentor, how to be a mentor, and what *not* to do once you've found your way. (People who send way too many emails to get someone's attention, I'm talking to you!) I am going to share what I go over with my high school and college mentees and professional clients, like Samantha.

MAP IT OUT

My client Samantha was a successful woman who works in finance. She thought she was spinning her wheels at work and felt her daily choices were reducing her as a person. When it came to work, she said:

+ She had forgotten why she once loved her current job.
+ She had forgotten what it felt like to be part of a team and make a difference.
+ She felt restricted by her boss.
+ She didn't know what she wanted to do next.

When it came to her personal life:

+ She couldn't remember the last thing she was truly proud of doing, creating, or achieving.
+ She didn't know what causes she wanted to support in her free time.
+ She didn't know why any nonprofit would want her.

+ She felt she didn't have enough time to go to her favorite cycling class or sleep.
+ She didn't have enough time to date or travel for fun.

Samantha's session fit right into the echo chamber of most of the people I meet, from college graduates and CEOs to people who are about to retire. She was lost. We needed to sit down together so she could recalculate her direction. The first thing I did with Samantha was turn these negative feelings into positive goals.

Under the job category, I asked her to:

+ Identify jobs she would enjoy doing
+ Identify companies she would want to work for
+ Set up informational interviews to learn more about those roles and companies
+ Reach out to friends, family, and mentors for moral support
+ Explore local networking opportunities like panels, conferences, and events

Under the personal fulfillment category, I asked her to:

+ Identify something she would feel proud to do/create/accomplish
+ Identify causes she would like to support
+ Identify what professional skills and personal gifts she has to offer
+ Purchase a spinning package for five classes for the following month
+ Put down a deposit for a trip to somewhere she would like to go

Under her dating goals, I suggested Samantha:

+ Read *Calling in "The One": 7 Weeks to Attract the Love of Your Life* by Katherine Woodward Thomas
+ Reach out to Project Soulmate, a matchmaking service based in New York City

Did Samantha do all the above right away? No! That would've made her go from lost to completely overwhelmed! The idea wasn't to change everything overnight, but to map out a plan she could work through little by little. Samantha started with booking an amazing trip and reaching out to her family, friends, and mentors to do some research on *herself*. This is a great exercise you can do, too, if you feel comfortable with asking friends and family for feedback. If you're not sure what to say in your email to your personal network, try something like this:

> Dear Raphaella,
>
> I am working on switching careers and working with a consultant to help me figure out what I would like to do next. Since I have been in this industry for ten years, I am trying to identify what I bring to the table. If you don't mind, can you tell me why you think I am a special person in your life? If you could also share five adjectives you would use to describe me, I would really appreciate it.
>
> Let's play tennis soon.
>
> Duckie

Samantha ended up taking on a new role within her company and kept her word that she would make more time for travel, exercise, and dating. After she rediscovered her happiness, Samantha reported feeling more connected to her life.

PARTNER UP

Another way to get to where you want to go is to find an accountability partner. My friend Peipei Zhou and I met at a summit at the United Nations. When we met, we each thought the other one was *really* intense. LOL. At the time, Peipei led a sales team on the Global Account Team at Facebook and I was about to launch my YouTube channel. We made plans to meet for lunch, and something just clicked. We both were in our own lanes, but we were very supportive of each other's goals and started to meet once a season to help keep us accountable to our professional and personal aspirations. It has been incredibly rewarding and exciting to be there for each other during life's milestones and career changes. It's also been comforting to have a partner in crime with whom I can be honest when I feel things are falling short. Yes, this is what family and friends are for, but it's important to have a business buddy you can do this with as well. Peipei and I always remind the other that it doesn't matter how long it takes you to reach your goal; what matters is that you keep going and don't give up on yourself. When patience isn't your virtue (it's not always mine), it really helps to have someone to help you stay focused. Find someone you can be raw and real with and who will be the same way with you.

You will find most people in your life will be happy to help you—you just have to ask for their help and be clear about what you need. If you're not sure where to start, look into finding a mentor.

WHY MENTORS MATTER

For everything you love—food, art, sports, medicine, theater, tech, science, fashion, reading, writing, photography, cooking, coding, you name it—there are ways to turn your passion into a paycheck, and having a mentor can make all the difference in helping you reach your goal. The best way for me to explain how vital mentors can be (especially when you feel you've lost your way) is by sharing something I learned at the eye doctor. Read the full story below.

#MYSTORY: Caution: Blind Spot Ahead

I sat down in the chair for my annual eye exam. "Rest your chin here for the visual field test and let me know whenever you see a flash of light," the doctor said. The flashes appeared one by one at different speeds. Sometimes there was a pause before the next flash. Other times, there would be one right after another. When I was done, I asked the doctor how many I got. "You got all but one! But that's normal," she said. "Everyone misses one because we all have a blind spot."

Unfiltered

OMG. Drop the mic. We all have a blind spot? Who knew?

It was around this time I was trying to figure out my brand. (Was I a journalist? Motivational speaker? Consultant?) Later that week, I had a meeting with one of my mentors, Evan Shapiro, former head of IFC, founder of Seeso, and now a TV producer (eshap.tv), and told him, "Evan, I can't seem to find a concise way to convey what I do for a living. This is my blind spot, and if *you* had to explain to someone what I do, I'd love it if you could share that wording with me."

Evan emailed me after his subway ride home. In ten minutes, he put down in words what I had been trying to convey for a year. Sometimes we can't see what's in front of us because there's an obstruction we don't know about. It's moments like this that mentors can really make a difference.

GUIDING LIGHTS ARE GIFTS

Evan had the advantage of being able to look at my situation from the outside in. He saw something I couldn't and offered me #unfiltered advice. Mentors can do that for you. Whether you seek out a mentor at work, at school, within your family, or in your community, you can rely on them for unvarnished advice when you're trying to find your way. Keep these points in mind as you consider why mentors matter:

+ *Mentors are amazing tour guides for life.* Whether your mentor is a dean, coach, older student, relative, or family friend, having a mentor provides you with a support system during your journey.
+ *A mentor can be someone you admire but don't know.* There have been times in my career that I needed some guidance, so I paid attention to what the people one step ahead of me were doing. I often got great ideas on how I could take my brand to the next level by learning from people I respected but had never met. Sometimes I had a mentorship moment while listening to someone speaking on a panel when I really liked what they said. Mentors can be people you meet with in person or follow on social media. However, in the event the person you admire is

Unfiltered

someone you really want to contact, do your homework before reaching out—and when you do, make sure you send whatever makes sense, such as your bio, resume, and links to your work, if applicable.

Approaching a Potential Mentor

When I gave a speech in New Orleans, a teenager named Ben Shapiro was in the audience. I saw Ben again while I was traveling the country on a speaking tour and had the opportunity to watch him lead a workshop for teens at a youth convention. I was blown away by his creativity and knew he was going to be successful no matter what he did in life. A year later, he reached out to me and asked if I was looking for an intern. He lived in Los Angeles and I was in New York City, so I told him I would mentor him through phone calls and emails, but other than that, I didn't have much to offer him at the time. For months, Ben emailed me and asked if he would be able to work on my YouTube channel if he flew to New York for the summer. He was so persistent that I felt bad saying no. His mom said she would rent an apartment in New York for the summer so Ben had a place to stay. He took classes a few days a week and worked with me on the others. Ben is a good example of staying in touch with someone you've met and not taking no for an answer.

If you are asking someone you don't know to be your mentor, make sure you're very clear, out of the gate, about why you are contacting them. Explain where you are in life, mention you are looking for a mentor, and highlight why they would be a great mentor for you. Here is what a young woman named Gabi Golenberg sent me out of the blue (see the letter on page 56).

At the time Gabi sent me this email, I had no plans to be in Los Angeles. My friend Pam had introduced me to a guy who lived there named Brett, but other than a phone call and some texts, we weren't in touch all that often. I explained to Gabi that my work was in New York for the time being, but that I would be happy to talk with her on the phone and keep her in mind for future projects. We were supposed to schedule a call, but I got busy with speeches and covering New York

Dear Jessica,

Hi! My name is Gabi and I am 15 years old and I live in Los Angeles. Through researching online as I was looking for possible mentors or admirable people who I can seek advice from about an internship, I came across your inspirational work with both your entrepreneurial skills and involvement in Jewish organizations. Those are two things that have been my passions and interests throughout my life. I attend an all-girls prep school here in LA and have spent the past two summers studying entrepreneurship and business at Columbia University. Your plethora of work in various different fields is something that I would love to strive for in the future and I really admire your achievements. My family and I are very involved in our synagogue and AIPAC. I will be heavily involved throughout the year and plan to attend conferences in DC. I also am drawn to SoulCycle and fashion week. :) It would be such an honor and huge opportunity to have the chance to speak with you at some point as your work mirrors my passions. I hope and look forward to hearing from you soon.

Thank you so much for your time.

All the best,

Gabi

Fashion Week and dropped the ball. This is how Gabi followed up (see the letter on page 57).

Notice how understanding Gabi was about the demands of Fashion Week and how sensitive she was of my time. Fast-forward four months. Brett came to New York City, and his sister-in-law, Debs, insisted he make plans with me. We met, hit it off, and started traveling back and forth between New York and Los Angeles to see each other. On one of my trips to California, I had the pleasure of meeting Gabi for coffee. She

Unfiltered

> Hi Jessica!
>
> I hope you are having a great time at NYFW. I have been following the shows and from what I hear and see, everything is fantastic as always. ;)
>
> I can only imagine how busy you are; I've learned and heard that fashion week is so time consuming. I'd love to chat with you, not sure if you are available at some point this weekend or early next week? Nevertheless, I would be thrilled to set up a time to chat with you.
>
> Best,
>
> Gabi

was even more impressive in person. We made a game plan for me to mentor her during her junior year and identified what projects of mine she wanted to help with.

Now, if you are writing to a family member, you don't need to be so formal, but setting up a time to connect does show you're serious and professional. For example:

> Dear Madison,
>
> It was great seeing you at Aunt Sylvia and Uncle Randy's anniversary party. As you know, I just started my pediatrics residency and am looking for a mentor. I admire the cutting-edge research you're doing and loved reading the recent profile on you in *The Garfield Express*. I know I could learn so much from you and your experience. Let me know if you're around this weekend to continue our conversation.
>
> Love you!
>
> Alexa

Have an Attitude of Gratitude

After your initial call, thank that person for agreeing to be your mentor and share what you got out of the conversation. Once they have signed on to be your mentor, don't bombard them with emails, calls, and texts. You want to be respectful of your mentor's time at all times, even if they're family. Whatever you do, if you send an email and your mentor doesn't respond right away, don't go into your SENT box, find that email, and hit FORWARD to make sure you've re-sent it. And don't send an email with just a question in the subject and nothing in the body like this (unless it's an emergency): "SUBJECT: Tony, did you get my text? THNX."

Just because you added THNX to represent "thanks" doesn't make your approach any better. Abrupt messages like this make you look disconnected from reality, which is: Tony has responsibilities other than being your mentor. So think twice before you press send.

Here are a few more tips to follow to make sure your relationship with your mentor stays positive:

+ *Meeting your mentor.* Once you set up a time to meet them, be clear about what you hope to get out of having a mentor. Are you looking for guidance? To shadow them at their job? Make sure your expectations match so there are no miscommunications.
+ *The mentor/mentee relationship.* Set the stage for how this dynamic will work early on. For starters, how should you get in touch if you need their advice? Does your mentor prefer phone calls, FaceTime, or emails? Do they mind if you send a text for something urgent?
+ *Plan ahead.* You'll also want to find out how often they can meet. Never leave a meeting without scheduling your next one. It is your job (not your mentor's) to keep the mentorship alive.
+ *The next ask.* If you have developed a nice relationship with your mentor over time, you may want to ask them to write you a letter of recommendation or be a reference for you if you're applying for an internship or job. Mentors are connectors. Your mentor may be willing to make introductions for you, too.

Making Connections

When your mentor makes a professional introduction for you, be sure to follow up in a timely fashion and keep your mentor in the loop. Remember, it is your job to reach out once your mentor has made the connection. Here is an example:

If your mentor, Brandon, introduces you via email to Debbie, the CEO of a company you really want to work for, be sure to Reply All to Brandon's email. Start by thanking Brandon for the introduction. Then mention how happy you are to connect with Debbie and go into what you want her to know about you and your interests. End by asking for the best way to set up a meeting or call. Debbie may reply and set up something herself, or she may loop in her assistant. In either case, be sure to follow up appropriately.

Before *and* after your meeting with Debbie, be sure to tell Brandon what's going on and thank him again for the introduction. He should not find out from anyone else that you and Debbie are meeting or that you *had* a meeting. After all, he is the one who opened the door for you. After you've met, don't forget to send Debbie a thank-you note!

+ *Keep in touch.* Mentor/mentee relationships can turn into lifelong friendships. Don't just make this about you and send updates about your life. Send your mentor a note from time to time to check in. Follow what they're up to. Congratulate them when you come across good news about their personal life (maybe their child got into college) or when you see an exciting update about their company. Send a holiday card or happy birthday note when appropriate. Not only does it show you're a thoughtful human being, but you also never know when they may have a position that would be a great fit for you, and it doesn't hurt to stay at the top of their mind.

+ *You can be a mentor, too.* Feel free to share how you can help your mentor. My mentees have been so helpful in teaching me about amazing apps, online tools, and the best ways to reach their demographic. For example, in addition to coming on shoots with me, doing research for segments, and weighing in on what we should feature on my YouTube channel, Allie Kory taught me about some cool newsletter programs, Nora Swidler showed me who I should follow on Instagram, Jamie Shapiro taught me how to vlog, and Ben Shapiro redid all my graphics and my website.

As you know, mentorship is a two-way street. It takes effort from both parties to have a meaningful outcome. If you've been thinking about becoming a mentor or just agreed to be one, there is a code of conduct for you, too.

Advice for Mentors

So you've agreed to mentor your college roommate's son or your neighbor's daughter. That's wonderful! If you're new to being a mentor, keep the following in mind:

+ Make sure you carve out the time on your calendar to fulfill your commitment to your mentee.
+ When you get together, don't talk about yourself the entire time. Remember, you're meeting to help this person grow, not because you need a new therapist.
+ Always meet in a professional setting.
+ Follow through on what you say you will do. If you say you'll make an introduction, do it sooner rather than later so you don't forget.
+ Your mentee knows you have demands on your schedule. When something comes up, notify them as soon as possible. Often your mentee will be traveling to you, and it's inconsiderate to have them show up at your office only to learn you can no longer meet.

- Support your mentee outside your meetings. My mentor Lora Dennis showed up every time I was honored at a gala and donated to every charity event I chaired. She even met her husband at an event I emceed. It always meant the world to me that she was there for me, so when I mentored Jamie Shapiro, and she told me she was in her high school musical, I knew I would do whatever it took to be there for her. She is an amazing young woman and I loved having her on my team. To show her how proud I was of her, I declined a work opportunity and traveled in a storm to attend a dress rehearsal. She couldn't stop telling me how much it meant to her that I showed up, but it meant even more to me to sit in that theater and see her shine.

Finally, remember that mentorship paves the way forward. If your mentee impressed you, do what you can to give them a hand as they start down their career path. They will not only appreciate it, but they will also be more likely to mentor someone else in the future.

Women Mentoring Women

If you are looking to support young women, check out GenHERation. As a University of Pennsylvania Wharton School of Business undergrad, founder Katlyn Grasso received the inaugural Penn President's Engagement Prize, which provides graduating seniors with $150,000 to develop projects that have the potential to change the world, and has led the company to empower more than 106,000 young women to date. According to GenHERation's website, through GenHERation Discovery Days, "high school and college women can visit the most innovative companies in America to meet female executives and identify role models to support their professional pursuits." To get involved, visit https://genheration.com.

Mentorship Starts at Home

The culture of mentorship is stronger if you incorporate it in your daily life, whether you want to be a mentor or are seeking a mentor to be your North Star. One way to start is by touting mentorship's benefits with your own family, friends, and colleagues. For example, if you are a parent, you can help your child talk to your colleagues or your friends who have jobs your child might like to learn about—or has already expressed interest in. Having a child, whether it's yours, a colleague's, or a friend's, shadow you or someone else in your professional network to see what that job entails is invaluable life experience. If a child is trying to start a new club, committee, or campaign, sit down with them and ask how the plan is coming together. Since most teens have to cope with their peers posting about their "perfect lives," it is important to support them in taking the steps they need to be proud of *their* path.

To build a culture of mentorship, help young people cultivate varied interests. If your mentee doesn't know what they want to be when they grow up, have them think about what activities make them happy and suggest they do research to find what activities already exist in their school or neighborhood.

Teenagers can learn a lot about being team players through sports, getting involved in the school play, or serving on a committee. And no, they don't have to be the quarterback, lead actor, or chairperson to make a difference. Sports teams need managers, plays need a stage crew, and committees need all kinds of members. Don't let your mentee talk themself out of giving something a try because they're afraid of getting

WATCH IT!

One of my favorite interviews I did for my YouTube channel was with then-eight-year-old Alexa Kahn, who taught me how to code. Her parents had learned about a program that taught creative entrepreneurship to kids and enrolled her. Years later, she's still coding, proving you're never too young to find your passion. You can see the interview I did with Alexa here: entm.ag/alexa out there. They can hone their ability to help others by tutoring, giving back to the community, or becoming a mentor, too. They can learn about different issues and how to plan an event by joining a club on campus. In addition to looking into what opportunities their school offers, recommend they check out what's going on within the religious institution they attend or what the community associations and nonprofits around them are spearheading. These establishments may offer a way for them to pursue their area of interest and find an internship or job.

You can also encourage volunteerism. Volunteering can help your mentee network for a job, find other role models, and learn a lot about themselves. Not only will they feel a tremendous sense of pride from helping someone else and seeing their hard work pay off, but there's also a sense of accomplishment that comes with contributing to the greater good that you don't get from other people's validation on social media. Yes, they'll still feel hurt when they see they weren't invited to that big party, but finding their passion and pursuing it will help them know their value, even when other people don't see their worth. As we know, this is a huge life lesson—no matter what age we are.

WATCH IT!

When Jason Tifford heard former Treasurer of the United States Rosie Rios talk about a nationwide initiative called Teachers Righting History (http:// teachersrightinghistory. org/), which is dedicated to highlighting historic American women who are often left out of history lessons, he was inspired to start a group at his high school called Students Righting History. In its first year, the club grew from two members to ten. Today, students in the club spend time auditing elementary, middle, and high schools to make sure their classrooms and hallways feature as many pictures of historic women as men. To learn more about Jason's story and Students Righting History, you can watch the interview I did with him here: entm.ag/righting history.

Helping Young People Turn Their Passion Into a Paying Job

In 2014, three TV executives were chatting: Alex Boylan, winner of *The Amazing Race*, TV host, and Emmy-nominated producer; Burton Roberts, *Survivor* contestant, producer, and world traveler; and Lisa Hennessy, an Emmy-nominated TV executive who helped build Mark Burnett Productions, overseeing hundreds of hours of network TV. They found themselves talking about how fortunate they had been to have the quintessential "dream job," and wondering what they could do to help young people find their own path to a dream career. That conversation launched DreamJobbing, a website that offers the coolest short-term opportunities in the world: being a photographer in Norway, a global giver for TOMS, a host for the Olympics, a wildlife volunteer in Thailand, a producer for CBS, and many others. People apply by making a 60-second video telling their story and why they are perfect for the job. Many of the chosen applicants ended up getting a full-time job at the company, so the trio expanded DreamJobbing into a platform that teaches students and young professionals the art of pitching themselves via video so they can gain the competitive edge they need to land an opportunity on their own.

To date, DreamJobbing has helped thousands of people tell their story and get in the door. The DreamJobbing team works with nonprofits, high schools, and colleges to help students network virtually, as well as give them the tools to land that important internship or job. If you're in Kansas and want to talk with an entertainment lawyer in Los Angeles, you can do that through the site. And, of course, you can always apply for one of their once-in-a-lifetime experiences. Take a look by visiting www.dreamjobbing.com.

Unfiltered

And don't forget to encourage your mentee to get into the habit of learning how to work hard and prioritize their mental and physical health. As we know all too well, this tug-of-war will only get harder as they get older.

REFLECTIONS

All hope is not lost, even when you feel like you've lost your way. Mentors can help us test our hypotheses on what makes us happy. If our data doesn't seem to be accurate, that's where a mentor can help us troubleshoot and draw a new conclusion. After reading this chapter, ask:

+ Who can be your accountability partner?
+ Who would you like to be your mentor?
+ If you need to go in a new direction, who in your network does something that interests you?
+ Can you connect with that person about a potential internship or ask to shadow them for a day?
+ What skills can you bring to the table?
+ If the people around you don't know what you're passionate about, how can you be better about letting people in and asking for guidance?
+ How can you become a mentor?
+ How can you better support your mentee?

As you've read, mentors can support you in a myriad of ways. They are especially helpful to bounce ideas off of if you're facing a setback or just made a mistake. In the next chapter, we'll address what you can do if you find yourself in either position.

Chapter 5

We All Make Mistakes

You wake up, and for a split second, you forget you've been fired. Today is the first day in your 15-year career you have woken up with no place to go. You find an old picture of you and your sibling and thank your social media stars that it's Thursday. You can post something innocuous and go back to bed. #tbt #goodtimes

Unfiltered

There are different kinds of professional mistakes. There are the ones that take us out of the running for a position, the ones that get us fired, and the ones where we realize we chose the wrong industry altogether. In my own story, a misspelled word cost me a prestigious fellowship and altered my entire career path.

I was in college and wanted to work at NY1 News in the worst way. While I was interning at *Dateline NBC* the summer before my junior year of college, I met someone who had interned at NY1 through this really cool program, so I decided to apply. The application process was long, and I made it through several rounds. In my final application, I had to submit nine pages of essays. One of the questions asked me to write about my favorite interview. I had just met Jon Stewart, so I wrote about that experience: "A crew from CBS was there working on a profile of Jon *Stuart*, and since they did not have a reporter, they shot my interview with him, using me as their field producer."

Accidentally spelling Stewart S-T-U-A-R-T ended my hopes for the NY1 internship. Have you ever read an essay or business presentation 100 times and somehow still missed a mistake? Have you ever showed that piece of work to your network—and realized everyone else missed the typo, too? #facepalm

While I was really upset at first, I ended up spending the summer interning at WMAQ, the NBC station in Chicago, and training for the Chicago Marathon. From that point on, I traveled to journalism conferences whenever I saw that someone from NY1 was speaking or holding a session to critique people's news reels. After graduate school, I got a job at the CBS affiliate in Burlington, Vermont, and sent a copy of my resume and reel to my contacts at NY1 every few months. It took me six more years to land a job at NY1, but I eventually got there.

Making a mistake like that can be devastating. How you take ownership of your actions is vital to recovering from setbacks (and there will be plenty of them). From job search mistakes and awkward moments in interviews to blowing your chance to land a big project at work or putting your foot in your mouth in front of the boss, mistakes abound in our professional lives. In this chapter, let's talk about some of those scenarios and how we can recover from them—or, at the very least, reduce the damage. First, let's take a look at what you can do if you perform poorly during an interview or mess up an application like I did.

BOUNCING BACK WHEN THE JOB SEARCH GOES SIDEWAYS

Whether you weren't prepared, got caught off guard, or knew your stuff but totally blanked, walking out of a bad interview is rough. Ian Saville is Facebook's learning and development partner, responsible for growing employees, nurturing an inclusive culture, and building learning programs. He says if you screwed up an interview because you rambled, his number-one piece of advice is to write out your responses to typical questions and practice reciting them so you're better prepared next time.

"Boil down the paragraph responses into concise bullets that you can speak to generally. You don't want to come across rehearsed," Ian says. "Define three to four key areas for which you can create value for a company in a specific role, and hit on those themes again and again across all interviews. You don't want to 'boil the sea' and say you're great at everything because people come away with nothing memorable about you when you try that approach."

If you really have your heart set on the job, make sure your thank-you note conveys what your interview didn't. You can mention briefly that your interview wasn't the best reflection of what you have to offer, but don't write a lengthy letter. Keep your note short and sweet. Be sure to highlight ideas or skills that support why you are right for the role or answer questions you stumbled on in the interview. The letter on page 70 is an example.

If you feel your note isn't enough, there's no harm in asking for another opportunity to talk with the person even if it's a five-minute phone call—and take Ian's advice into consideration. Learn from your mistakes, organize your thoughts before the call, role-play with a friend or colleague, and don't harp on this setback forever.

Unfiltered

Dear Morgan,

It was a pleasure meeting you on Tuesday. I enjoyed our conversation and learning more about Silk City Studios. When you asked me about a time I missed a deadline and how I recovered, I failed to recall when I worked at Emily Brooke Productions and received an order that was mislabeled. When I opened the shipment, I noticed that the shirts that said "large" on the tag were really mediums and every medium was really a small. I called the manufacturer and learned that they ran out of the sizes my client needed, so they just used what they had in stock. I called another company that agreed to remake the order and called the client right away. I explained that the manufacturer had mismarked the entire line, that I had found a new company to do an emergency order, and that we would absorb all the rush fees. My client was not happy that he was not going to receive his products on time, but he was grateful that I called him with a solution instead of just calling with a problem. I hope this example does a better job of showing you how I recover from mistakes and think on my feet.

Thank you again for bringing me into your office to discuss your head of sales position. I look forward to staying in touch with you.

Sincerely,

JR Matthew

To prevent submitting an application with a typo, try reading everything you wrote out loud to see if you catch anything new, and then send it to one more person to proofread. Whenever you're writing an important email, don't put an email address into the SEND TO line until you're actually ready to send your note. This will help you avoid hitting SEND too soon.

Now that we've addressed some ideas you can implement if you've made a mistake that kept you from getting the gig, let's look at what you can do to stay positive if you made a mistake while you were on the clock.

HOW TO RECOVER WHEN YOU'VE MADE A MISTAKE ON THE JOB

If you just made a big *This could get me fired* mistake on the job, you are allowed to be upset. In fact, research shows that happy people don't bury negative feelings, so there is no need to post about how amazing your life is today. Research also shows that happy people embrace where they are and take ownership of their actions. We all make mistakes at work—it's part of learning and growing. After all, we're not perfect. Don't consider yourself a failure and wallow in a sense of inadequacy; instead, take note of what went wrong and resolve to do better. Options include asking your boss for a short chat about ideas for how you could handle the situation differently, crowdsourcing friendly advice from one or two close friends who work in the industry, or asking an industry organization you belong to to chime in with their suggestions. Avoid getting consumed by your negative thoughts for too long because you may need your energy reserves to find a new opportunity and network like it's your full-time job. It's an attitude Jim Curtis adopted after he made the biggest mistake of his career. Read the full story below.

Jim's Story: A Bad Move That Cost Millions

After Jim Curtis (http://jimcurtis.us/) graduated from college, he got what he had worked for so long to achieve: his dream job on the floor of the American Stock Exchange. He had made it all the way to Wall Street from Brockton, Massachusetts, and he was feeling quite proud of himself. However, he quickly found he didn't love his job. In fact, he wasn't even sure he liked it. For Jim, the work didn't incorporate what he was best at and it didn't create a sense of flow or passion for him.

One day, Jim made one of the largest daily trades on the exchange. In a matter of seconds, millions of dollars had been traded. All the traders were in a frenzy, trying to make sense of what was happening: Was it a merger, a takeover, or a random act of God? The truth was, Jim had electronically traded the wrong stock, at the wrong price, for the wrong amount. As soon as he realized what he had done, after a few seconds of what he calls "stomach-dropping dread," he took ownership of his mistake.

"I went to everyone I traded with and asked them—well, begged them—to let me out of the trade," he says. "At that time, you could do this. It wasn't digital to the public. Because I had developed great relationships with the people who worked around me, everyone let me out of the trade. I realized that I was better suited for a different role, one where I could focus on building personal relationships, and I knew I had to find something I was passionate about."

Jim went on to work for a company he had covered on the exchange, OnHealth.com; it was later sold to a very young digital health company, which became WebMD. He played a leadership role in taking the company to IPO before helping develop the health site Everyday Health. According to Jim, the company's combined verticals, which include print publications, Berkeleywellness. com, healthcentral.com, thebody.com, remedyhealthmedia. com, healthcommunities.com, the liveboldlivenow platform, the intelecare.com adherence platform, and other assets, have helped the company grow to be the third largest in reach second only to WebMD Everyday Health. The company is tops in reach for patients with long-term chronic conditions according to Manhattan Research, comScore, and other print circulation audits. Jim says his passion for his work comes from his own experience battling a mysterious chronic illness for more than 20 years.

In his book, *The Stimulati Experience: 9 Skills for Getting Past Pain, Setbacks, and Trauma to Ignite Health and Happiness* (Rodale Books, 2017), Jim helps people transform their struggles into their strength. "You may think that because of an illness, you are not good enough, or you might feel shame as if it is your fault," Jim says. "I had all these issues when I was 'undiagnosed' with a strange neurological condition. It presented much like MS or the ever-expanding Lyme disease, and I went into survival mode—simply dealing with the issue at hand and not making any plans for the future."

WATCH IT!

To learn more about Jim's story, you can watch my interview with him here: entm.ag/jimcurtis.

Jim believes that survival mode is important at the "point of impact" to get you through those first weeks but says we must break out of it to truly become healthy and successful. How do you get out of survival mode? First, Jim says, you have to realize that you are still good enough and that whatever your diagnosis is, it's not your fault. "Cars break down all the time and we don't shame them—we fix them," he says. "Staying positive and continuing to work toward your goals as best you can will help you get well faster or learn to manage your condition better." If you are experiencing a setback due to poor health, Jim suggests this mantra: "My pain is my power—there is nothing I can't do!" Finally, Jim suggests sharing your story to help someone else in your position—which will help you, too.

WHAT TO DO IF YOU CHOSE THE WRONG CAREER PATH

While Jim's mistake on the trading floor helped him discover his passion, you may find the idea of changing careers terrifying. You could be where you are for a long list of reasons. Whether you were pressured to pursue your current career path or didn't have any other options, once you know you're in the wrong place, suddenly your head is flooded with questions and doubts:

+ What am I going to do?
+ How am I going to tell my parents?
+ How is my spouse or significant other going to react?

The anxiety can become a tidal wave, but there are things you can do to make a plan before everything falls off the rails.

Before you start thinking about what you want to do and how you'll break the news to everyone, take the time to remember who you are. If you feel so lost that you can't even do that, reach out to those closest to you and ask them for help, like we talked about in Chapter 4. Ask your "grand jury" of peers and loved ones to describe you in a few words. Ask them what they think you're good at. Ask them to recall when you have seemed unhappy or not yourself.

When I forgot what made me *me*, Jennifer (my North Star) suggested I write a personal tagline in as close to six words as possible so I could have a quick way to remember who I was at my core. Think of your tagline as your email signature or Instagram bio. After thinking about hundreds of buzzwords, I came up with:

Jessica Abo

Journalist by Day

Social Entrepreneur by Choice

That seemed to encompass everything I was doing at the time. Now it's your turn: Take out a piece of paper and write your name at the top. Make a list of your buzzwords and see which ones jump out at you. They could be anything from author, speaker, and philanthropist to father/mother, boyfriend/girlfriend, daughter/son, volunteer, etc.

In addition to the six-word test, Jennifer also asked me to watch Simon Sinek's TED Talk on how to find your why, write my eulogy from a friend's perspective if I died at my current age (I was 32 at the time), and then write another eulogy from the perspective of either someone I knew or someone I

> ## WATCH IT!
>
> You can see Simon's TED Talk here: www.ted.com/talks/simon_sinek_how_great_leaders_inspire_action

didn't know 60 years later. I wrote that eulogy as though my husband was reading it after I died at the age of 92. If you choose to do these exercises, the TED Talk is fascinating. It will force you to ask yourself some tough but awesome questions.

The eulogies will:

+ Help you find a little more clarity about who you are and what you want

+ Help you have a better sense of what you are chasing after
+ Help you find your brand

The best part about doing these for me was the opportunity to hold a mirror up to myself so I could explore more deeply why I was doing what I was doing. They helped me create a filter for gauging what I was going to spend my time, energy, and resources on so I could make decisions that were more in alignment with what I really wanted.

Once you've gone through these exercises, try another exercise I suggest to my clients. Think about what your perfect job would look like and write a full job description for it. If you need some inspiration, go to LinkedIn, look up people you admire, and read how they describe their work. Those key terms may help you find the right language. After you've done that, think about how you want to feel in that job and add that at the bottom of your page.

The goal of all these exercises is to help you face your fears around switching gears, like Simon Huck did when he realized he wasn't meant to be a lawyer.

HOW TO SWITCH CAREER GEARS

Simon Huck knew he loved all things pop culture from the time he was ten. He loved watching all the award shows on TV so much that his parents bought him a subscription to *US Weekly*. In college in Canada, he was working at a part-time retail job, flipping through his beloved *US Weekly*, when he saw an article about PR guru Lizzie Grubman. Simon started to cold-call her office and continued to do so for three weeks.

The bold move got him an internship with Grubman and made him realize that he could not continue down the path he was on. He called his parents and told them that he wanted to switch gears and that he no longer had plans to attend law school. Simon admits that was a tough time for him and says his parents lost faith in how he would make a living. But in time, he showed them that he could follow his passion *and* pay his bills. After working for Grubman and veteran publicist Jonathan Cheban, Simon became the principal owner of Command Entertainment Group (www.commandentertainmentgroup.com). Today, Simon brokers deals between major Fortune 500 companies and celebrities. His work has appeared in more than 70 countries and reached millions of consumers through TV,

WATCH IT!

To see my video with Simon, you can go here: entm.ag/simonhuck.

social media, and other digital platforms. Simon's advice for anyone hesitating to take the leap is to do whatever you need to do to push yourself forward and get over your fears, "whether it's listening to a podcast that motivates you or finding a mentor."

You may not feel as comfortable as Simon when it comes to making a bold move like cold calling. You may be thinking, *Cold-call someone? That's so scary!* And you're right. Cold calling can be awkward, especially in a world where most people communicate screen to screen. But the person you want to contact may not know you want to talk with them—or even that you exist. If you're really serious about turning your mistakes into opportunities like getting an internship, a different job, a meeting with a possible mentor, or even a second chance with a co-worker, you have to be willing to put yourself out there.

You are going to need to dig deep and leave your disappointment behind you so you can be quick and creative with your approach. Not all your attempts are going to be successful on the comeback trail, so get comfortable with rejection. Some things to keep in mind before you pick up the phone:

+ *Rehearse what you want to say and set a timer.* Whatever your reason for calling, write it down and practice your pitch. You should be able to say why you're calling in sound bites. Don't overwhelm the other person with too many details.
+ *Be prepared for the person you're trying to reach to actually pick up the phone.* Let's say you hit the jackpot and the person you're calling actually picks up! Maybe their assistant stepped away or they always answer their own line. Who knows? Don't waste time being caught off guard. Acknowledge your good fortune and get to the point. It also can't hurt to have a few pointers up your

sleeve. Use your time wisely and efficiently by saying something like, "Thank you for talking with me. I'm so glad I was able to reach you. I want to talk with you about [describe the situation briefly] and how I could handle this better in the future" if you've made a mistake on the job. If you are cold-calling a company like Simon did, tell the person why you are calling, such as "I read a lot about you and your company and mission, and I am interested in working for you as part of your amazing team."

+ *Dress the part.* You may find it helpful to actually get dressed before making your cold calls. Getting in work mode can help you get to work! But if you're happiest in your pajamas, that's great, too. Do whatever you need to, whether it's smiling before picking up the phone, looking at pictures of your loved ones, or getting out of bed to make your best first impression. Give yourself every boost you can so you feel like you could do absolutely anything!

+ *Follow up.* As soon as you hang up the phone, send a thank-you note or email to the person you spoke with and then do whatever you said you would. If you said you would send your request via email, send it. If you're supposed to call another number, call it. Don't lose momentum. Go right back to hitting the ground running.

+ *Take a time out.* After you've made your call(s) and completed your follow-up tasks, take a few minutes. Get some fresh air, turn on some music, give yourself some time to regroup—and remember to acknowledge and congratulate yourself for having the courage to make the call(s) and take the first step toward switching career gears.

REFLECTIONS

I hope you're feeling better even if you just messed up on an application or in an interview, made a mistake on the job, or realized you picked the wrong profession. When we see people's posts, it often looks like everyone became successful overnight. For most of us, there have been many bumps and ego bruises along the way. Remember the following tips to get you past the rough patches:

+ Always remember who you are.
+ Try one of the exercises Jennifer had me do to find your tagline and discover your why.
+ If you know what you want to do next, make a list with all the numbers you need, and don't be afraid to pick up the phone. Your new job may be only one call away.

If you got to the person you wanted to reach and they rejected your pitch, your product, or your proposal (or you), we will delve into how you can *still* turn things around in the next chapter.

Chapter 6

Sometimes Being Rejected from Something Good Is Directing You to Something Better

You come out of a great workout and feel like the day is yours.

You check your email on your way out of the gym and stop in

your tracks. *You didn't get the job.* All you have to show after six

rounds of interviews, an all-day presentation, and a group dinner

that made you miss your girlfriend's opening-night performance

is a two-sentence email explaining they went in another direc-

tion. You post to social media: Current Mood: poop emoji. You

know by the time you get off the subway your mother will have

left you 12 voicemails to find out what's going on. #winning

Unfiltered

Getting a job or promotion, getting into college, or hitting any other big milestone isn't an exact science, but in this chapter, I want to help you avoid feeling like you could've done more. With that said, a theme I will repeat throughout this section is this: If you did your best, then that employer, admissions office, or other decision-maker just did you a favor. No matter where you work or go to school, you have skills to offer this world that only you can contribute. So don't forget your value—no matter how many times you get rejected.

HOW YOU CAN TURN REJECTION INTO RESILIENCY

There are universal truths when it comes to rejection. For one, not getting the job or promotion doesn't define who you are or dismiss all you have accomplished. If you got passed over, it means the company or your boss needs more information before they can know if you truly belong there and in that position. It's also possible that you just weren't the right fit for this particular position at this point in time. The first question I ask people who got passed over for a job or promotion is: What did you do outside of your application to let your interest in the company or position be known? From midcareer clients, I often hear, "I got three callbacks, then didn't get chosen. Was it something I said *or didn't do*?"

SMH.

The competition for jobs and promotions today is fierce, especially if you've been stagnant for a few years. You have to be memorable and make a case for yourself. How do you do that?

When you need to convince a company or boss that you're the best candidate, make sure you cover the basics:

+ Include your experience, from your days in the office to your time in the military.
+ Submit solid references.
+ Be clear about why you feel you are the best person for the job or promotional position.

The more of these boxes you can check, the easier it will be for a company or boss to understand how much you want the position. If

Unfiltered

you're missing items from this list, getting the job isn't impossible. You just need to work that much harder. You also may need to potentially give yourself more credit for your life experiences that relate to the skills required for the position. Here are some ideas:

+ *Write down your relevant skills.* Think about the skills required for the position you want. Now write them down and add some information about where you acquired each of the skills and what experiences you had to develop them.
+ *Create talking points for your meeting, phone call, or other interactions.* A great way to get a sense of what's happening in the company is to check out its social media and publications, like its annual report (if it is a publicly held company), white papers, law review, or medical journal. Read up on what's making headlines, not just for that company but also in the industry, so you can have a thoughtful conversation or digital interaction that goes beyond the mundane stuff.
+ *Follow up.* After your meeting, send the people you met a *hand-written* thank-you note. Often, the person you met will put it in your file.
+ *Curate your file.* When you work at a company, the HR department creates a file for you. Your annual reviews and any other information about you go into it. Be aware that there may be notes or items in your file you don't know about. Keep copies of all your annual reviews so you can refer to them as you apply for promotions and other jobs outside the company.

You have to be willing to go out of your comfort zone. An HR representative or even your boss may not be able to pick up on the amazing person you are through your application, so make sure that your file and everything you present say what you want that person to know about you.

Another universal truth about rejection: It's not always about you. It could be about them. Your boss or the HR person hiring for the position may have had someone in mind—and you don't fit the avatar they envisioned. They could also have met three people before you that fit their idea of the perfect candidate, so by the time they got to you, they were already done looking. They just wanted to see who else was out there so they could confirm they had made the right selection. They could also have had a quota to meet for the number of applicants they had to interview prior to making their decision. The truth is you'll most likely never know why they didn't select you.

Not taking it personally when you don't get hired is a real challenge for many people. However, it is essential to learn so you can rapidly move on to addressing another opportunity that might actually be better for you in the long run.

If you really feel like you need to know why they didn't hire you, you can always ask. Some will tell you; others won't. If you can find out why they didn't select you, it may shed light on some areas where they felt you need to improve. Keep in mind not everyone will be willing to share these insights with you, so if you don't receive a response to your inquiry, don't take it personally. Move on.

Another universal truth: personal satisfaction matters. So you didn't get the first job or promotion you went for. Does that really mean you are a complete failure? Not at all! In fact, it may be a sign that you should step back and evaluate why you even wanted that job or promotion in the first place. More than a raise or better-paying job, personal satisfaction in our professional lives is more important than ever in today's fast-moving world. The more satisfied we are at work, the more confident we tend to feel in our relationships at home, the sports we play, and the other activities we get involved in. Make sure you are going for a new position for the right reasons so you can increase your satisfaction, not just your bank account.

#MYSTORY: Planes, Trains, Automobiles, and a Cardboard Ellen

Forty-three. That's how many jobs I applied for while working in a toxic environment in Vermont. While I met some of the most talented, loving people on the planet during my two years at that job, there were a few people who went out of their way to let me know they did not want me there and who on more than one occasion tried to sabotage my work. After I reached the

Unfiltered

one-year mark, I spent my second year trying to move on. Those 43 job interviews were in different markets, so I was in my car or on a plane every chance I got. While I was a finalist many times, none of those opportunities worked out. I was so desperate to get out of that newsroom that I decided to apply to law school.

My schedule was brutal. I woke up at 2 A.M. for the morning show and often got sent on assignments that wouldn't get me back to the newsroom until around 4 or 5 P.M. I would run home to eat dinner, go to Kaplan for my LSAT course, and be home and in bed around 10 P.M. During that time, I also applied to the White House Fellows program. I spent months working on my application and essays and was one of the youngest people in the country to make it to the regional finals, but I didn't make the final cut. During this miserable time, I couldn't let go of the TV dream. Since I really wanted to be a talk-show host and pursued a news career to help me get there, I decided it was time to use my reporting experience in a different way.

I had learned *The Ellen DeGeneres Show* had stronger ratings in Los Angeles than it did in New York, so I emailed every member of her staff asking if I could meet with them when I was out in Los Angeles. One producer responded agreeing to meet. When I got out to Los Angeles, I told her my idea, and she said she loved it. She told me to put a pilot together and send it to her. She introduced me to other producers in the office and told me all about her career and a book she wrote. We walked out of the lot together, and before I walked back to my rental car, she said, "You're going to be a star." Suddenly, I felt elated and was ready to fly back to Vermont to start planning the production of my pilot.

The next step was driving from Vermont to New York City with an extremely tall cutout of Ellen that barely fit in my car. I recruited my old videographer, Bill Evans, and my cousins, Matthew and Eric Rosenberg, and we hit the streets. Matt held a boom box and played music from a playlist I made. Eric got people's names and asked for their permission to be in my pilot video.

Unfiltered

I nearly passed out when *Ellen*'s executive producer called me after I got back to Vermont. "Jessica, your DVD is the buzz around my office. What are you looking to do exactly?" I explained that I wanted to be Ellen's New York correspondent and how I could bring the cutout of her to premieres, red carpet events, you name it. He asked me if I had any plans to be in Los Angeles and I said yes, which was a total lie. I had just been there for a friend's wedding and was making $25,000 a year. I called my parents and told them I had to fly back to Los Angeles. My mom has always been my biggest cheerleader and told me not to worry; she and my dad would take care of it. I flew out to Los Angeles and stayed with my friend Brad. Every morning, I called the executive producer's office and was told to call back at a certain time. When I called back, I would be told to call at another designated time. This went on for the three days I was in Los Angeles.

On my last day there, another producer was nice enough to take my call and offered some advice on how to get into the talk show world. I asked her if she would be willing to meet me, even for five minutes, and she said she couldn't leave her office. The woman who told me I would be a star completely blew me off. I had even bought and read her book.

Then I was back on the plane. By then, I had gotten into law school, been rejected from the White House Fellows program, and left completely crushed by the *Ellen* experience. I sent the DVD to everyone I knew in the business, including mentors, former professors, people I interned for at *Dateline NBC*, and family friends who "knew people" in the business. One day, a network executive called and asked if I had watched *Ellen* that day. I had worked a double shift covering a fire, so I missed it. He told me he saw the episode out of the corner of his eye and saw the show had taken my idea—they just didn't take me with it. I was able to connect with a producer to see what had happened. "I'm so sorry," she said. "At least you know you're on the right track. Don't give up." I think that made me feel worse. If you want to see the video, it's on YouTube. Just search my name and Ellen DeGeneres. If you can click now, you can watch it here:

▶ entm.ag/ellen

Fast-forward a few years. I left *Ellen* behind and finally got that dream job with NY1 where I spent the next ten years. After I did well on my current events quiz, the person interviewing me said she was impressed I knew so much about the people running New York and the events NY1 was covering. Her quiz was about five pages long. The practice test I made for myself the night before (and studied all night long) was more than 12. She asked me for a copy of my test to give to future job candidates. Shortly after that, I finally started working at NY1.

HOW TO HOLD ON TO YOUR HAPPINESS WHILE YOU'RE WAITING FOR YOUR BIG BREAK

So while you busy yourself with turning your lemons into lemonade and creating something positive out of your rejection, remember that all is not completely lost. Just because one area of your life is not looking anything like your friends' posts about how they're "crushing it" at work doesn't mean you don't have a lot to be proud of in other departments. Different aspects of our lives ebb and flow—sometimes you'll have a great day at work or get the big break you've worked so hard for. Other days, your personal life will shine while your career just sort of exists in the background. Some days, it all sucks. Some days, it all rocks. What's most important is that you can find joy somewhere—even while you're waiting for the tide to turn in your direction. Take my friend Jonah Platt, for example.

By all accounts, both on social media and IRL, things are working out for Jonah Platt. From 2015 to 2016, he starred in the Broadway hit musical *Wicked*, and on Easter Sunday 2018, he was part of the live performance of *Jesus Christ Superstar* on NBC. While these life-changing opportunities came through, he will tell you there have been hundreds of other times that he's struck out. "I'm two steps down the road out of the 100 I need to take to get where I want to be," he told me during an interview on a rehearsal break.

Jonah says his career path has taught him how to handle what we covered in Chapter 5: how to overcome when you've messed up and how to course correct when you find yourself in the wrong place.

Unfiltered

During his senior year at the University of Pennsylvania, Jonah decided he wanted to be a TV writer and worked on a script. He shared it with a family friend who was an agent, and that got him a meeting. "I sucked in the meeting," Jonah says. "I wasn't prepared. I was so green. I didn't know how to sell myself and didn't get that job." Jonah says when you find yourself in a similar situation, you have to learn from it. "You also have to remember that you had enough talent to get the meeting in the first place, so blowing an interview doesn't mean you're never going to work in that industry," he adds. So if you're still recovering from a major interview fail, remember you have skills—you just need to polish your interviewing ones.

After he graduated, Jonah landed his first writing job. "I worked on two shows that got canceled after six episodes," he says. "I worked on another show that was so successful that there wasn't room for me to show what I could do." No matter what industry you want to work in, sometimes it all comes down to luck. In TV writing, Jonah says, "You have to be at the right place at the right time. You have to have the right showrunner who gives you opportunities. If you have a boss that's not willing to elevate you, you have to ask yourself how long you can be happy in a subordinate position."

Jonah knew it was time for him to pivot after five years in the business. He was working on a show and a lightbulb went off. "I was pitching jokes that people thought were funny, but that wasn't enough. When you sit in a writer's room, it comes down to, "Can you *sell* your joke?" It doesn't necessarily matter if your joke is the funniest. Because I was young, and at the assistant level, I didn't have everyone's trust, and I knew I'd have a better shot at getting my jokes scripted if a more senior writer pitched them. That reality was too frustrating for me, so I decided to put a career writing for someone else on hold," he says.

While he spent time figuring out his next move, a childhood friend called and said he was doing a reading for a musical and the lead male had just dropped out. Jonah got the part, and several more lead roles followed. With more confidence and a bigger profile, Jonah began spending 10 percent of his time writing and 90 percent acting. His next break came when he got a job performing in *Hair* at the Hollywood

Bowl. He was the only noncelebrity to be cast as a lead, and he met his wife, Courtney, during that production, too. Jonah says he's been fortunate to have some incredible experiences, but as an actor, social media can destroy you if you let it.

This goes back to what I said earlier: Know your worth. Just because things don't always go your way doesn't mean you are a complete and utter failure. It's important to make sure you are looking at yourself through the right lens, not comparing and despairing over what everyone else is posting about on social media or saying around the water cooler at work. Some days you'll feel like you're on top of the world. Other days, you may feel like you just won a first-class ticket to the cellar, and you'll have to find a way to stand back up, brush off your knees, and keep moving forward.

If you think that's hard in a corporate job or as an entrepreneur, think about how difficult it can be for actors. Audition after audition followed by rejection after rejection makes it more and more difficult to muster the confidence to try again and have the patience and courage to keep going after your dream.

HOW TO BE THE STAR OF YOUR OWN LIFE

"Nobody knows how frustrating it can be to be on Instagram more than an actor," Jonah says. "You might have blown an audition in the morning and then see your friend on set, working, and think, 'I'm terrible. I'm never going to make it.'" Jonah says the key to his success has been understanding his journey is his own. "I'm in a unique position because of who my brother is [Ben Platt, best known for his Tony Award winning role in *Dear Evan Hansen*]," Jonah says. "I'm where I'm at, while my brother's career is exploding at the same time. It's one thing to ignore your friend's career; it's a different story when it's your sibling."

Jonah says to hold on to your happiness, you have a choice: You can be happy for your friends/family and know your time will come, or you can let it send you into a deep spiral of self-doubt and hatred. "I never wanted to be a bitter brother or unsupportive friend, so to be able to separate myself and have my own journey has been helpful," he says. "It solidifies that I'm doing my own thing and that it will take as long as it takes, but I'm confident that I'll get to where I want to be." In other words—do your thing on your own terms. It doesn't matter how long it takes to get there, just keep going.

REFLECTIONS

In this chapter, we discussed why you have to be ready to make your case to earn a place at your dream job. We also went into why it's important to consider being rejected as resiliency training. Let's review some things you can do to prepare:

+ What are you most proud of? Is that story part of your application or interview notes?
+ What have you done to go above and beyond to show a company that you want to work there or want that promotion? This is the time to share what you've done, but don't overdo it!
+ Have you asked the best people you know to write you a letter of recommendation for a new job or position? Have you notified your job references that they may receive an email or call?
+ If you're making a pitch for a promotion or new job (or auditioning for a role), have you practiced with anyone?
+ If you've been rejected, did you give yourself some time to be upset? Are you at the point where you need to pick up the pieces and move on? If the answer is yes, who or what can help you figure out your next move? If you're not sure, do a search on LinkedIn to see who in your network is doing exactly what you want to do (or at least something close to it).

When you feel there is something you just *have* to do, you will stop at nothing to do it. So if you can't imagine your life without something, never stop working for it. No matter where you are in this process, keep your head up. If you can't seem to do that these days because you're facing social rejection on a daily basis, the next chapter is dedicated to how to cope with a bully.

Part Three

Taking Back Your Happiness

Chapter 7

How to Outsmart Your Bully

You're sitting at your desk when your colleague walks into the office. She says hello to everyone but you, says she's doing a coffee run, and asks everyone what they would like—except you. She starts to talk to another colleague in a whisper. They both look at you and laugh. You post a picture of you and your awesome family. #loved #lucky

Unfiltered

If you're being bullied at work, at home, or in your social circle, it's easy to hide your pain on social media because you usually only showcase the parts of your life you want people to see. Every now and then, you will see someone post that they're having a bad day or going through a hard time, but, sadly, in most of the news stories about a bullied person taking their own life, the people around them say they had no idea things were so bad. In the cases where people did know and try to help, we're reminded we have so much work to do to protect victims of bullying. What's crazy to me is that unlike outgrowing other things from childhood, some adults don't ever seem to give up bullying.

While I believe that certain people are placed in our lives for us to learn important lessons, no one deserves to be bullied. I combed through hundreds of articles and interviewed experts to help you outsmart the bully in your life, but there isn't a tried-and-true formula that will work for every situation. The same goes for your legal rights because anti-bullying legislation varies depending on where you live.

ARE YOU BEING BULLIED?

According to the Centers for Disease Control and the Department of Education's federal uniform definition of bullying for research and surveillance, the core elements of bullying include unwanted aggressive behavior; observed or perceived power imbalance; and repetition of behaviors or high likelihood of repetition. There are several types of bullying, so let's use the Bullying Behavior Assessment in Figure 7.1 on page 93 to identify what you, or someone you know, may be facing.

The first step experts recommend is to share what is going on with someone you trust or you feel is trustworthy. Depending on what's happening to you, the bullying behavior may be ruled unlawful or fall into criminal categories, such as harassment, hazing, or assault. If you want to know your legal rights, you can look up your state's anti-bullying laws since they vary. "For example, New Jersey has one of the most comprehensive definitions in the country," Danielle Reiffe, a licensed clinical social worker, says. "It includes gender identity, but not every state includes gender identity/expression." Wherever you live, and whatever the case may be, you don't have to suffer through this alone.

Unfiltered

FIGURE 7.1: **Bullying Behavior Assessment**

Put a check in the yes or no column when answering the following questions:

	Yes	No
1. Is someone saying or writing mean things about you?		
2. Is someone teasing you and/or calling you names?		
3. Is someone making inappropriate sexual comments to you or about you?		
4. Is someone taunting you or threatening to hurt you?		
5. Is someone hurting your reputation and/or relationships?		
6. Is someone leaving you out on purpose?		
7. Is someone telling other people not to be friends with you?		
8. Is someone spreading rumors about you?		
9. Is someone embarrassing you in public?		
10. Is someone physically hurting you or destroying your possessions?		
11. Is someone tormenting you by hitting, kicking, or pinching you?		
12. Is someone spitting at you or on you?		
13. Is someone tripping you or pushing you?		
14. Is someone taking your belongings?		
15. Is someone being mean or making rude hand gestures?		
16. Is someone being verbally aggressive with you online?		
17. Is someone sending you threatening messages or harassing you online?		
18. Is someone spreading rumors about you online?		
19. Has someone modified, disseminated, damaged, or destroyed your privately stored information?		
20. Has someone made a fake account on your behalf using your private information?		

For this chapter, I asked Danielle and other experts to weigh in on what we can do to prevent a bully from getting the best of us, as well as how we can support someone who is being bullied, whether it's our

FIGURE 7.1: **Bullying Worksheet,** continued

Identify the Bullying Behavior

If you answered "YES" to any question from 1–4, you may be the victim of verbal bullying.

If you answered "YES" to any question from 5–9, you may be the victim of social bullying.

If you answered "YES" to any question from 10–15, you may be the victim of physical bullying.

If you answered "YES" to any question from 16–20, you may be the victim of cyber-bullying.

---

child, a student, or a colleague. I will highlight the roles empathy and self-compassion play in bullying, what we all can do to be upstanders, and stress (again) how you have the power within you to access your gifts to power through this pain point.

#MYSTORY: Keep Your Head Up

In seventh grade, I started a new school, and the two most popular girls did not like me from day one. In school, I was miserable, but I smiled through it every day. Every week, we attended a chapel service. Even though I am Jewish, I loved the school itself because I had great teachers, learned so much about leadership, and liked participating in the chapel services. But while the student body was joined in prayer, I was busy thinking up ways I could miss school so I would not have to feel so heavy-hearted. I thought if I fainted and hit my head on the pew, I could end up in the hospital and be out for a few days. While my classmates were listening to the liturgy and scripture, I was calculating how I could make myself faint.

The worst parts of the school day were walking in the hallway between classes and dumping my tray at lunch. I tried to time my day so that I would not have to see anyone from this clique and the mean comments, echoing laughter, and stares. My mom was determined to help me get through this experience and come out a stronger person: "Jessie, go stand in the garage and walk into the house. I will sit here and stare at you, OK? You have to walk by me and keep your head up. If you put your head down, you have to go back into the garage and try again."

After many attempts, I managed to keep my head up during her "stare" exercise, but while her intentions were good, things in school did not get better. This group of girls left mean notes in my locker. They called my house at bizarre hours of the night and breathed heavily into the phone before hanging up. They made fun of me the minute they saw me and would call me names like "fat pig" when the most popular boys were around. One day, an older sister came to pick up some of the mean girls from school. When she saw me cross the street to get to my mom's car, she stepped on the gas as if she were going to hit me. A few people from my class saw what happened, which made it even more humiliating.

Since my parents knew about everything that was going on, they asked me every day if we could have a meeting with school officials. I made them promise that they would not do anything because I was already so embarrassed that I was 12 years old and the target of someone else's torment. Somehow, these monsters made me feel that asking for help would make me even smaller. Somewhere in all this, I was ashamed that I could not handle it on my own. My parents and I finally ended up having a meeting with school officials, which helped a little. I got through that year by focusing on the people and activities I loved.

STAY IN YOUR OWN LANE

To survive the mean girls' bullying behavior in middle school without crumbling into a million pieces, I learned that I could control what I chose to focus my attention on. I spent a lot of time with my sister, Alyssa. She always had thicker skin than I did and tried her hardest to make me a stronger person. I also spent hours on the phone with my camp friends, Jill Hollander and Jessica Poznik, who lived hours away from me. I found high school easier because I was president of my class, got involved in the school musicals, and played sports. Instead of focusing on everyone else, I had learned how to stay in my own lane. Over time, the mean girls stopped being mean, and we all moved past seventh grade and became friends. And that's what you might need to do as well to get through a rough patch of bullying.

After spending years on the road talking to teens and professional adults around the country, I have heard many stories that mirrored my own. In many cases, what I went through is nothing compared to what some teens and adults have shared with me. Social media gives mean people a bigger opportunity to access us individually and reach into our personal worlds. It is scary. So I want you to know three things:

1. If you are a victim of someone else's pain, this is temporary.
2. If you are a bully, you can't fix yourself by breaking someone else.
3. This experience may influence your life's work.

Keep your eyes forward on what you want to do and where you want to go.

Open Up Wednesdays

While working in TV news for 15 years, I often gravitated toward the underdog stories. However, any time I covered a bullying story or read that another teenager took their life, I always felt sick to my stomach.

Our world has made many advances since I was a teenager, but when it comes to being kind, we still have so much work to do. I will never forget the day I covered the story about a student at Rutgers University who took his own life. Tyler Clementi's roommate had used a webcam to capture Tyler kissing another man and posted the encounter online. Tyler killed himself by

Open Up Wednesdays, continued

jumping off the George Washington Bridge. It pains me to know so many people are hurting and that ending it all seems like their only way out.

I started my YouTube channel, JaboTV, so it could be a positive resource for people who were looking to turn their struggles into strength and to be an answer for people asking: Am I the only one who feels like this? The first series I did was called, "Open Up Wednesday," (OUW), and I kicked it off with YouTuber Tyler Oakley. I had no idea who he was, but teens I interviewed before launching the channel told me I *had* to interview him. My friend Robyn Fink happened to be at a PR agency that was hosting an event with him, so I showed up with my crew, and he and his publicist, Lisa Filipelli, were more than happy to support my new channel even though I didn't have a single subscriber yet. Tyler talked about how he got through high school and shared his advice for other teens. Every week I asked athletes, celebrities, CEOs, changemakers, and influencers to share an OUW moment (pronounced ow!) and how they POUWERed through it.

We all have our OUW moments and go through experiences that make us forget how much we have to offer. If you are carrying around the mean things people are saying about you or doing to you, I beg you to remember, and celebrate, everything that makes you *you*.

You can see my full interview with Tyler Oakley here:

▶️ entm.ag/tyleroakley

START WITH KINDNESS

There are several ways to break the cycle of bullying. First, know your worth and help others cultivate that sense in themselves. In addition to being aware of what makes us worthy, clinical psychologist Tara Cousineau (www.taracousineau.com) says being empathetic is the number-one way we can support the people around us. "Our empathy muscles are like the muscles we work hard to strengthen at the gym. They need training and practice in order to work at their peak when we need them," she says. But, she adds, it's not a surprise that our empathy muscles need more attention.

"Today's societal pressures and attitudes reinforce independence, competition, social comparison, self-absorption, and personal achievement—hardly the seeds for empathy," Cousineau writes in her 2018 article, "Leading with a Kind Mind" (www.leader-values.com/wordpress/leading-with-a-kind-mind-tara-cousineau-phd). In her book, *The Kindness Cure* (New Harbinger Publications, 2018), Cousineau addresses how narcissism is on the rise and empathy is on the decline. Since we live in what she calls a "cool to be cruel culture," she says that now more than ever, we all need remedial training in empathy and mindfulness. "I call it kindfulness because I think it's really about sort of being aware in the present moment with *heart* vs. just being aware in the present moment," she says.

It's a practice she says falls off the grid early in our lives. While we all think it's a good idea for young children to be kind, Cousineau says some parents assume other people are teaching their children kindness or they're seeing kindness happening in their community. Unfortunately, she says, the emphasis on being kind stops around third grade. Instead of promoting a culture that's empathetic and positive, all our attention goes toward *not* engaging in negative behaviors, like drinking, doing drugs, and being a bully. While these lessons are extremely important, Cousineau says spending so much time on preventing negative behavior keeps us from teaching others, and ourselves, positive behavior like how to be compassionate to others and ourselves. "Research on helping shows it's a great preventive for teens and risky behavior. When teens engage, even just an hour a week, in helping somebody outside their family, it prevents them from getting involved in substance abuse or unprotected sex and things like that because it takes them out of the 'me' mode and into the 'we' mode," she says.

That's why Cousineau believes that teaching kindness is just as important as any other life skill we impart to our kids, campers, students, employees, or mentees.

"We have to be intentional about where we direct our attitude toward helping. We need to be intentional about being thankful and what we appreciate," she adds. She suggests starting your day by committing to doing one nice thing for someone and one thing to better care for yourself, whether it's getting a good night's sleep, calling a friend, getting some fresh air, exercising, or eating healthy.

Aviva Goldstein (whom you read about in Chapter 1) has done extensive research on bullying. She counsels parents and children in schools and through her private practice. When it comes to seeing someone being bullied, whether around a board game or in the boardroom, she says empathy plays a big role in leading people to stand up to bullies. "What's fascinating is that when one person stands up and intervenes or provides support (emotional or physical) to the victim, others almost always follow suit, which leads the victim to find her/himself surrounded by people trying to help and a reduction in feelings of isolation," Goldstein says. Besides being a good, supportive person, she says there are other benefits to being what's called an "upstander." "If you are known as someone who helps others, then if a time should come that you need someone's help, there are collections of people who feel connected to you and might be more likely to come to your assistance. Without knowing it, the one action of sticking up for someone can have a long-lasting domino effect of creating community and cultivating connection."

It's clear from what Cousineau and Goldstein have to say that we need to be more kind to the people around us and to ourselves to become more empathetic on a daily basis. But they say it's also important to understand the motivations of a bully and the environments that might breed their behavior.

ARE YOU CREATING A TOXIC ENVIRONMENT?

Goldstein believes we would all benefit if we invested more in constructing human foundations that led to people moving away from being passive bystanders and toward being productive upstanders. Here's what she wants you to ask yourself if you're in charge of kids or managing adults:

+ What am I doing (passively or actively) to promote a culture at home, school, or work in which bullying is tolerated?
+ What am I doing (passively or actively) to promote a culture at home, school, or work of bystanding?
+ What am I doing (passively or actively) to promote a culture at home, school, or work of upstanding?
+ Have my children/students/colleagues heard me say nasty things about others?
+ Have my children/students/colleagues seen me keep silent when others have said nasty things about others?
+ How have I responded (in voice, body language, and action) when someone has confided in me that they've either experienced or witnessed bullying?

If you can identify ways in which you are passively or actively promoting negative behavior and a toxic environment, Goldstein recommends doing something counterintuitive and unexpected: Make it about you. You might think that the emphasis should be on the victim or the perpetrator, but by inserting yourself into the scenario, you give yourself the nudge you might need to take responsibility for changing the current dynamic. She suggests engaging in conversation with a victim of the toxic behavior and/or environment and making statements of awareness, empathy, inquiry, and action. Try statements like these:

+ *Awareness*: I recognize that what's been going on isn't OK. I realize that [specific behavior] has made you/others feel uncomfortable, and that has to stop. Everyone has the right to feel safe at home/school/work.
+ *Empathy*: I am so sorry to hear about your experience. Thank you for trusting me with your stories. I will be here to support you.
+ *Inquiry*: What can I do to change this? Who should I bring into this conversation? What do you need/want from me?

+ *Action*: I am committed to playing a role in changing the situation. I am capable of . . .

By emphasizing the "I" in each statement, you take upon yourself the authority to do whatever is in your power to adjust the problematic paradigm.

How This Bullied Teen Became a Teen CEO

Valerie Weisler grew up in a suburban home. Surrounded by a white picket fence and friendly neighbors, she will tell you her early years looked pretty normal to any outsider. But inside her home, life revealed a different story. A few days before her first day of ninth grade, Val's parents sat her and her brother down and told them they were getting a divorce.

In the days that followed, Val went from being a happy teenager who never stopped talking to being painfully shy and quiet. That was all it took for a group of girls in her school. "It was like something out of a Disney Channel Original movie," Val says. "They would wait for me at my locker every morning. I'd come in, and they'd watch as I'd open my locker and notes would come pouring out, telling me I shouldn't have even come to school."

At first, Val says, she felt sorry for herself. "They called me a mute."

Then one day, Val saw a boy getting bullied at *his* locker.

"It was like I woke up from a really long nap I wasn't supposed to take," she says. "And I went up to the boy and said two words that would change my life and save his life. I said, 'You matter. We are going to get through this together. I am in the same boat.' He started to cry and told me he had been bullied all his life but

How This Bullied Teen Became a Teen CEO, continued

that someone coming up to him and saying, *Hey, I see you; you're not invisible,* really validated him and gave him this new hope to go on. This made me realize how lucky I was. Yes, my situation was truly tough, but at the end of the day, I had an incredible support system from my community. Some kids went from being bullied at school to the same hurt at home. Hearing this boy's story ignited a fire inside of me. I had a choice. I could let the bullying drown me, or I could use this struggle to do something about it. When I got home from school that day, I googled how to make a website. I sat at my kitchen table for six hours designing The Validation Project (TVP)."

At 14 years old, and still too scared to talk, Val emailed back and forth with other bullied kids from her school. Her makeshift website went from being a place where kids from school emailed her to a place where bullied kids from all over New York started to reach out. Then came emails from all over the United States and then kids in Israel and Poland and Spain and Uganda.

"They were coming with many different struggles—not just bullying. Some didn't like the way they looked in the mirror, some didn't have a school to learn at, and some didn't have a family. But one thing that each kid always came with, no matter where they were from or what they were going through, was a passion—something that kept them going and inspired them," she says.

That is how it all started: Google, a website, and countless emails. In five years, The Validation Project has become a global organization that works with 6,000 teenagers in 105 countries, turning passions into positive action through unique mentoring

How This Bullied Teen Became a Teen CEO, continued

and community service programs. The Validation Project ultimately designed a pro-kindness curriculum that teaches educators and students how to work together to solve problems in their communities. It is taught at more than 1,000 schools around the globe. Val has spoken at the White House and served as an ambassador for the U.S. State Department during the Obama administration. She is making the world a safer place by being willing to find answers for herself and anyone else who needed to be validated, too.

REFLECTIONS

You don't deserve to be hurt, humiliated, or harassed by *anybody*. If the person you tell doesn't do anything to help you, find someone else who will. Keep trying to get help until someone does listen! While we can't control a bully's behavior, whether it's a parent, child, colleague, stranger, neighbor, or troll, we can choose where we put our energy. I know it may seem hard to pivot and focus on something good like an activity you love, volunteering, or spending time with different circles outside your negative environment, but sometimes it's on us to choose something positive to focus on—even during the darkest times. If you want to be proactive, remember:

+ Be an upstander.
+ Look at the culture you're perpetuating.
+ Make sure you make empathy part of your daily routine.
+ Pay attention to the new person in school/at the office.
+ Keep a record of what's happening to you or whoever is being bullied.
+ Talk to someone you trust about how to solve the problem.

Unfiltered

When there doesn't seem to be a solution, do your best to focus on the good things in your life. If you're in a situation where you feel you're being harassed or discriminated against, I want you to know what resources are available. In the next chapter, we will look at different laws and a sampling of workplace scenarios to help you understand your rights.

Chapter 8

Know Your Rights in the Workplace

You meet your friends after work, and they ask if everything is OK. Everyone agrees you haven't been yourself lately. You say you're just tired. How can you tell them your boss tried to kiss you? Will they even believe you, or will they think it's your fault? You post a picture of your group raising your glasses in a toast so everything looks normal. #girlsnightout

Unfiltered

There are many reasons a person may be unhappy at work. When you go online and see pictures of other people's lives, they may remind you just how awful your work situation is. If you're being harassed at work, I want you to know your rights. Knowledge is power, and you are entitled to feel safe at work.

In light of all the courageous people across the globe, from actresses to athletes, facing to their bullies and speaking out about sexual harassment, many took to social media to share their #MeToo stories. Maybe you shared yours. Actor and activist Alysia Reiner (http://alysiareiner.com) was motivated to join hundreds of celebrities behind the Time's Up movement (www.timesupnow.com), working to ensure safety and equality for all in the workplace. "Our first initiative was to launch The Legal Defense Fund (www.timesupnow.com/#resources-anchor), which raised more than $20 million in less than a month," she says. "It allows women and men to get free legal counseling pertaining to sexual harassment in the workplace. It is not just for people in Hollywood; it's for anyone and everyone facing harassment: farmers, hotel workers, accountants, sanitation workers, bankers, etc. While the fund was raised with Hollywood awareness, its purpose is to bring aid and awareness across all industries."

For Alysia, the movement is personal. After reading the #MeToo stories and news headlines, she says her own bad memories have resurfaced: "How many deeply inappropriate situations I was in, how I blamed myself, and those where there was borderline sexual assault." That's why she's so committed to helping people get the space they need to heal and the tools they need to process what they've experienced. "Taking action and being part of the solution is part of my healing," she says. "I don't like to talk about things too much—I like to get to work changing them." Right now, she wants to figure out how we can all come together around this problem. "We have the potential at this moment to make outrageous change," she adds.

But for some people, the change has to start at the micro level. If you feel you're facing workplace harassment or discrimination, educate yourself so you know what steps to take to change your situation.

KNOW YOUR RIGHTS

Regardless of whatever else is going on, you have the right to work in a safe place. Unfortunately, that doesn't mean you won't come across a co-worker, supervisor, or manager who is an asshole. You know—the kind of person who turns your office into a hostile and intimidating place for the entire team, not just you. "Working for a boss who is always in a bad mood and shouts curse words at everyone means you're working for an Equal Opportunity Asshole," employment lawyer Tom Spiggle says. He left his job as a federal prosecutor to start The Spiggle Law Firm (www.spigglelaw.com), which specializes in sexual harassment, wrongful termination, and pregnancy and caregiver discrimination. While working with a jerk is awful, "in order for you to have a harassment claim, someone's behavior must violate Title VII of the Civil Rights Act of 1964, or a host of other federal laws,

which make it illegal for someone to be targeted based on a protected class," he says. "For example, age and disability are not protected classes under Title VII. Your age is protected by the Age Discrimination in Employment Act and someone's disability is protected by the Americans with Disabilities Act (ADA)."

I asked Spiggle to walk me through the different types of protected classes. Check out the categories in the "Harassment Worksheet" in Figure 8.1 on page 108 to see if you are possibly being harassed.

Spiggle says if you answer "Yes" to any of those questions, you may have an actionable legal claim and should talk to a lawyer to make sure you understand the law. "Political affiliation and marital status are not

TIP

In addition to the forms of harassment and discrimination listed above, Spiggle says you should be aware that unwanted touching is a separate claim: "That falls under assault and battery, which are crimes that should be reported to the police." They can also be the basis of a civil action that you can bring in court. Spiggle recommends talking to a lawyer ASAP if you are being inappropriately touched at work.

FIGURE 8.1: **Harassment Worksheet**

Put a check in the yes or no column when answering the following questions:

	Yes	No
1. Is someone harassing you based on your race?		
2. Is someone harassing you based on your national origin?		
3. Is someone harassing you based on your political beliefs?		
4. Is someone harassing you based on your religious beliefs?		
5. Is someone harassing you based on your gender?		
6. Is someone harassing you based on your gender identification?		
7. Is someone harassing you based on your sexual orientation?		
8. Is someone harassing you based on your age?		
9. Is someone harassing you based on your physical or mental disability?		
10. Is someone harassing you based on your marital status?		
11. Is someone harassing you based on your veteran status?		
12. Is someone harassing you based on your reporting illegal behaviors?		

directly protected by Title VII, though marital status could be implicated under Title VII if, for instance, an employer fired unmarried women with children but not men. There are a number of state and even local ordinances across the U.S. that do make illegal discrimination and harassment on the basis of political affiliation and marital status," which is why Spiggle recommends you seek legal help. If you feel you can't afford an attorney, Alysia suggests reaching out to the Time's Up Legal Defense Fund (https://nwlc.org/times-up-legal-defense-fund/).

While writing this book, I expected to come across people who had been on a bad date, gone through a friendshift, or didn't love their job. I never expected to interview so many men and women who feel they have no support at work or are afraid of their employer. The majority of the people I interviewed felt there was no point in reporting an issue to HR because HR could not be trusted or they feared retaliation. In other cases, a company was so small there was no HR department, so employees were left to fend for themselves.

So what are your options?

HOW TO REPORT BULLYING AND HARASSING BEHAVIORS AT WORK

The Equal Employment Opportunity Commission (EEOC) is the federal agency that enforces Title VII. Spiggle says whether or not you have a legal case depends, in part, on where you live because the case law on what constitutes a hostile work environment can vary from state to state. Since federal law doesn't make a distinction between bullying and harassment in the workplace, you must refer to your state's anti-bullying and anti-harassment laws to see what your rights are, though Spiggle notes that anti-bullying laws generally only apply to school or a school-related setting. That said, familiarizing yourself with both anti-bullying and anti-harassment laws is a useful exercise if you are unsure of how to approach a strategy. Other resources to check can be local and state law. "For instance, the DC Human Rights Act covers a broad range of workplace conduct; therefore, an employee working in the District of Columbia has legal protections that exceed federal protections," he says.

Here's Spiggle's advice on the steps to take if you think you're being harassed or discriminated against based on your protected class.

1. *Keep notes.* Make sure you have a list of what happened, where, who it involved, and when. Keep track of who witnessed the behavior, and save all paper or electronic trails related to your case (emails, texts, pictures, etc.).
2. *Consult your company handbook or employer's code of conduct.* It's important to know what behavior your company addresses so you know if someone, at the very least, is violating company policy.

Unfiltered

3. *Call your company's hotline.* You can report a hostile work environment or harassment claim through your company's 1-800 number or another method for reporting harassment. The mechanism for reporting can usually be found in your handbook or similar guidance.

4. *Protect yourself from retaliation.* If you work in a company with 15 people or more and go directly to a decision-maker—or you put a claim in writing—saying, "I believe I am the subject of harassment against a protected class . . ." you may be legally protected from retaliation. Even if what you were subjected to is deemed not to be harassment, the fact that you reported it protects you by law. If you work in a company with less than 15 employees, this protection may not apply to you, so check your state law or ask a lawyer. If you are looking for an attorney who represents employees, the National Employment Lawyers Association (www.nela.org) is a good place to start. Avvo (www.avvo.com) or asking your county bar association about their lawyer referral program are cost-effective options, too.

5. *Your claim is time sensitive with the EEOC.* If you want to file a claim with the EEOC, you have to do so within a certain time frame. You will lose your right under federal law to sue forever if you miss that window. The EEOC's website (www.eeoc.gov) is a great resource, or you can call your local EEOC office to find out how much time you have to report an incident and file. You can now file a charge electronically called a Form 5. A lot of counties have an office of civil rights, and you may be more likely to get someone on the phone if you call them. If you file at the state or local level, they may have a form-sharing agreement and cross-file with EEOC, so check to make sure you're covering all your bases.

Many people who confront their bully find the behavior worsens or find themselves out of a job. "HR doesn't have the political capital to stop this behavior sometimes, or they're just out to protect the organization," Spiggle says. "It takes a lot of guts and fortitude, but you can have a lawyer help you behind the scenes. Your company may be in the 10 percent of companies that do the right thing. If they're not, you may be entitled to severance and a resolution of your claims. If you're going to leave your company, you may as well make your employer pay and ensure both parties sign a nondisclosure agreement that makes sure you won't bad-mouth the company and they won't say bad things about you. You can negotiate what is said about you in the event your future employer calls your company for a reference—as well as who says it." Spiggle says while going to court is a significant commitment, you should know all your options so you can decide what course of action is best for you.

IS YOUR BOSS AN ASSHOLE OR A HARASSER?

In a 2017 survey by the Workplace Bullying Institute, 19 percent of participants said they had experienced bullying at work, and another 19 percent said they had witnessed bullying. The survey also found 61 percent of bullies are bosses. By now, most of us have seen the studies that show working with a bad boss increases our chances of having health issues. Yet, according to TalentSmart, a provider of emotional intelligence (EQ) products and services, more than half of the people who have a bad boss stay in that position. Only 27 percent of people quit as soon as they have a new job and 11 percent quit without knowing where their next paycheck will be coming from. In conducting interviews for this chapter about what makes a bad boss, it seemed most fell into one of eight categories:

1. The Mean-Spirited Egomaniac Boss
2. The Inept Boss
3. The Combative Boss
4. The Money-Hungry Boss
5. The "Buddy-Buddy" Boss
6. The Micromanaging Boss
7. The Inappropriate Boss
8. The All-of-the-Above Boss

Not sure what to do if you're working for one of these bad bosses? The following sections detail some of the classic "bad boss" scenarios, as well as some advice on how to navigate your working relationship with them.

Unfiltered

THE MEAN-SPIRITED EGOMANIAC BOSS

Toxic bosses come in all shapes and sizes. When I posted to Facebook that I was looking to share people's "toxic boss" stories, Robert was the first to reach out about his experience with this kind of boss. Here is Robert's story in his own words:

> I once worked at a higher education company with a very highly skilled manipulator whose only focus was getting himself further—even at the expense of his team and business. It was scary to see how much pleasure this man got out of embarrassing people and being mean. He would throw people under the bus in front of everyone. He never took ownership of anything. He talked about what I would consider personal HR matters with everyone and played favorites. If you weren't on his good list, it wasn't good for you. He would pit others against each other, saying: "Someone told me YOU said this." Or "A little birdie said YOU said that . . ." He did not just humiliate people about their work in public; he also would comment about people's personal lives and relationships. He made fun of one colleague for being a vegan and for going to the mountains on the weekends. He made fun of another colleague for breaking up with someone and told a married woman, "Oh, you must have a ton of money; why don't you stay home?"
>
> Our office culture was too afraid to speak up. Most of the team said they felt like they were in an abusive relationship. When our boss wanted to be charming, he was really charming. He was the best manipulator I have ever met, hands down. One minute he would be bringing in snacks and talking you up behind closed doors. The next he would tear you apart in front of the team. He would invite us to concerts or out to dinner, but he would use whatever he learned about you when you least expected it.
>
> There were times I thought he was my friend. He didn't have a ton to pick on me about and I didn't fall for his shit because it wasn't my first job. I wanted to call the CEO (who was based in another state) and tell him what was going on in the office. But it would have been clear it was me who placed the call, and my boss would have retaliated against me and made my time there worse. While I'm a confident guy and a good judge of character, this boss totally tricked me.

Unfiltered

I eventually left and couldn't be happier. Most of the people I worked with have left, too.

If you're dealing with an egomaniac boss, Robert says his tough time taught him some useful lessons that are worth remembering and applying to your own experience:

+ You are not crazy and it is not your fault.
+ Sometimes the best thing you can do is leave, even if you love your work/co-workers.
+ If you can't leave for financial reasons, stay until you have a new job.
+ Keep reminding yourself you are a good person and a good employee and find your support system within the job until you can get out.

Spiggle's Take

Does Robert have a legal claim? Most of what he describes would not likely make for a winner in court. His boss is a jerk, but for the most part, an even-handed one—anyone at any moment could be up or down. There is one place that this boss is skirting close to a law violation: Telling a married woman that she must have a ton of money and wondering why she did not stay home is a form of gender stereotyping, which can be illegal under Title VII. If the boss had, say, demoted her after making this comment, that could be the basis for a lawsuit. Even Robert could have a case if he had been punished for standing up for her. If she had been demoted and Robert wrote an email to the CEO saying that he believed the married woman was punished because of discrimination, then he likely would also be protected from retaliation under federal law.

THE INEPT BOSS

It's hard to work for a boss who isn't qualified to hold the position. Lianne shared this experience:

When I was working at a law firm, the executive director left. Up until his departure, we were a small office of six lawyers with a great work environment. When the new person came in, she acted like she was righting a sinking ship. None of us could understand why she was so determined to make so many changes. She had the ear of the board of directors and terminated three women in her first week. She then got rid of the program we were developing to help poor people. We came to learn she was insecure about her role because she had never been a boss. As a result, she undid a lot of good work we had done before she started. Instead of looking at us as resources to help her navigate the office, she saw us as a threat to her authority. She had no desire to learn what was working and what could be changed. It was a frustrating situation because she made a lot of mistakes. She once sent out 1,500 letters with a spelling error. She would spell the names of judges, lawyers, and courts wrong and hated being corrected. We fixed whatever we could and moved on because no one wanted to be embarrassed. She was fine when we did our work, but if anyone took an approved vacation, she would barely say hello on their first day back.

I loved the work and didn't want to leave, so that's why I stayed. It was a complete shock when she fired me along with two other employees on the same day. We should have nipped things in the bud after she was on the job for a month by going to her and voicing our concerns. I think the board tolerated her because her role was not the easiest job to fill. Plus, the board was a bunch of volunteers, so they did whatever they could to avoid going through another candidate search. She was very good at recruiting lawyers and getting people to show up for parties, but that was pretty much it.

Lianne advises that protecting yourself and considering all your options are important ways to navigate the messy terrain of working with an inept boss. She also suggests that you:

+ Write down everything.
+ Don't assume that you're in the right and that everything will work out in your favor.
+ Put whatever energy you can into your job search. Make sure you have copies of what you want from your current office and that your resume or LinkedIn profile is up-to-date. You never

know if this person will make an irrational decision and let you go, and you may get to a point where you're fed up and decide to leave.

Spiggle's Take

Lianne's probably right: There's not much to suggest a strong case as a legal matter. First, this is a small firm under 15 employees, the threshold at which most federal anti-discrimination law kicks in. If Lianne were to come to me, I'd want to know what state she worked in. For instance, in DC, she would be covered by the DC Human Rights Act. In Virginia, no such luck. Assuming that an anti-discrimination law applied, I'd want to know more about the fact that she fired mostly women. Keep in mind that a member in a protected class—in this case, a woman—can still violate the law by discriminating against others in the same class. The fact that Lianne's director is a woman does not give her a get-out-of-jail-free card to discriminate against other women.

THE COMBATIVE BOSS

Some stories people shared with me included bosses who lost their temper, ranging from those who got angry from time to time to other scenarios where a boss had full-out temper tantrums. No matter how old you are, seeing someone lose their cool can be scary. In Cindy's case, it actually affected her health. Here is Cindy's story:

> I worked for a nonprofit with a boss who loved to turn people against each other and asked employees to weigh in about people who worked at their same level. He often made snide comments that he presented as a joke, but no one could go to HR because we knew nothing would happen. Our office was a chatty one, and you knew if you went to HR that the HR person was going to call everyone and share what you said. There was no anonymity. Meanwhile, my boss was so combative. He fought with people and berated them in public all the time. I developed a lot of anxiety being around him because I never knew when he would turn on me.

Unfiltered

As I matured, I became the office therapist and found myself being a buffer between him and the rest of our team. "What he's trying to say is . . ." is a sentence I said often to younger employees who didn't know how to navigate someone with no boundaries.

If you have a combative boss, take heart and take notes. Cindy says that keeping good records is important. In addition, remember:

+ The nonprofit world can be a tough one because it's not run as a corporate business. You have to create strong emotional boundaries for yourself and document everything.
+ You have to remind yourself daily, "This is not about me," because chances are the minute you leave, your boss will treat your replacement the same way.
+ If there is a way to capture your boss's combative behavior, make that part of your case.

Spiggle's Take

Again, this is mostly a case of bad management and immature personal behavior rather than the stuff good lawsuits are made of. Cindy's situation is still instructive for how to use the law to protect yourself at work. First, it is sadly common that HR departments do more harm than good when it comes to protecting employees from a bad boss. When people come to my office for help, and I think there is arguably illegal behavior going on, I counsel people to put themselves in a strong legal protection and report illegal behavior. This then potentially gives them another claim—retaliation—if the company takes action against the employee. Even if you never plan to file a suit, it's better to have more than one potential claim to bring. It makes for a bigger lever to negotiate with. Second, Cindy mentions that she developed anxiety. This is important because the Americans with Disabilities Act (ADA) can cover temporary conditions like depression or anxiety if diagnosed clinically. If Cindy had clinical anxiety disorder, even if temporarily, and she told HR and then got fired, she could bring a lawsuit—or threaten one to get severance—under the ADA. The EEOC enforces the ADA, and its website has some great information. Keep in mind that, like other types of federal discrimination claims, you must file a charge of the last discriminatory act with the EEOC—a simple, no-cost process—within either 180 or 300 days, depending on the state you live in.

THE MONEY-HUNGRY BOSS

We all know the boss has to worry about a company's bottom line. But as Lucas shares, some bosses are willing to have better results at the cost of their own employees. Here is Lucas' story:

I was the national sales director at a small company. We started with 13 people and grew to 50. I loved the brand, most of the people, and had tremendous respect for the CEO and founder, but she was loyal to a fault. She was working at a publication when she started doing designs at her kitchen table for her new company. Once she left her job to start her baby soft goods company, she brought her former assistant with her and made him the COO. He had no business experience and had never managed people. She would say things like, "I know no one likes him and he's horrible," but she empowered him to do everything. We were such a close team that we just picked up the pieces where we needed to. I would even walk his dog if he were in a meeting and he never once said, "Thank you." That's the kind of guy he was.

It got so bad our CEO brought in a business coach, and I raised awareness about how awful the COO was treating the team. It ended up hurting me even though he got destroyed by nearly everyone in the company. I faced retribution for being honest and regret not having everything the CEO told me in writing. She always assured me I had nothing to worry about and that when she sold the company, she would "take care of me." I brought in millions of dollars in revenue for the company only to find out she gave other people in the company money after she sold it. I never saw a penny and was sick to my stomach for two weeks. I waited for something good to come, and it never did. She was out for herself more than I realized.

Lucas says the main takeaway here is that the end of a job isn't the end of your life, even if you lose out on money owed to you in the process. He also suggests the following:

Unfiltered

- Don't let money hold you hostage or be the reason you fear getting fired. Once you have six months of your salary in the bank, start looking for another job.

- Don't take whatever job comes your way. Wait for a job you really want.

- Document everything! This is especially necessary with internal conversations, and follow up with an email recapping what was said. It's not rude; it's responsible.

Spiggle's Take

Not much to be done legally here. Promises like, "I'll take care of you," usually are not enough to support a claim that you have a stake in the company. Don't count on it if it's not in writing!

THE "BUDDY-BUDDY" BOSS

Most people go into a job wanting their boss to like them. Not only does it feel good to have your boss' respect and support, but it also helps you feel like you have a bit more job security (even if you don't). When a boss doesn't like you, it can be awkward. When a boss doesn't like you because you don't treat them like your bestie, that's just bizarre. Consider Blake's story:

> I worked in a newsroom with a boss I knew was going to make my life difficult. Most people didn't have the training she did, which made her feel great about herself and her own talent because everyone worshipped her. I had the most experience out of everyone in the office and couldn't understand why she was so much harder on me than everyone else. She constantly criticized my work and often made me redo assignments other supervisors thought were excellent. What made things worse was she partied with my colleagues. Since I didn't go out for drinks or do drugs with her, I became even more of a pariah. The person who hired her asked everyone to write an anonymous review so he could gauge her work. I wrote my letter, printed it out, and placed it in his mailbox as he instructed. I had known this man and worked closely with him for years. He called me into his office and told me he couldn't believe

what I wrote. He said I wasn't who he thought I was because my letter was so mean. I was crushed because my letter didn't rip my boss to shreds by any means. It simply stated how I felt. I ended up taking another job and was so happy to get out of that environment.

Friends are great to have in the office, but it can be tricky when that friend is also the boss. Blake shares these key takeaways to help you stay on the right side of your professional relationship:

+ Sometimes you do have to play the game and show up to work events like holiday parties, birthday parties, or farewell events. However, you should *never* do anything you're uncomfortable with for the sake of a job. If you feel like your safety, morals, values, or ethics are being compromised for your job, find a new job.

+ When a supervisor asks for your honest opinion, you have to be prepared to stand behind your word. If you're not willing to rock the boat, then say as little as possible. If you believe in how you feel and want to share those views, trust your gut and say what you must. Just be prepared for any outcome.

Spiggle's Take

Ugh, this sounds like a terrible experience but not one involving illegal behavior by the boss. It's poor management, but not illegal for a boss to prefer those whom he or she hangs out with after work. However, it can raise flags if the boss likes hanging out with only a certain type of person after work—for instance, only men or only workers without children. Also, if the boss fired you because you refused to do drugs with him or her, that might be an illegal form of wrongful termination because he or she punished you for refusing to take part in an illegal act. These claims are usually a matter of state and not federal law.

THE MICROMANAGING BOSS

Some micromanagers are awesome at their job because they have great attention to detail. Others are a pain to work for because scrutinizing everyone's work validates their power trip. In David's case, his boss was a micromanager who liked to get a little too close for comfort. Here is his story:

> I worked in the worst environment with a series of back-to-back bosses. One boss was known for micromanaging everything. She would hover over everyone, and when she would come check up on me, she would stand behind my chair and massage my shoulders. Numerous times, I told her it made me uncomfortable. I'm 6'4" and weigh 300 pounds and felt helpless. She told me I would get used to it eventually, but I never did. There was no HR to go to, and the person who had previously been the head of HR was the wife of the CEO, so we never had anyone to talk to. When I told the CEO what was happening, I asked if our conversation could be kept confidential and he said no. She ended up getting fired for negligence but blamed everything on me. The biggest lesson I learned is how to be a better boss and manager and how never to treat an employee. I eventually left the company.

Nothing is worse than being micromanaged and feeling like you're always doing your job the wrong way (especially when you know you're doing it correctly). David reminds you to practice vital self-care by doing the following:

+ Focus on the work at hand because that's really all that matters.
+ When your work environment takes a toll on your mental health, you have to make a change. It may be scary, but be prepared to leave the company or start seeking new employment.

Spiggle's Take

There is almost no situation in which it can be legally acceptable for a boss to stand behind a subordinate and massage his or her shoulders, especially when the subordinate has made it clear that he does not want to be touched. Not only could this be the basis for a hostile work environment claim, but it also can be the basis for a civil or criminal assault and battery charge.

Here's what you can learn from this. First, sexual harassment laws apply equally to men and women. That means that it is illegal for a woman to sexually harass a man.

Unfiltered

Second, the size differential—David being much bigger than his boss—is mostly irrelevant. If the sexually inappropriate conduct is either severe or pervasive (the standard under federal law), it does not matter that the person doing the harassing is physically smaller.

Third, unwanted touching is a violation of assault and battery laws in most states. Of course, not every unwanted touching will result in the police coming to make an arrest. But here the manager continues massaging David after he explicitly told her to stop. Not only did she ignore him, but she told him that he would "get used to it." Ouch. Another thing to keep in mind about assault-and-battery laws is that they often apply to all employers regardless of the company's size. So even if the employer here had fewer than 15 employees, and therefore was not covered by federal sexual harassment law, assault-and-battery laws still apply.

Finally, it is not clear here that David was retaliated against for reporting his boss' behavior. But if he did get demoted or fired after reporting her inappropriate touching, he likely would have a separate claim for retaliation against his employer. If I were the attorney representing this company, David's story would make me break out in a cold sweat.

THE INAPPROPRIATE BOSS

Maybe you have a boss who insists on brushing her hair at your desk, leaving strands of hair all over the place. Or your supervisor clips his nails whenever he's bored, which is both annoying and disgusting. Here is what Eric shared about his inappropriate boss:

> I worked with a boss who used to take off her shoes even though she had a full-on foot fungus. Her feet were literally rotting. The way our desks were set up, we faced each other. She would always take her shoes off and never wore socks. No, it wasn't illegal that she made the office reek of her feet, but it was extremely uncomfortable.

While gross feet aren't necessarily a reason to quit your job, they certainly can make your workday unpleasant, as can other off-putting behaviors. If you are faced with a boss who behaves inappropriately by having poor hygiene, making you suffer through their bad/crude jokes, or subjecting you to other awkward nonsense, Eric suggests you try the following:

* If you can work from a different area, move.
* If you are confined to that area, consider going to your boss' boss and saying something.

Spiggle's Take

Yep, Eric's right. There's nothing illegal here. But gross! Worth noting, however, is that in some instances, unsafe working conditions can be a violation of Occupational Safety and Health Administration (OSHA) regulations, which can be reported to that agency or its state equivalent. Stinky feet, however, probably aren't covered.

THE ALL-OF-THE-ABOVE BOSS

If your boss is mean, that's difficult. If your boss belittles you, that's rough. If your boss is inept, screws you over, makes advances or inappropriate comments, or wants to be best friends, you have my sympathies. If your boss is all of the above, you'll be able to commiserate with Christopher. Here is Christopher's story:

> I work at a company with a mean-spirited, micromanaging, money-hungry, inept boss who sometimes wants to be buddy-buddy with you, depending on what his agenda is for the week or the day. He learned I have anxiety and mocks me for it. One day I was making tea, and he asked me if it was chamomile to calm my anxiety and suggested I drink two cups instead of one. I took offense at someone making fun of my mental illness. I think my anxiety has helped me succeed because I cross every "t" and dot every "i," and it helps me achieve my goals. With that said, it's no one else's business to talk about.
>
> Another day, he walked into the office and saw me sniff a little bottle of lavender I keep at my desk to help me relax. In front of the entire office, he shouted, "What are those, poppers?" Poppers are known to be a recreational drug used by men to enhance sex. I think because we're

both gay and because a lot of gay men work at the office, he thinks he can say what he wants to the community. While it was pretty offensive, no one said anything.

Since I love our company's mission, I don't want to leave. I took a more direct approach because HR is looking out for the company more than the employee, so I don't want to go that route. I told my boss we had to have a serious conversation and explained I didn't feel like I had a support system. I made sure I wasn't disrespectful or angry. He was extremely combative and told me to "shut the fuck up" when I expressed my feelings, but at least I did my part. He's inappropriate with how much he compliments people and makes promises that are always empty. Sometimes, he butters us up so much and then knocks us down the following week. He takes advantage of everyone's emotions when we're stressed at the end of a quarter for the sake of his own goals.

Christopher says, "As long as I do good work and have success, that's all someone will see on my resume, so to me, that's all that matters." If your situation is really that bad, he suggests you:

+ Talk to co-workers you trust but don't gossip about the problem.
+ See if anyone else feels the same way you do and make sure you're not being overly sensitive.
+ Talk to someone outside the company and get their advice on what to do.
+ If it negatively affects you every day, look for other opportunities. Otherwise, try to stick it out.

Spiggle's Take

I understand that Christopher does not want to leave his job, and he's clearly correct that raising any improper behavior will not likely result in a change in the organization or his treatment. But, depending on the size of the company, Christopher may, because of his anxiety, be covered by the Americans with Disabilities Act (ADA). And one of the big obstacles for these kinds of cases, proving that the employer knows of the disability, does not exist here; his boss clearly does. It is also clear that his boss treats him differently because of it. If his boss fires or demotes Christopher, he should see a lawyer about pursuing a claim under the ADA. Another issue raised by what has happened to Christopher is the issue of a hostile work environment based on sex. Here his boss made a comment about "poppers," which—as far as Christopher is concerned—has a sexual connotation. To have a successful sexual harassment claim, the behavior must be either severe or pervasive. A single comment like the one made here most certainly would not constitute the basis of a sexual harassment claim. However, if the boss were to repeat this behavior, it could constitute pervasive harassment.

REFLECTIONS

You have the right to work in a safe, nonhostile, and nondiscriminatory environment. If you've started resenting everyone who posts to social media about their work or avoiding social settings because people might ask you what you're up to these days, this is a good time to look at what the problem is and how you can fix it. Knowing your rights is a great place to start, but that might not be enough to change your situation. Ask yourself:

+ Do I have a legal claim?
+ Whom can I confide in for support or contact for legal counsel?
+ Are my notes ready to go? If they aren't, start to organize your timeline of events so you're prepared.
+ If I am an employer, how can I improve my office culture to create a safer work environment?

If you choose to leave your current workplace for any reason, you'll find ideas on how you can pursue your passion in the following chapter.

Part Four

Building What Makes You Happiest

Chapter 9

Starting Your Side Hustle

Your friends ask if you're around this weekend. You say you're working on a project and ask for a rain check. No one knows your "project" is binge-watching *Shark Tank* because you dream of seeing your amazing idea on the show one day. You post an inspiring quote about success, which looks like you're trying to motivate your network, but you're really motivating yourself. #everydayimhustlin

Unfiltered

If someone gave you a million dollars, there's a good chance you'd spend some of it trying to take that idea you've always had in your head to market. Since winning the lottery or receiving a million dollars from a stranger may never happen, you're in luck. There are plenty of other ways for you to become an entrepreneur. Maybe you have thought about doing something on top of your full-time job, or maybe you already have a side hustle that has proved it can be a viable business. In this chapter, you'll find tips to get your hustle up and running, questions to ask before you give your two weeks' notice, and a glimpse of what to expect when you're flying solo.

If you have been sitting on an idea and feel it's time to pursue it, be ready for the amount of time and energy it will require. If you can work a full-time job *and* get your side hustle up and running (before or after work, on the weekends, and on your vacation), you may find that road to be best. If you're not in a position to work a full-time gig and start something on the side, you can still make this work.

In the next sections, you'll meet two entrepreneurs who got off the ground by taking different paths.

SHAWNA'S STORY: STARTING A BROWNIE COMPANY FROM SCRATCH

Shawna Lidsky had been working in the TV business as a sports broadcaster for more than 12 years and could feel the tide shifting in local media. More cable channels were popping up, and job security was low. She knew it would be a tough job when the time came to start a family since sporting events mainly take place at night and on weekends. She also wanted more vacation time and flexibility, but her news station in Vermont required her to work there for 15 years before getting a third week of vacation time. Shawna says the job was a great gig in her twenties and early thirties, but she couldn't envision doing it forever.

While she had only made brownies from boxes, she thought it would be cool to source local ingredients and make a product that Vermonters could be really proud of and enjoy. "I love the Vermont lifestyle and had the crazy idea of capturing that in a brownie," she says.

Unfiltered

How to Hold Down a Job While Starting a Side Hustle

Sometimes the best way to incorporate a side hustle is to blend it with your day job. You can't always draw stark lines between the life you have now and the life you want. When that happens, think of ways you can test your ideas for the new gig while maintaining the status quo at your day job.

For example, Shawna started playing with different brownie recipes before and after her news shifts and on the weekends. With an exhausting work schedule, no business background, and no professional baking experience, it seemed like the perfect recipe for disaster. But the key to her success was not biting off more than she could chew. She didn't have a business idea one day and quit her job the next. Instead, she brought every batch of brownies she made into the newsroom for everyone to try. Her colleagues were happy to eat the brownies and give her unsolicited feedback, and she was thrilled to turn them into an informal focus group. No one knew she was starting a business, so she stored away their opinions. When Shawna got laid off from the newsroom due to budget cuts, she had a decision to make: apply for another TV job or pursue her business full time. She decided it was brownies or bust, and the Vermont Brownie Company (www.vermontbrownie.com) was born.

What You Should Ask Yourself Before Starting a Business

Long before you start thinking about quitting your full-time job, Shawna recommends asking yourself these five questions:

1. *Do I have the time and money my idea needs?* Shawna was willing to spend all her free time in the kitchen, but she didn't want to burn through too much money too soon. At first, she even mixed the brownies with a spoon because she didn't own a mixer! Her then-boyfriend (now husband) attached a wire hanger to a drill to make her one. Disclaimer: Do not try this at home.

2. *Have I read books or spoken to entrepreneurs to find out what I'm really getting myself into?* Shawna admits she was so concerned about not knowing how to bake that she almost threw in her apron before she even started. She dug into reading books on

entrepreneurship and found a resonating theme that marketing was just as powerful a skill as baking, if not more so.

3. *Can I handle extreme highs and extreme lows?* In Shawna's case, she almost put herself out of business before she began. She asked friends and family to have a few people over to their homes and sample different flavors, and gave everyone who attended a coupon for 50 percent off. One woman gave her coupon card to her husband, who then ordered $4,000 in corporate gifts. Shawna couldn't produce $4,000 in product for $2,000 when she was just getting her company off the ground. She went from being excited by such a big order to nervous her business would be destroyed. Luckily, VBC survived this snafu, and Shawna had the stomach to handle the stress.

4. *Am I OK not getting a paycheck the first year?* "You have to be willing to sacrifice the exact things you hope to gain back over time; making money is one of them," Shawna says. There are the expenses you plan for and the ones that pop up. You need to be aware of what you have to spend while knowing you won't be making bank deposits into your account any time soon.

5. *Am I comfortable working with people who are better than I am at certain things and who are often smarter than I am?* "Ignorance on fire is better than knowledge on ice," Shawna says. "There was a whole lot of ignorance on fire during the startup phase, and working with people who were experts in marketing and packaging was vital to VBC's success."

Shawna's Advice

In addition to testing different recipes in the early days, Shawna also made sure that no one had registered the name Vermont Brownie Company in the state of Vermont. Capitalizing on the Vermont cachet was key. She suggests that once you register your business, you should get a web domain and business cards. She also encourages you to:

+ Surround yourself with great people.
+ Remember there are very few problems that don't have solutions. You just have to go out and find them.

+ Forget the idea that others have it easier than you. Your business is not the only one struggling! Every business model has flaws unique to its industry or product.
+ Keep in mind transition is scary (even when it's good!).
+ Always remember the most challenging and scariest opportunities often reap the greatest rewards.

Unlike Shawna, who worked a full-time job while getting her brownie business off the ground, Erica Mandy had to go a different route.

ERICA'S STORY: POWERING UP YOUR PODCAST

Shawna had the advantage of creating a side hustle that didn't directly compete with the tasks she performed in her day job. As such, she was able to test her ideas without upsetting her managers. But what if you can't do that? Many people want to start businesses that are an outgrowth of what they do every day. It's natural to want to apply your expertise in a meaningful way to grow your business, but employers aren't always thrilled to foster a potential competitor. When your side hustle has to fly under the radar, you have to get creative.

After ten years of working her way up in TV news, Erica Mandy had made it to the second-largest news market in the country before she turned 30. But a few years after checking that career-goal box, she looked around and realized her *next* goal was no longer what she wanted—and perhaps just as important, it was no longer what much of her audience wanted, either. She kept hearing from people how news is too "depressing," "biased," or "takes up too much time," and she was uniquely positioned to be a credible yet casual and upbeat voice giving you the day's news in a quick, convenient way.

Starting a news podcast on top of her full-time job wasn't an option because she was under contract with her TV station and was not allowed to do anything else. If you can't start your side hustle while working full time, Erica recommends doing some research on it: reaching out to knowledgeable people, reading blogs, listening to podcasts, and even running a survey using a service like SurveyMonkey (www.surveymonkey.com) to get feedback about your idea. Once she took those steps, she checked her finances and gave herself one year to pursue her dream job. The only thing left to do was sit down with her boss and break the news that she was leaving.

What to Ask Yourself Before Leaving Your Full-Time Job

Erica says that before giving your notice, you should know that feeling discomfort, taking risks, and embracing innovation are necessary parts of any business for the *entire* life of the business. "If you're thinking about packing up your desk and turning in your ID card, think back to the past and ask yourself how moments of discomfort made you feel," she says. "Was it the good type of stress that helped you rise to the challenge? Or did you feel depleted? When you start a business, you have to be ready for different obstacles that may come out of nowhere." If you don't feel ready to get on that roller coaster, you may want to prepare a little more before leaving the security of your 9-5 job and riding into the Wild West.

How to Launch Your Company with Confidence

You can help nurture your side hustle by harnessing the power of your network. Seek out mentors in your industry and look to them for advice or feedback. Erica also turned to professional help when launching her podcast, *theNewsWorthy* (www.thenewsworthy.com). She met with an accountant to determine if she should be an S corporation or an LLC and used a website called 99designs to help her with her initial logo and cover art. Don't leave friends and acquaintances out of the mix, either. They can often operate as objective, informal focus groups to provide feedback from a consumer perspective. Erica also asked her social network for help when she needed it. "You must be willing to put yourself out there and then don't stop with just the people you know," she says. "Follow up with those potential connections and friends-of-friends."

Doing your homework is key. Research, research, research. That's exactly what Erica did—she researched other key players in the industry. The first time *theNewsWorthy* was featured on a popular podcast app, it started with a LinkedIn message. She reached out to five people she found through LinkedIn who likely made decisions for the feature she wanted. She didn't know them personally but paid for a month of LinkedIn Premium to message them anyway, and one of them responded. About two weeks later, *theNewsWorthy* made the cut and she got the feature she wanted. That helped her podcast grow by 600 percent in the first couple of months and gave her the credibility she needed to get even more features.

Finally, if you don't have a tribe, create one. Attend industry events; reach out to potential clients, vendors, and mentors on LinkedIn; and support other people in your industry. Erica attended conferences and talked to everyone she could. She met a tribe of supporters within the industry that later brought in cross-promotion opportunities and even media coverage.

While all these steps helped give Erica the confidence she needed to launch her business and survive all the ups and downs entrepreneurship brings, she says the main reason she was able to sleep at night was because she had a financial plan in place. Knowing she had savings for a year helped her take the risk in the first place.

But what can you do if you have an idea but no money? Karen Cahn, CEO and founder of crowdfunding platform iFundWomen, says you should consider a crowdfunding campaign.

HOW YOUR FAMILY, FRIENDS, AND FOLLOWERS CAN HELP YOU FUNDRAISE

There are several crowdfunding platforms for all different kinds of projects, from personal charities on GoFundMe to creative projects on Kickstarter. Crowdfunding is when you, the creator of the project, go out and raise small increments of money from lots of people to accomplish your goal.

Karen Cahn decided to create a crowdfunding platform just for women-led startups and small businesses after experiencing firsthand how challenging it can be to raise venture funding. "Women only get 2 to 6 percent of venture funding dollars, and most businesses will actually never be appropriate for venture investment. All most companies need is a small amount of seed cash to see if there's even a 'there' there, and to prove there is demand for their product or service, before wasting time on a business idea that's not going to work," Karen says. It was this insight that led her, a former Google/YouTube executive, to found iFundWomen, a fundraising ecosystem for women's businesses. Since she started the site back in November 2016, tens of thousands of funders have backed hundreds of startups and helped raise millions of dollars in seed cash to help these businesses prove demand and take their ideas to the next level.

In addition to helping women raise the money they need to start and grow their businesses, iFundWomen's coaching staff provides free campaign coaching to every entrepreneur who wants to learn how to crowdfund effectively. They also have a production studio where they take the burden of a campaign video off the entrepreneur, speeding up their time to market. "Entrepreneurs who do the homework and use our coaching tools raise 4.5 times more money than those who DIY it," Karen says. iFundWomen also has an Accelerator Pool, which benefits entrepreneurs with lower-income personal networks. "iFundWomen is the only crowdfunding platform built exclusively by women for women, and we have a pay-it-forward model where we reinvest 20 percent of our profits from standard fees into live campaigns on the site," Karen says. "Second, with our local strategy, we are a one-stop shop for people who wish to support female-led startups and small businesses in their own local community."

Whether you start with a simple ask to family and friends or choose to participate in a crowdfunding campaign online, remember that you don't have a lot to lose when you seek funding in this way, so it doesn't hurt to try. Remember the old adage: If you never ask, the answer is always "no."

WATCH IT!

I sat down with Karen to discuss her crowdfunding tips for any woman who wants to apply. You can watch our interview here: entm.ag/karencahn.

Gillian Stollwerk Garrett is one woman who launched a campaign through iFundWomen. For years, Gilly self-funded her organic skincare line, Gilly's Organics, but she wanted to scale and upgrade her packaging. Her iFundWomen campaign not only raised funds but also raised the bar for her brand. "I was a little hesitant to do a campaign and ask people for money, but I got over that really quickly," Gilly says. "I got so much exposure from doing this. People started buying my products, and angel investors and VCs started reaching out to me."

WATCH IT!

You can hear more about Gilly's story and her advice if you're thinking about running a campaign here: entm.ag/gilly.

MANAGE YOUR SIDE HUSTLE MONEY

Whether you use a crowdfunding campaign like Gilly or have savings in the bank like Erica and Shawna, it's important to know how you will manage your money. So how do you get your financial plan together?

To help you avoid that gnawing feeling in your stomach that you're about to run out of funds, certified financial planner Brittney Castro says to make sure that before you start, you have a game plan to pay your personal bills for the first *one to three years* you'll be building your business.

"The reality is a lot of businesses are not cash flow positive until years three-plus," she says. "That means you have to have a game plan for your income source for those years. Make sure you are clear on how much income you actually need from your business every month. Even if you don't take a 'paycheck' right away, this is your goal, and when you are clear on a goal you are that much more likely to achieve it." Brittney says if no money will be coming into your business for a while, and you aren't working a full-time job, you need to know how much you can afford to pull from your savings before you get started.

In addition to being a certified financial planner, chartered retirement planning counselor, accredited asset management specialist, entrepreneur, and speaker, Brittney is also the founder and CEO of the Los Angeles-based financial planning firm, Financially Wise

Women (www.financiallywisewomen.com). Through her work, Brittney teaches her clients how to manage their money. She also advises them to consider hiring a CPA to help them figure out how to set up their business and bookkeeping and sort through the best approach to paying their taxes. "As a financial planner, I usually recommend that my business owner clients have a separate tax savings account and shave off at least 20 percent from gross business income every month and transfer into that tax savings account," she says. "That way when their quarterly taxes are due, they have the money ready to go and won't be stressed."

The reality is most businesses acquire debt whether it be a business loan or personal debt. "If you find yourself with debt from your business, the best approach is to create a game plan to pay off that debt in the most efficient way. Review your business budget and determine how much you can make in additional debt payments every month," Brittney says. "Start with the debt with the highest interest rate, and pay the minimums on the rest until that one is completely paid off. This is the most efficient way to pay off your debts as it will save you the most in interest over time."

While it isn't easy, Brittney encourages you to stay motivated—even when you're staring down a huge pile of debt, which is, let's be honest, the case for a lot of us. "Remember that the debt helped you start a business and learn a lot about money, so in the moments you feel overwhelmed or stressed by it, switch your mindset to gratitude, as that will help you stay inspired and motivated to pay off the debt and enjoy the journey of doing so," she says.

Last but not least, Brittney says to be prepared that your business may take longer to take off than you might hope. "While most people say you don't make money until your third year, every business is different," she says. "I would say on average most businesses are not fully profitable and consistent with cash flow until year five." To keep your head above water as you scale your side hustle into your dream business, Brittney suggests setting realistic goals and being mindful about how you approach money. Here are three of her top tips for financial success:

Unfiltered

1. Be clear on what your long-term vision for the business is. Are you building it fast to sell for a profit, or do you want to grow slow and steady and maintain the business for more than ten years?

2. If you are committed to put in the hard work day after day, it will eventually pay off. But that doesn't mean you won't tweak and learn and pivot along the way. When you start a business, you have to stay as lean as you can so you can make those changes when needed.

3. Review your financials every month and learn how to read a balance sheet and P&L statement so you can learn what it takes to run a profitable business.

When your financials are in order, it makes your business much more likely to succeed. And make sure to hire a great bookkeeper, CPA, and financial planner. When you have the right financial professionals on your team, you can learn how to run a financially successful company that supports your life vision and income goals. Who doesn't want that?

All these tips and stories highlight the fact that both input and outcome matter in business—it's not just about the bottom line.

WATCH IT!

As Brittney pointed out, starting a business can take longer than you expect, and it can take quite some time before you see a profit. Philip Wolff and Chief Behr are two of the most sought-after hairstylists in the world. When they decided to expand their brand, they started by offering classes to people in the industry and then moved into creating their own product line. "There have been parts when we thought, *this is just too hard*. We were traveling and even losing money sometimes. But we believed in it so much, we didn't let that knock us down," Philip says. He adds that to be successful, you have to know who you are and what you are about and be patient. To watch my interview with Philip, you can go here: entm.ag/philipwolff.

#MYSTORY: Big Dreams, Bigger Bills

Around the time I came up with the idea to start a production company and my YouTube channel, my news director in New York told me my unit was being eliminated to save money. At the time, I had no savings because during my first three years in that newsroom, I made less than $50,000 a year. In my second three-year contract, I made less than $70,000 a year. Given New York City rent, transportation, food, medical bills, taxes, donations to charity, and my social life, my salary didn't get me very far. I always lived from paycheck to paycheck and even started to accrue some debt. My parents were extremely supportive of my career and did what they could to help me, but I never told them how much debt I really had—especially when I started my business. They had already done so much for me (like pay for all of my education); I wanted to do this next chapter of my life on my own.

I decided to stay in the newsroom as a freelancer, making $250 a day. I worked five additional jobs to cover my expenses and save enough for my YouTube launch. For a year, I juggled different jobs, often working three jobs in a day and sleeping two to three hours a night. Here's a look at my insane workload during that time:

+ I freelanced in the newsroom.

+ I consulted for a tech startup.

+ I was the event planner for a nonprofit gala.

+ I contributed to a digital platform.

+ I traveled the country on a speaking fellowship.

This was a very stressful and unpredictable path. During that year, I also needed major oral surgery and, due to complications, needed eight more procedures. I was always in pain, but I couldn't take a break because I was determined to see my channel come to life—and I had to pay my bills.

I knew how much I could spend on each video to have enough content for six months. My plan was to see what the response was to those initial videos from viewers and then evaluate whether I needed to find investors/ sponsors or go back to a full-time job. Despite having more than 100 meetings with experts, entrepreneurs, influencers, accountants, and attorneys, I still made so many mistakes in structuring and sustaining my business. The biggest ones were:

+ *Not knowing that business owners must pay quarterly taxes.* This one really screwed me because as I got paid, I would pay off my debt. I assumed that by the time April came around, I would have enough jobs to dedicate solely to my taxes. My parents offered to help. Having to take them up on their offer felt just as mortifying as making this mistake in the first place.

+ *Not being able to count on my cash flow.* I didn't take into account that although I was working six jobs to cover my expenses, I wouldn't always get paid on time. Even though I had signed agreements for every job, you'd be surprised how many people you have to chase down in the freelance world to get them to pay you for work you have already done!

+ *Not making profitable choices.* Given my TV news background, I wanted my videos to be perfect. In the end, I had beautifully shot and edited content without enough power to market them through paid advertising. In hindsight, I should have spent 80 percent of my time and money on marketing and 20 percent on production and managed my content calendar so that my videos would have lasted a year, not six months.

+ *Not watching my small expenses.* Another thing I don't necessarily consider a mistake, but that hurt me financially, was paying for every coffee, breakfast, lunch, dinner, or drink when someone agreed to meet me and let me pick their brain. It was important to me then, and still is to this day, to show my appreciation for people's time, advice, and introductions. While this practice made me feel good, it took a toll on my finances.

Most entrepreneurs will tell you the money side of any business is really stressful. There were days I had more green and pink envelopes than white ones—I had reached the point where credit card companies sent me those scary letters that said, "This is your final notice!" It feels awful to be so far behind, but I prayed a lot and picked up whatever freelance jobs I could to make sure I never got to the point that collections called me. After a while, the money started to come in because what I built had value and I could start to charge more for my company's services when someone hired me to consult, produce content, do media training, or give a speech.

You Have to Be Healthy to Have a Healthy Business

Above, I mentioned how I went out regularly to network over coffee, breakfast, lunch, dinner, and drinks. It's so tempting when you're starting a business to devote your entire life to it! But business performance expert James Nicholas Kinney says you have to "pay" yourself first. He believes in order to set yourself up for success, you need a psychological and physical anchor to help you stay grounded. "Whether it's walking, yoga, boxing, painting, or any modality that you're into, you really need to have balance in order to increase your business performance," he says. "If you don't invest in yourself, the business will suffer. Money is not the only metric of success. A sick leader equals an unhealthy bottom line." As a bicoastal professional known for starting with $200 and building a seven-figure business group, James knows how important it is to network and nurture relationships. He suggests meeting your colleague or potential client for a walk or some other activity to keep you healthy while creating meaningful connections. "An authentic opportunity will help you develop a relationship that will differentiate you vs. your competitors," James says. For more advice from James, you can watch the interview I did with him here:

 entm.ag/jameskinney

Unfiltered

FIGURING OUT WHAT TO FOCUS ON

As you can imagine, when I met someone and they asked what I did for a living, it took ten minutes to explain I was a news anchor/reporter/ motivational speaker/consultant/media trainer/event planner all rolled into one. Oh! And I was starting my own digital platform while working on a book and merchandise for my brand.

When I met Bill Shaw, Entrepreneur Media, Inc.'s president (he was the chief revenue officer back then), we talked about how I could contribute to Entrepreneur.com. Before I left his office, he said he was impressed with my ability to work hard and build a credible brand on my own, but he thought an industry strategy expert named Kathleen Griffith might be able to help me narrow in on what could make me the most money so I didn't need to run around in so many directions. I am forever grateful he made that suggestion.

Kathleen is the founder of Grayce & Co (https://grayceco.com/), a marketing and business consultancy that works with both Fortune 100 and media companies. She is also the founder of Build Like a Woman (www.buildlikeawoman.com), which helps female founders scale their businesses. I had spent my entire career supporting people in some way, and for the first time, I had the ear of someone who wanted to sit down and help me.

Kathleen and I taped our four sessions so people like you can go through the same boot camp I did. The episodes will walk you through how I chose what to focus on and how I developed my brand strategy and marketing plan. While I knew bits and pieces of what I needed to do, Kathleen helped me get everything buttoned up the way I needed to in order to scale. You can watch the episodes (Branding Boot 1, 2, 3, and 4) or go through the exercises in the following sections.

▶ entm.ag/bootcamp1

▶ entm.ag/bootcamp2

▶ entm.ag/bootcamp3

▶ entm.ag/bootcamp4

Phase One: How to Defeat Fragmentation

If, like me, you're working several jobs to keep your head above water, that can hurt you in the long run. "To defeat fragmentation, you have to figure out what the main job is that you *want* to focus on," Kathleen says. Write down all the jobs you're doing and circle the *one* you want to be your priority.

Phase Two: Your Brand Strategy, Purpose, and Values

Kathleen says that once you know what you want your main job to be, the next thing to do is define your brand strategy. If you can answer the following questions, write them down here. If you can't, figuring out those answers is a good place to start before moving on to Phase Three. Ask yourself:

+ What service do I provide?
+ What problem do I solve?
+ Functionally and emotionally, what makes what I offer different from others?
+ In a world full of competition, why should someone hire my company over another company offering the same services?
+ What is the ultimate promise I "will deliver to the world? We will refer to this as your brand purpose. This is the essence of the business' goals and the philosophy underlying them," Kathleen says.
+ What are my three core values? Examples of values are: inclusive, fair, persuasive, empathetic, transparent, relatable, authentic, and committed.

Kathleen advises that it is important to have a brand with a clear purpose and consistent values because at the most basic level, a "brand" signals value to consumers and gives them a reason to pay the price you're asking. Without a brand, your product is in essence an interchangeable commodity. Brands give people something to remember and help you stand out from your competition.

Unfiltered

Phase Three: Identifying and Reaching Your Potential Partners, Clients, and Customers

With your brand in place, it may be tempting to cast a wide net to reach your target audience, but now is the time to think about exactly who you are going after. For example, are you going after Millennials? Baby Boomers? Men? Women? Once you know who you want to reach, you'll be able to craft how you will communicate with them. Answer the following questions to identify your target audience:

+ Who do I want to partner with?
+ Who do I *not* want to partner with?

Once you identify who you want to reach, the next step is to nail your tactical marketing plan. Marketing will help you scale what you are known for in the world. Your brand logo and guidelines for all marketing must be consistent, and your content must speak from a place of honesty and authenticity. Every visual must be stunning and carefully chosen, and all copy (headline, call to action, subject line, descriptions, teasers, video titles, tweets) must stop people in their tracks.

Most important, part of your plan is activation. You want things to be *actionable*, *measurable*, and *repeatable*. First, determine your top three marketing tactics to focus on for the next six months in priority order.

1. _____

2. _____

3. _____

Once you have established your brand strategy and marketing plan, you can create a pitch deck. "The pitch deck will help sell your offering to potential partners, investors, or sales targets by telling a story about the problem you're trying to solve in the world and highlighting why your company is well-positioned to solve it," Kathleen says. "Good pitch decks show a clear, cohesive vision of the offering and the company and show that there is a realistic, convincing upside to addressing a consumer need that's currently not serviced by what's existing in the market." A typical pitch story arc follows:

1. Outline the problem that your business is trying to solve. Make sure to outline *who* has that problem, which will tee up what consumer segment your business is targeting.
2. Expand on what the market opportunity is and how the market is growing.
3. Describe what currently exists in the market that is attempting to solve that problem, with a nod to why those are falling short.
4. Introduce your solution, positioning, and what makes it uniquely suited to solve that market problem. Explain why this solution will bring about better results for the client/customer.
5. Include any relevant press clippings, previous partners you've worked with, testimonials, and/or case studies.
6. Conclude the pitch deck with a contact page for follow-up meetings.

Finally, list 20 pitch targets and how you plan to reach them.

Phase Four: Go to Market

One theme that has repeatedly cropped up in this book is the importance of being flexible when it comes to business. You may know your audience and how you want to communicate with them, but you have to keep track of what's working and what you need to adjust as your business evolves. To stay on top of things, make sure you:

+ *Have a timeline.* Determine milestones and set up weekly reviews for completion.
+ *Assemble a tribe.* Identify who can help support you. Assemble a "board of experts" for your own life because iron sharpens iron.
+ *Pass it on.* Share resources with other entrepreneurs and plug into a new community.

Unfiltered

Now that you've been through Kathleen's branding boot camp, if you have a strong brand and stunning materials/product/content/you name it and you still struggle with your reach, next up is some advice to help you dissect your social media strategy from social media marketing experts Stephanie Cartin and Courtney Spritzer.

HOW TO REACH THE RIGHT AUDIENCE

You may not be fluent in hashtags, filters, and memes, but that doesn't mean your business doesn't need a digital strategy. Inside social media marketing agency Socialfly (www.socialflyny.com), you will find a group of young, creative, and driven Millennials who share a passion for social media, marketing, and working with influencers. Cofounders Stephanie Cartin and Courtney Spritzer created their company to help entrepreneurs reach the right audience online when there's already so much competition for people's time and attention.

"Social media changes so fast," Stephanie says. "You can try to map out your plan for six months to a year, but in that time, algorithms can change, new platforms can pop up, and you have to be prepared to keep asking yourself where you want to spend your marketing dollars."

For business owners who are not selling a product but a service, like doctors, lawyers, consultants, or tutors, the same rules apply. "You can't just post something to social media every Sunday and expect a huge boost in your business," Stephanie explains. "You have to make sure you're sending out the right message, at the right time, to the right people. While Socialfly is a social media and influencer marketing agency, the same rules apply to us, too. We started our company reaching people through social media and blog posts. Then we wrote a book and, most recently, started our own show on Facebook Live called SocialLive. You have to keep evolving in today's world."

Here are some questions the Socialfly team recommends you ask yourself to help figure out your plan:

+ *Where are your potential consumers spending their time?* If you don't know, the best way to find out is test and learn. Put up the same post on every digital platform, and see where you get the most engagement.

+ *Do you know how to create compelling content?* Maybe you're a chef who can post videos of yourself making easy recipes. Maybe you're an artist who can show your work coming to life. If you're a health coach, maybe you can share health tips. People love behind-the-scenes posts and useful information.

+ *Are you not sure what to share or how to create compelling content?* In that case, you may want to hire a team to help you craft and produce your story. Socialfly has an in-house team to help with photo and video shoots and graphic designers and copywriters to help with branding. They also help their clients work with macroinfluencers and microinfluencers.

+ *Does working with macroinfluencers or microinfluencers interest you?* If you're looking to collaborate with talent, that may boost your image and reach, but you need to make sure you're part-nering with the right person and not spending more than you can afford. Whether you work with someone who has millions of followers or only a few thousand, you need to make sure you have an agree-ment with a clear set of guide-lines so your influencer knows what his exact role is and what he's contractually obligated to produce.

> **WATCH IT!**
>
> For more tips, you can watch the video series I did with Stephanie and Courtney here:
>
> entm.ag/socialfly1
>
> entm.ag/socialfly2
>
> entm.ag/socialfly3

+ *Do you have a budget for ads?* Advertising on social media is import-ant to the success of any campaign. It's pay to play, especially on Facebook, but the good news is the targeting is so precise that you can reach your ideal customer with exactly the right content to move them. Once you start using ads, it's even more import-ant to analyze how they perform.

TIPS FOR BRANDS AND THE INFLUENCERS WHO WANT TO WORK WITH THEM

If the founders of Socialfly have inspired you to work with or become an influencer, there are many ways to make this happen, but not all brand-influencer relationships are successful. Claudine DeSola created the Caravan Stylist Studio to connect brands and influencers in an authentic relationship that helps both sides. "We create programming throughout the year for our brands that includes providing services to influencers, product sampling, and organized events," she says. "We help actresses get ready for red carpets, TV appearances, photo shoots, and other major events. The studio is also open to creatives who want to come in and have a 'me' day. Our hope is that after guests visit the studio they feel they 100 percent understand the products we use and share information about the brands via word-of-mouth to friends and family. We have seen 70 percent of the people who come into our studio share something about the brands via social chatter because it's all authentic—no one is being paid to comment or share content."

In the following sections, Claudine shares her tips and best practices for how you can amplify the message of your brand and reach a wider audience.

Create a Cost-Effective Strategy

There are many brands working on influencer marketing, but they are typically short and expensive campaigns. To help create a cost-effective strategy, Claudine suggests the following:

+ *Take your online offline and back to human interaction.* Claudine believes organizing an experience that guests will do insta-stories about, or creating short video clips talking about the benefits of your product or service, is more valuable than a photo of someone holding a product and saying they love it without really telling us why.

+ *Focus on bigger programs and strategies.* Paying one person to post one time can produce beautiful content, but Claudine says creating an ongoing program allows for continuous content and authentic interactions.

+ *Be different.* "You see the same influencers getting paid by all different companies, sometimes in the same genre, which is a big 'oops!' I don't find it very believable when I know someone is being paid by a hair care brand, and they are talking about one hair care product that they love so much one week and a totally different hair care brand the next," she says. "Brands need to be more careful with the influencers they are choosing to make sure they really do love the product and their reviews are honest." Claudine encourages brands to think out of the box and support new talent, especially creatives like fashion designers and artists who should be seen as influencers and content producers.

The key to a successful campaign is research: Make sure you find the right person to elevate your brand. Know your metrics of success going into any relationship, and communicate your objectives before you have an influencer sign on the dotted line. If your number-one goal is an increase in sales, that's very different from raising awareness about a new product. The best campaigns are the ones where everyone involved is on the same page.

So You Want to Be an Influencer

If you have millions of followers and aspire to become an influencer, it can be tempting to take any deal that comes your way, but Claudine says saying "yes" to every brand can dilute yours. "Being authentic is everything," she says. In order to do that, you can:

+ Test products and learn if you like them before you agree to a campaign.
+ Engage with entrepreneurs who might not have a large budget but will help you find out about your favorite popular product and possibly something new as well. "You also never know what brand you might discover that might start off with a smaller budget that you might be able to grow with over time," she says.

+ Use resources like Caravan that can help you create more editorial content.

Keep in mind that earning bank as an influencer only happens if you work hard. There is no magic formula. Next, we'll talk to some influencers who have made the hustle lucrative.

Influencer Insight

Making a living as an influencer takes time. Picking the right person or charity to promote your brand can also be a process. Here is some expert advice from top influencers to help you succeed. Think of this as your own personal expert roundtable.

Mick Batyske (http://mick.co/) is a DJ who has spun for many celebrities' private parties. A tech investor and influencer, he's become the go-to consultant for many brands. His number-one piece of advice for today's influencers is to stay flexible. "To me, branding is a constant evolution," he says. "Oftentimes, people spend so much time building a brand that they quickly outgrow it and never course correct. You change. Your personal brand changes. The marketplace changes. Everything is in flux, and you have to be able to adjust all while staying true to yourself. It's not easy, but it is possible. I've reinvented myself twice in the last ten years, but both times were logical and holistic evolutions from who I was into who I am becoming and where I want to go."

Daniel Greenberg's love for tech and working with influencers has led him to work with major brands such as Vita Coco and the Video Music Awards. His number-one tip for companies is to pay close attention to microinfluencers. "A microinfluencer is someone with less than 25,000 followers. Chances are when that person posts something, their fans will actually pay attention because they trust that person and engage with them regularly."

Lisa Filipelli runs Flip Management (www.flipmgmt.com) focusing on her long list of clients, including Tyler Oakley, Ingrid Nilsen, and Amanda

WATCH IT!

To watch my interview with Daniel, go here:

entm.ag/danielgreenberg

WATCH IT!

To watch my interview with Lisa, go here:

entm.ag/lisafilipelli

Steele. Her number-one piece of advice is to consider collaborating with digitally native content creators to boost a brand's bottom line. "Creators are their own writers, directors, producers, marketers, and publicists," she says. "Influencer marketing accounted for $1 million to $2 million in budget five years ago. Now it accounts for $2.4 billion. These creators have influence."

When Danielle Finck was 25 years old, she had a job she loved, but several side opportunities kept popping up. With so many friends starting social impact and nonprofit projects, she decided to help them get their messages out to the media. Her side hustles turned into a full-time job, so Danielle decided to quit and start her own PR firm. For the past decade, she has been running Elle Communications (www. ellecomm.com). Danielle's Los Angeles and New York offices focus on highlighting companies and individuals who care about their mission as much as their margin. Elle supports nonprofits, social enterprises, corporate social responsibility teams, ethical brands, and activists and change makers like UNICEF, Rock the Vote, The Little Market, Biossance, Cora, Justin Baldoni, Amanda de Cadenet, Alexis Jones, and the Kind Campaign. Her advice to both brands and influencers is to "make sure your impact strategy is authentic. Impact has become such a trend, and it's wonderful that more people are adopting impact strategies in their businesses. But don't force an unnatural relationship. People can tell whether it's genuine or a marketing gimmick."

George Brescia (www.georgebrescia.com) is an author and style expert. He says whether you're shooting a video, trying to seal a brand deal, or getting together with your in-laws, how you dress sets the tone for everything. "You cannot wake up in the morning and open your closet and be like, 'Ugh! I hate my clothes!'" he says. "It's not going to work. How are you going to have a good day? You

WATCH IT!

To watch my interview with Danielle, go here:

entm.ag/daniellefinck

have to have clothes in your closet that make you feel good. So you want to have what I call a closet full of 'tens': the right color, the right silhouette, clothing for you."

WATCH IT!

Watch my interview with George here:

entm.ag/georgebrescia

LEGAL ADVICE TO SET YOURSELF UP FOR SUCCESS

All the side hustle and startup talk in this chapter means nothing if you don't protect yourself and your brand on the legal front. Not only do you want to be sure you retain control of your intellectual and business property, but you also want to be sure you aren't infringing on anyone else's trademarks or business ideas. And, for some industries, there are complex systems of certification and licensing in place that may affect how you do business (trade industries are notable examples). To protect yourself and the future you are building, making sure you are covered legally is paramount.

When I started my company, I always said:

+ There are things I know.
+ There are things I don't know.
+ And there are things I don't know that I don't know.

I pretty much lived in the last category and was constantly trying to play catch-up in the business and legal world. I was always behind the eight ball, trying to make sure I had all my legal boxes checked—and I often didn't know what those boxes were. In the following section, let's talk about some resources I found helpful and get some words of wisdom from legal experts who can help you keep going on the days you want to quit.

Gather Your Legal Go-To Experts

The pool of potential lawyers is as wide and deep as an ocean. Where do you start? Who is the right lawyer for your business? To begin your search, try pinging your network of mentors and colleagues for recommendations.

I did just that. Using social media for *good*, I crowdsourced resources when I first started my company. When I posted something about needing legal help, a girl I went to sleepaway camp with messaged me to contact her husband. Thanks to Aaron Wright, an expert in corporate and intellectual property law and the founder/director of the Tech Startup Clinic at Cardozo Law School, I got a ton of legal guidance, support, and the documents I needed, like nondisclosure agreements and video releases—for free. I am indebted to the students who worked with Aaron on my company's needs and encourage you to see if there are any free clinics in your area.

Once you've got a pool of potential lawyers in place, think about what your business' specific legal needs are. For example, I knew I needed to speak with a lawyer who understood YouTube agreements. I had attended a digital summit and met someone from YouTube who put me in touch with someone on her team so I could become a YouTube partner. The jargon was new to me and I didn't know my rights. I asked dozens of people for help, but all the lawyers people connected me with didn't have experience with YouTube or wanted thousands of dollars in legal fees. Just as I was running out of time to return a signed agreement to YouTube, I met an attorney named Andy Lee who took me on pro bono. His daughters had been bullied and he wanted to help other kids by helping me start my channel. Thanks to Andy, I was able to sign an agreement I understood without signing my life away. Ask anyone and everyone for help when you're getting started. You never know who will give you a break because they share your mission and vision.

Next, educate yourself on legal matters that pertain to your business. While you likely shouldn't act as your own lawyer, you can and should know enough about the legal aspects of your business that you can be proactive about protecting your assets. For example, when it comes to protecting

> **WATCH IT!** ▶
>
> Once my channel was up and running, I did a profile on Andy's daughter, Nina. We discussed her music career and her incredible anti-bullying anthem. You can watch the episode here: entm.ag/ninalee

your brand, you will want to educate yourself about intellectual property law. I watched videos on the U.S. Patent and Trademark Office's website (www.uspto.gov), which I thought were very helpful for understanding trademarks and copyrights.

To break down what you need to know, IP attorney Scott Sisun says, "It's good to invest in your IP portfolio. Investors down the road, or possible companies looking at your business, will ultimately ask about the IP portfolio and the protections that are in place. Along those same lines, you must always monitor, protect, and enforce your mark, brand, or IP against others, or you could potentially lose it." He also urges everyone to be careful when it comes to using images found online. "I just always tell people not to 'borrow' anything off the internet. The internet's not the public domain, and it's highly likely that whatever you're borrowing, whether it's images, drawings, literary works, whatever it might be, it's likely owned by someone else."

WATCH IT!

To learn how to register and clear your IP and the differences between a trademark and copyright, you can watch my interview with Scott here:

entm.ag/scottsisun

REFLECTIONS

From how to start and fund your passion project to how to protect your intellectual property, we covered a lot of ground this chapter. Let's review the main themes:

+ Do you have an idea you want to launch? How can you make this happen?
+ Do you have a strong brand and know your target audience? How will you communicate with that demographic?
+ Are you using social media to engage consumers?
+ Are you making smart choices when it comes to your brand as an influencer? Are you working with the right influencers to elevate your brand?

Unfiltered

+ Have you done everything you can to protect your assets?

With your awesome platform and products in place, let's talk about what you can do if you're about to step into boss territory.

Chapter 10

How to Act Like a Boss

You have the corner office, the nameplate, and the business cards. But you've never been a CEO before, let alone managed other people. You've been building your business from your apartment/basement/garage, and now shit is about to get real. You've assembled a rockstar team who is about to arrive at their new jobs. You post a picture of your new office space. #dayone

Unfiltered

Whether you are the CEO of a business you've built or just got tapped by your employer to be the CEO of your current office, the role can be intimidating. Suddenly the buck stops with *you*. You are steering the ship—and you have passengers who depend on you. You are the boss—so now you need to act like one.

While being the CEO can be scary, stressful, and overwhelming, it can also be thrilling. As film industry vet Sherry Lansing says, this is a really exciting time for you, too. Sherry became the first woman to head a major film studio when she was named president of 20th Century Fox back in 1980. In 1992, she became chairman and CEO of Paramount Pictures. In her 30 years in the movie business, she participated in the distribution, marketing, and production of more than 200 films, including Academy Award winners *Braveheart*, *Titanic*, and *Forrest Gump*. If you're having anxiety about your new role, Sherry says her number-one piece of advice for you is: Know you're not stuck.

"I think what happens so often in business is a CEO gets to that position after years of doing the actual job and then misses the previous work," she says. "Being the executive in charge of everything gives you the ability to collaborate and to help other people fulfill their vision." If you find you miss doing the work you used to do, Sherry suggests finding ways to make your role more involved in the day-to-day. When she ran Paramount, she thought of the studio as one big production company. "I used to say to the executives, because I loved being a producer so much, 'Think of us as being executive producers on every movie,'" she says. "We have to be involved. We have to read all the scripts—every draft of the script—we have to look at the dailies, we have to go to the set, and we have to go to every sneak preview. So in many ways, that was the way I continued my love. I didn't spend as much time, perhaps, as I should have on maybe what the commissary looked like or on meeting with the banks. But I also had a partner. So we could split it up."

Sherry says if that's not feasible and you really miss your old job or you really don't like being the CEO, then you should pivot. "If you find that you've gotten promoted out of what you really care about, then you should take a beat and go back. There's nothing wrong with that. Or start your own company, which allows you, maybe, to be more hands on."

In this chapter, I'm going to give you some ideas to help you thrive in your new leadership role. From how you treat your employees to how you reach your demographic, this section is packed with tips from people who believe being kind has a place in your workspace. You're the boss—own it.

WATCH IT!

To watch my interview with Sherry, and hear her advice on the one thing everyone needs to succeed, you can go here:

entm.ag/sherrylansing

BE AWARE OF YOUR UNCONSCIOUS BIAS

You may think you are an open-minded person. You may be proud of the fact that you have such a diverse group of people on your team. That doesn't mean your experiences or outside influences won't affect the way you view the world. Most of the time, we don't even realize when we're being biased. Consider these examples:

+ Have you ever been at a restaurant when the service is slower than usual? Your server is a different race than you, and under your breath you mumble, "Ugh. Why do they hire these people?" as opposed to simply asking if your order is almost ready.
+ Have you ever interviewed someone with a foreign accent and found yourself speaking louder when really you meant to slow down your speech because you're known to be a fast talker?
+ Have you found yourself getting extremely annoyed that an elderly person or someone with a cane is taking too long to exit an airplane?

Whether you don't like someone and don't really know why or today's headlines have made you more biased, we could all benefit from a self-audit. You can find quizzes online to help you discover your biases or just start asking yourself if you're making skewed decisions based on

Unfiltered

your inner thoughts and beliefs. But here's the deal. It's 100 percent OK to go to a female doctor if that makes you more comfortable. It's not OK to assume that between two partners in a practice, the male doctor will be smarter and have more training than his female colleague.

I want to pause here for a minute because I'm fascinated by this research when it comes to gender bias. In an op-ed for *The New York Times*, "She Gets No Respect" (www.nytimes.com/2014/06/12/opinion/ nicholas-kristof-she-gets-no-respect.html), Nicholas Kristof looked at a study (www.pnas.org/content/early/2014/05/29/1402786111) that found "female-named hurricanes kill about twice as many people as similar male-named hurricanes because some people underestimate them. Americans expect male hurricanes to be violent and deadly, but they mistake female hurricanes as dainty or wimpish and don't take adequate precautions." What struck me the most about Kristof's piece was "women were as likely as men to disrespect female hurricanes."

Kristof makes the point that people "often assume that racism or sexism is primarily about in-your-face bigots or misogynists, but research in the last couple of decades—capped by this hurricane study—shows that the larger problem is unconscious bias even among well-meaning, enlightened people who embrace principles of equality."

That's partly what drove Gail Tifford to create a movement for men and women in the marketing and advertising world (read more about it later). Gail is Weight Watchers International's chief brand officer and someone who has dedicated her career to creating change from the inside out. Before joining Weight Watchers, Gail served as Unilever's vice president of media and global digital innovation. In that role, she started a national campaign to prevent gender bias from inaccurately portraying women in the media. "I think one of the most important things we can do is to understand ourselves and our own biases, which may be very different from everyone else's. Bias exists in all of us and may take different forms—gender bias, religious bias, disability bias. Only when we can understand what our biases are can we set out to change," Gail says.

How #SeeHer Is Disrupting the Advertising and Marketing Industry

Gail Tifford set out to change the way women are characterized in ads, in movies, and on TV, but the entire #SeeHer campaign came out of a conversation with her (at the time) 14-year-old daughter and her friends. "We were in the car driving, and I was asking them what they wanted to be when they grew up. My daughter said she wanted to be a detective because she was so inspired by the lead character in *Law & Order: Special Victims Unit*, and another young girl said she wanted to be a doctor because of *Grey's Anatomy*." Gail was struck by how influential female characters on TV were—and realized just how few role models they had.

The first thing she did was take that car conversation to two friends: Megan Smith, who at the time was the chief technology officer of the United States under the Obama administration, and Shelley Zalis, founder of The Girls Lounge/The Female Quotient. They shared her concerns. Megan was worried there were not enough young girls going into STEM careers, and Shelley was concerned about women's equality in the workplace. When they really dug into the causes of these problems, they agreed girls didn't have enough positive role models and that most of our media perpetuates negative stereotypes of women. "We also acknowledged that media didn't only reflect culture; media creates culture, and that's when we decided to enlist thousands of brands through the Association of National Advertisers (ANA) to help create a culture where women and girls are accurately portrayed," Gail says.

Gail has found one of the reasons #SeeHer has been so successful is because it's rooted in the belief that this is not a "female" issue.

How #SeeHer Is Disrupting ..., continued

"This is a social and economic issue," she says. "Men and boys' participation and awareness are critical to our continued success. We have more than 1,000 brands onboard worth more than $50 billion in U.S. advertising spend committed to furthering the accurate portrayal of girls and women in media and advertising by 2020. We have engaged all major networks and content creators and have started to see many fruits of this labor already on air, such as at awards shows and at the Olympics."

HOW DOES YOUR COMPANY MEASURE UP?

Gail says there are clear markers companies can study to ensure they're keeping their bias in check. "We created what's called a GEM score (Gender Equality Measure) to help advertisers measure the bias in their ads," she says.

Here are some questions Gail says all advertisers should be asking themselves when developing an ad:

WATCH IT!

To learn more about #SeeHer, you can watch my interview with Gail here:

entm.ag/seeher

+ Do I think highly of how women are presented in the ad?
+ Are women presented in a respectful manner in the ad?
+ Is it inappropriate how women are featured in the ad?
+ Are women presented in the ad in a manner where they can be seen as good role models for other women and young girls?

For the team behind #SeeHer, it all comes down to making executives more aware and holding them more accountable. It's also about ensuring the work they produce and distribute meets a new standard that the #SeeHer community hopes becomes the norm.

Unfiltered

WHY BEING NICE MAKES YOU A BETTER LEADER

One of the things Gail and Shelley both say is: "If you can see her, you can be her." For Fran Hauser, that means if you can see a nice boss, you can be a nice boss. For far too long, being nice has been mistaken for being weak, and this startup investor and longtime media executive is on a mission to change that.

There are plenty of women who believe being a bitch helped them succeed, but Fran says you don't have to be a bitch (or a jerk) to be the boss. That's why she wrote *The Myth of the Nice Girl: Achieving a Career You Love Without Becoming a Person You Hate* (Houghton Mifflin Harcourt, 2018): to challenge the notion that you cannot be both kind and successful. "In reality, niceness is an essential quality of leadership for the world we're living in. It's a superpower that can unlock all sorts of potential and possibility we're currently missing," she says. "There's actually something very wrong when kindness isn't part of the picture when it comes to our leaders. When kindness isn't modeled and celebrated, we find ourselves in a workplace environment that is, at worst, toxic, and at its best, fails to allow us to reach our full potential and share the best of ourselves with others. And people are clamoring for a better, more human, nicer style of leadership."

> **TIP**
>
> Remember that being kind does not mean you should be a pushover. Hold firm to your convictions, be direct, and maintain clear lines of reporting with your employees.

Fran knows all too well how it feels to be criticized for being nice. When she was in her early twenties, she was working at Ernst & Young, one of the biggest professional services firms in the world. She was young, ambitious, and extremely hardworking and was doing well in her job there. In her quest to be agreeable above all else, she says she was overly deferential, a "people pleaser," and admits she was easily intimidated by clients. "I especially remember an imposing older man who was a VP at Coca-Cola who was the central casting version of the smart, tough, demanding leader—and I was a bit like one of those pull-string children's toys," she says. "In client meetings, my line of choice was 'That's interesting,' no matter what subject was being discussed. We could have been talking about what to get for lunch, and if someone suggested sushi, my response would have been, 'That's interesting.' It got so bad my boss pulled me aside and told me, 'Fran, you're yessing the client to death.' It was the start of a long tug-of-war, both within myself and in conversations with managers and colleagues, about how to strike a perfect (and elusive) balance between kindness and strength."

If you're a boss, Fran suggests taking the lead on creating an environment rooted in respect, trust, and kindness.

If you think being nice will keep you from succeeding, you may be surprised to learn the results of a Google study. "When Google set out to study what makes the best-performing team, it found that the most effective teams showed respect for each other, creating environments where people feel comfortable being themselves," Fran says. "And *Harvard Business Review* found that, when deciding whom they'd want to work with, people value likability more than competence. Those whom *HBR* termed 'lovable stars'—those who are both likable *and* competent—have the exact combination of likability and ambition that so many women are struggling to achieve."

But how do you achieve likability without being seen as a kiss-up?

HOW YOU CAN BE GENUINELY NICE WITHOUT BEING A BROWNNOSER

When Fran was at Time, Inc., Mitch Klaif was the chief information officer. As the head of technology, Fran says he was under a lot of pressure to keep the infrastructure running, and in many ways, it was a thankless job. Many of the people coming to him were unhappy because their email wasn't working or they didn't have the funding they needed for a project, but Fran took the time to get to know Mitch as a person. "I asked about his family and listened when he was frustrated about something," she says. "I got along with Mitch really well, while many of my colleagues had a hard time getting him to prioritize their initiatives. At one point, my team needed to accelerate a product launch, which meant we'd need a lot more resources from Mitch's team. I assumed my boss would ask him directly, but instead she said, 'Fran, you need to ask Mitch. He can't say no to you.'"

Sure enough, when Fran walked into Mitch's office, he was happy to help her team, but it wasn't magic: "Mitch was inclined to say yes to me because we already had a relationship. In other words, I didn't just go to him when I had a problem or needed something. As a so-called 'nice girl,' being empathetic came naturally to me, and it simply worked to my advantage when it was time to negotiate or ask for something."

Below are Fran's five ways you can be nicer and stronger—and get better results—in your role as a leader.

1. *Speak up.* By hiding behind a facade of agreeableness, Fran says you're hijacking your own effectiveness and not leaving a great impression of your strength and value. In the end, that can turn you into a people pleaser. "It's OK to push back if you do it respectfully. The key to disagreeing respectfully is staying positive—don't just say it's a bad idea. Instead, suggest a better solution and your reasoning behind it. Also demonstrate that you invested the time to understand the other person's point of view—this is usually a good way to defuse the situation."

2. *Give feedback.* When you build a strong relationship with your team and care deeply about them and their careers, it can be a struggle to give tough feedback. But Fran says avoiding delivering negative feedback can make you seem like a pushover and, frankly, a bad mentor or boss. "You're also doing a disservice to the employee who would benefit from constructive criticism ('constructive' being the key)," she adds. "Give feedback that is nice and direct by presenting the information in an empathetic and supportive way. Position it as helpful advice rather than harsh critique." Fran suggests starting on a positive note about the person's performance—something that is true and meaningful, and that doesn't feel like a throwaway. For example: *I'm really impressed by/with how thorough your analysis has been.* Then move on to the "issue." Say: *I want to be helpful and better understand what is driving the problem*

(e.g., missed deadlines). Fran says don't get personal: focus on the facts. Give specific examples and paint a broader context. For example: *Sloppy financial reports can give people a lack of confidence in your numbers*. "Ask questions and make it a dialogue, not a one-sided lecture. When you leverage your kindness to give feedback empathetically, the conversations become more pleasant and effective for everyone involved."

3. *Negotiate.* The fact that women have a hard time negotiating for themselves is a major factor in the gender wage gap. But Fran says you should never be afraid to ask for what you deserve. "Use your relational skills to negotiate strategically in a way that is good for you and the company," she advises. "Focus on the company's goals and the true value you add to the organization instead of all the reasons you feel you want a higher salary. Data talks—gather as much as possible to use as backup. This can be data about your accomplishments or salary data from peers at other companies. Sometimes the value you've added is not tied to a specific project but that you've created a culture for your team that has resulted in improved morale and retention. Also, women tend to negotiate better when they are negotiating on behalf of someone else. Think about yourself and your value in the same objective manner."

4. *Network.* "Career success is increasingly defined not just by how many hours you spend at your computer but also your ability to connect to others, to incorporate outside perspectives, and to navigate groups. These are essential skills in today's ultraconnected world because no one and nothing exists in a vacuum. This means connecting the dots between ideas, businesses, and people. As a kind woman, you have an advantage here *as long as you get away from your desk* because a lot of this connection requires the very people skills that you have spent a lifetime developing," Fran says. If you aren't investing in yourself and networking, she adds, you won't acquire the experiences and insights that will lead to connecting the dots.

5. *Make decisions.* As a leader, you need to be able to make decisions that might upset others. "Yes, it's essential to think everything through from multiple perspectives and get buy-in and advice from colleagues, but at the end of the day, a leader has to be able to stand in her own shoes, make a clear decision, and then own the results of that decision," Fran says. The trick, of course, is to strike a balance between being empathetic and being unable to call the shots because you're so worried about how your decisions will affect others. "To avoid overempathizing to the detriment of your own success when making a decision, ask yourself what you would do if all the people in your life supported your decision," she suggests. "Once you make the decision, thank everyone you've consulted for his or her input. Acknowledge that your decision isn't going to make everyone happy, but express that you feel strongly that it's the right direction. It's better to make a decision swiftly to avoid being perceived as wishy-washy and so you can all move forward."

As an employee, you also have to be prepared to stick up for yourself if you have a boss who takes advantage of your natural inclination to be a team player and go above and beyond. "Saying no is one of the hardest things to do, but it's critical to set boundaries," Fran says. "First, if it's a situation where your boss hands you a last-minute project (again) or makes an unfair request, be honest and push back." Say, "I've been struggling with how to talk to you about this. Over the past two weeks, I've had to change my personal plans three times at the last minute to stay late. I wonder if this is a good opportunity for someone else on the team to pitch in." More often than not, your boss doesn't realize the dynamic that has been created. If it's a situation where you are overextended but have a hard time saying no to a coffee date or meeting request, Fran recommends writing down your top career priorities (she calls this her Four

> **WATCH IT!** 🖳
>
> To watch my interview with Fran, go to:
>
> entm.ag/franhauser

Setting Stronger Boundaries

As Fran highlights, it's important to set boundaries. And while it's smart to protect your time, self-defense expert Jennifer Cassetta wants you to be smart about protecting yourself, too. In her book, *Hear Me Roar: How to Defend Your Mind, Body & Heart Against People Who Suck* (Promoting Natural Health, 2014), Jennifer breaks down the ABC's of self-defense. When it comes to setting boundaries, Jennifer says everyone has a different comfort level when it comes to personal space, but "setting physical boundaries is crucial to protecting your body from a potential predator."

To learn how to use a strong tone, powerful vocabulary, and commanding body language, watch the interview I did with Jennifer here:

▶ entm.ag/jennifercassetta

Square), and if an ask doesn't align with these priorities, respectfully decline.

CREATING A POSITIVE OFFICE CULTURE

As Fran points out, being nice can create a more positive work environment for you and the people you're leading. It can also help the people on your team have the confidence they need to perform at their best. Kindness is so important to Craig Dubitsky that he built an entire company around the idea and incorporated it into his title: friendly founder of hello products.

Craig came up with the idea of a naturally friendly oral care company when he was looking for toothpaste in a Manhattan drugstore. "I looked at the shelf, and I saw these products that literally had pictures of extracted teeth on them," he says. "I really love brand and design and form and shape and all sorts of visual cues. I kept thinking, if you're trying to sell me toothpaste, why on earth would you ever show me an extracted tooth?" When he looked at the ingredient list, things didn't get much better. "There were, in some cases, ingredients that had been banned from other consumer products years before. Yet we were putting these things in our mouths, and in our children's mouths, a few times a day. I thought that was crazy."

The first thing Craig did was work with a formulator who became the head of research and development for hello. Once they had the "goop," as he calls it, figured out, and had determined how to make hello a profitable business, he turned his time and attention to his company's values and the people who would represent them. "I think if you're starting a company and you have this concept you want to bring to fruition, you've got to make sure that you're trying to stand for something," he says. "One of the first things most people connect with is the name of something—it can either be instantly, 'Wow!' or kind of forgettable. The naming thing is really key. For us and our brand, I dreamt up this word 'hello' because I was trying to think of the friendliest word I could think of simply because everything else in oral care seemed remarkably unfriendly."

Office Culture Tips

If you want to create a company that engages consumers and the employees working hard to serve them, here is how Craig does it:

+ *Believe in generational wealth.* Craig says starting a business gives you the opportunity to "choose your family." Since everyone works together, everybody is an equity stakeholder. "We're owners of the business. That, to me, makes a big difference. The idea is you should feel motivated and excited about what we're doing, and know that we care as much about each other as we do about the brand. It's part of our values to create value and to offer value to people. If we create value for our stakeholders, they should all do well." Craig says making every employee a stakeholder has a dramatic impact because the benefits last for generations. "There's a ripple effect," he says.

+ *Believe in an open environment.* Craig says when you tell someone who works outside the marketing department that they can't come to a marketing meeting or someone who isn't a designer that they can't weigh in on a design, you're making a mistake. "Good ideas can come from anybody," he says. "That's the kind of environment we want. That's the culture we have. No one has sole dominion over good ideas. We don't ever put anybody in a silo as that is demotivating and unfriendly—and it doesn't allow folks to create their biggest impact."

+ *Shine a light on everyone's talents.* No matter what business you're in, if you're working with at least one other person, Craig says it's imperative to know what skills your partner has outside your company. "The idea is to make sure you find a way to let those talents shine and come through and help your business. If you're running a larger organization, figure out new ways to tap into the talent that's sitting right in your midst."

+ *Hire people who are passionate about things outside of work.* "I think people make the mistake of thinking, 'You just have to be passionate about my brand—just about my brand.' It feels really good to think folks are passionate about the brand, but we're trying to be sure people have outside passions because it shows a level of emotional depth that's really critical." Craig says when you're starting a business, it's going to be an emotional roller coaster. "To know that people have the ability to pull back into a place of passion, emotional excitement, and security and then, hopefully, aim just properly and let that go, you're going to slingshot into the future to a better place."

+ *Go out of the way to take care of your team.* "We have a great CEO. We have a great head of sales. We have a great head of marketing. We have a great head of finance, as well as a great head of supply chain, and a great R&D lead. Everyone really punches well above their weight. Part of my job is to magnetize the company to attract the best people, energize the brand, then basically, get out of the way so that the smartest, best people can do their smartest, best work," Craig says. Last but not least, he adds, you should strive to create an environment where people love what they do: "You

WATCH IT!

To watch my interview with Craig, you can go here:

entm.ag/craigdubitsky

have to put the magic above the math. If you get the magic right, the math takes care of itself." Yes, creating a company that's good for your stakeholders and shareholders is critical, but so is taking care of the people who show up to work with you every day.

Now let's say you have an awesome product, a happy team, and a thriving company. Whether you want to cash in on that success or have simply reached a point where you want to move on, it's important as a founder to think about your exit strategy.

WHAT TO DO WHEN IT'S TIME TO SELL OR CLOSE UP SHOP

Many entrepreneurs will tell you they started their company out of necessity. Perhaps they needed a product that didn't exist, so they created it. Perhaps they needed a solution to a problem. They couldn't find one, so they invented one. For Pamela Mirels, spending five years working at a company as an analyst, senior analyst, and chief of staff taught her that she loved managing large projects. "I really enjoyed being in sales, operations, and finance at the same time," she says. "I knew I wanted to start my own business, but it wasn't like I knew I wanted to make Spanx or something specific. That's why I went to business school. I wanted two years for creative play. I experimented with a lot of ideas. I explored a food truck and a wedding registry, but neither was 'it.'"

In 2012, Pam was inspired to plan an event after seeing the movie *Searching for Sugar Man*. The film tells the story of U.S. musician Sixto Rodriguez, who became a huge hit in South Africa in the 1970s. Rumors circulated for years that Rodriguez had died; but two fans from Cape Town made it their mission to find out *what really happened.* (Spoiler alert: Rodriguez is alive.) Pam decided she was going to find Rodriguez and invite all the South Africans she knew to a concert in New York. Once she found his booker, she booked Rodriguez on her credit card for $30,000. "I booked flights for his band and his family before selling one ticket," Pam told me in our interview for this book. "I did all this in October and planned the concert for April. I decided then that I wanted to build a company that let people 'horde' their culture. I thought we could bring together people who love art in New York City and provide premium experiences and access for them since you often need to be on the inside of all these organizations to get to go to all these cool events. That was the kind of audience we were playing to. It took six weeks to build a demo website, and I lumped in a company membership with my ticket price."

The Rodriguez event sold out, and within four years, CultureHorde had more than 1,000 members. Once Pam reached a point where she thought she had grown the company as far as she could in New York, she says the natural next step was to expand CultureHorde to other cities and have a general manager for each location. But she was getting married and didn't want to travel anymore.

She thought about her next move for at least a year before she sold. She asked her COO if she wanted to take on more responsibility, but the COO didn't feel that was the right route and declined Pam's offer. Pam also met with an entrepreneur who focused on sponsorships and spent months talking about what CultureHorde could become. "What you have to know about moving on from your company is that it's like dating," Pam says. "You have to investigate every opportunity because if you created something of value, people will try to BS you into a deal. Researching your options can be a huge time suck until you find *the one.*" Ultimately, Pam chose another experiential company to acquire CultureHorde.

Before you sell your company, Pam says there are a few things you should do:

* Look at your options and don't rush the process.

+ Educate yourself on what selling your company entails, both legally and financially.
+ If you don't get a term sheet, or letter of intent, from a potential buyer between four to six weeks of meeting them, that's a red flag.
+ Make sure you feel comfortable with the deal and with what will happen to your database.
+ Be prepared for some trust to erode between you and your buyer. Even if you're friends, going through an acquisition can make the best of friends question the other side's motives. You have to remember that it's a negotiation and everyone wants a better deal.
+ Outline your transition before you finalize the sale.

When it's all said and done, don't be surprised if you have mixed emotions. "Look back at what you built and know the future is yours," she says.

REFLECTIONS

I hope after reading this chapter you feel empowered in your role and have the tools you need to empower the people you're leading. Whatever you do, don't forget you're never stuck. Remember:

+ When it comes to leading a team, spend some time thinking about your life experiences and how you see the people around you.
+ Try not to let old habits cloud your judgment and never tolerate intolerance.
+ Embrace kindness in your role and your workplace.
+ Create a culture where people want to come to work every day.
+ When it's time to move on, educate yourself on all the steps you need to take.

If you, your company, or even your exit makes for a good story, the next chapter will explain how to go about getting press or getting published.

Chapter 11

Expanding Your Reach and Platform

You can't afford a publicist yet, but you want the world to know your company exists. You ask your nephew if he's interested in running your social media and doing research on who to contact in the press for potential interviews. He's excited to make some extra cash during his senior year, and you're relieved you don't need to learn how to use Snapchat. You wake up on Monday morning and see comments and likes under your nephew's creative post. #MondayMotivation

Unfiltered

After spending so many years reading pitches from publicists, I can tell you there is a right way and a wrong way to pitch. I always appreciate people who take the time to look at my work and familiarize themselves with what I cover. My biggest piece of advice: Don't email me a pitch and then later that day hit the little arrow or FWD on your screen so it reappears in my inbox. Give me a few days to get to it before you follow up.

Some people send me pitches that have my name in the subject. For example:

"Jessica—I Have an Entrepreneur You Have to Meet."

I usually open those because I'm intrigued, but I loathe the emails from people I don't know that say: "Dear Jessica: It's been forever. How are you? I want to pitch a client I think you will love . . ."

Don't lie. Instead, say:

> Dear Jessica,
>
> We haven't met, but I'm familiar with your work. I recently saw your piece on Roth, Tooch & Tova and thought you would be interested in my client, who started a company that (explain the company here). Attached you will find a press release and talking points. Please let me know if you have time for a call and we can discuss story angles. I would love to share our client roster with you as well.
>
> Sincerely,
>
> Jordana Nadine

To help you get the coverage you're looking for, I asked Jason Feifer, the editor-in-chief of *Entrepreneur* magazine, to share his thoughts on the subject.

Jason started as a community newspaper reporter and has worked as an editor for *Boston* magazine, *Men's Health*, *Fast Company*, *Maxim*, and now *Entrepreneur*. He has freelanced for *GQ*, *ESPN the Magazine*, *New*

York magazine, *The New York Times*, *The Washington Post*, and more. And he has two podcasts: *Problem Solvers* and *Pessimists Archive*. He always wanted to be an editor-in-chief, though he says he would have been OK not achieving that goal: "I'm a big believer in setting goals but being fine finding something different along the way. As it so happened, this worked out."

Jason says the hardest part of his job is also the most exciting part. "Media is an ever-shifting industry, so we have to be constantly thinking of new ways to be relevant to our audience and to go beyond the basic content products we've relied upon for so long," he says. "A strong media brand needs to be so many things. I think we're only at the beginning, which means when you send a pitch, you have to keep in mind what media companies are looking for today beyond just filling space in a magazine or airtime."

Since getting the right coverage can help you engage with consumers or sell products or services, here is what Jason has seen work best:

+ *Sometimes you're not the story.* You may be pitching outlets hoping for an entire feature on you and/or your company. If no one is biting, you may have a better chance at being mentioned in a bigger story. While fancy features are great, consider pitching trends in your industry that no one seems to be talking about and how you can contribute to that discussion. It's really important to know *why* you want coverage before going down the time-consuming (and sometimes expensive) path to getting press. Identify your goal, and whether or not media can help you reach it—then focus on the publications that make sense. Perhaps the bigger feature on your personal story or your company's success will come later.

+ *Fascinating and compelling stories are always welcome.* Reporters are always happy to learn something fascinating, and if you have a compelling story to support your pitch, that's a win-win. Even if a reporter isn't working on that topic at the time, most save the really good pitches to revisit when they need a story that can run anytime. For example: Have you failed and made a major rebound? If so, how did you do it?

+ *Don't throw a dart in the dark*. Spare yourself the disappointment, and a reporter the agony, of having to go through pointless emails. Be specific and share one or two things that the journalist *needs to know*. Or better yet, try establishing a personal connection with the reporter so you have an idea of the subjects they cover.

+ *Repetition is an editor's worst nightmare*. You may be putting your best work forward by sending an email with a newsworthy subject line. But if you're pitching a story that's been done a million times, you have to be more creative. Think about what really sets you apart. If you don't know, spend more time on that question before you pitch.

+ *Read my mind*. Before sending a pitch, spend time looking at the pieces that publication publishes and how their content is formatted. Reporters really appreciate when you pitch something that will surprise and interest their audience and fills a need in their next issue or broadcast at the same time.

> **WATCH IT!** ▶
>
> You can watch my interview with Jason here:
>
> entm.ag/jasonfeifer

Now that you have a sense of what you need to do to get press from an editor, next are some tips from PR gurus who work with clients morning, noon, and night.

GET THE MEDIA TO BITE

If you do some research, you will find most publicists cover different areas. Some focus on beauty brands, while others only represent authors. Whoever you choose, you want to make sure they have experience pitching your kind of company to the right contacts. You don't want a publicist representing your lipstick line who only works with home and gardening editors and reporters.

If you choose to pitch to journalists on your own, Gwen Wunderlich has some advice. She has spent more than 20 years raising awareness for some of the biggest brands in the fashion, beauty, luxury, lifestyle, and celebrity industries. The CEO and cofounder of Wunderlich Kaplan Communications (http://wkc.rocks/), Gwen is an expert at crafting messages that gain the attention of the media, investors, and retailers. If you're not working with a PR firm, Gwen says, "Stop with the long, drawn-out stories. When pitching via email or phone, make it a fast, hard sell and straight to the point. Never lie, never falsify; but sensationalism sells. So the question is, how are you giving a real wow factor to your story/brand or message?"

If you are working with a publicist, Gwen advises to sign on the dotted line *only* when you're sure you have the money to pay the firm's or publicist's retainer for six months to a year. "Sometimes press hits overnight and sometimes it takes a while," she says. She adds you must know *why* you're hiring a person or agency to help you: "Press is to build brand awareness—not to generate sales. Although it does almost always, don't expect your PR person to drive sales home for you. This isn't their job. Make sure you give your publicist the tools they need to succeed. Scrimping, saving, and being a tightwad harms no one but you in the end. Whether this means books, clothes, or beauty products to send to editors, many times the media needs to see the products before they review them. So send it. Make sure you allow for that in your PR budget. Also, get back to your publicist in a timely manner. They are pitching their hearts out for you. Don't make them lose a story because of a tardy reply. Treat them with kindness and grace, and appreciate their wins. They are your cheerleaders every single day. Don't you want them to be pumped up about you? Of course you do. Authentic excitement wins every single time," she says.

Last but not least, Gwen says people can use PR to empower themselves. "You are a brand in the making," she says. "Your life is a story to be told. Think about how you want to be perceived to the world. Create that. You can press restart at any time. Create your sellable story. Use it to network, score the gig you want, and create the life you've dreamed of. The power of PR is magic!"

With your PR tools sharpened, here's what you should keep in mind if you dream of being published.

GETTING PUBLISHED

Writing a book is a lot of work, but there are benefits to being a published author. Most authors want to write a book because they have something to share and find personal satisfaction in knowing they will make the world a better place in some way. While that's true, most will tell you publishing a book didn't make them rich or famous. However, in addition to checking an item off your bucket list, publishing a book can help you acquire credibility, get more leads, gain more exposure, and take your speaking engagements to the next level.

Before you go down the rabbit hole of spending your days, nights, and weekends attached to your keyboard, I asked Jennifer S. Wilkov, my North Star whom I've mentioned earlier in this book, to share her expertise. Jennifer is an international bestselling award-winning author, an award-winning freelance writer, and a respected book and business consultant. You can learn more about Jennifer by visiting Your Book Is Your Hook (http://yourbookisyourhook.com).

Jennifer's Advice to Help You Get Published

Over more than a decade as a consultant for a variety of projects, encompassing nonfiction, fiction, and children's books, Jennifer has seen and heard a lot. "I have enjoyed the pleasure of writing books and love sharing them with multiple audiences through many different marketing techniques," she says. "I have met many people when I have taught at conferences and festivals and work with those who have not only book projects but screenplays for film and TV too." Jennifer says she knows what works and cringes when she sees aspiring writers making common mistakes. Here are Jennifer's quick tips to keep you on the straight and narrow path to success with your project:

+ *Know your audience and make it relevant.* Understand for yourself first why you want to write your book or project. Get clear about the audience you want to talk to and make sure your language reflects them including age and other demographic considerations. Avoid jargon so you don't turn off your audience and lose them.

+ *Don't write for the trends.* They will be over before you finish. Write what you love and can relate to. This will make the project that much more fun for you, and your joy will translate to the project and make it more enjoyable for your readers.

+ *For fiction, finish writing your book before you seek a publisher or literary agent.* Fiction books must be written and edited and in the highest and best state when you present them to the publishing industry and your audience. Make sure you get your project in the best condition you can.

+ *For nonfiction, put together a book proposal.* You won't need the book manuscript to be completed right away. However, you will need to know the full table of contents for the project and the chapter titles. A book proposal is the "sales brochure" for your book. It requires that you present your knowledge of the audience you're writing the book for and the competitive titles that are already out in the marketplace as well as your credentials and your intentions for marketing and promoting the book. You will also need to include at least one or two completed chapters to show that you can write.

+ *Consider what you want your experience to be.* The publishing industry tracks all books using an ISBN number so they can see the sales of your book as soon as it is released. This is important because whether you choose to self-publish or get a literary agent or publisher, the number of books you sell in the first six weeks or so is an indication of whether you can market and move your books to an audience. This factors into business decisions about any other books you want to publish later. Self-publishing will speed up the publication process of your book. Going with a literary agent or publisher will slow it down. Make the right decision for the right reasons and be aware of the ramifications of your choice.

Finally, remember that every author and book needs a platform. "Platform, platform, platform" is what you will hear from the publishing industry. What's your platform? Whether your project is fiction or nonfiction, you need to provide a solid online and off-line presence—or platform—that the industry professionals can easily find. This is more than just a website. It includes your social media activity, your in-person appearances, and much more. The further you cast your web of marketing and influence, the more publishers will be interested in your project. After all, at the end of the day, it is a business decision about who can move the most books.

WATCH IT!

You can watch my interview with Jennifer here:

entm.ag/yourbook-isyourhook

REFLECTIONS

Getting your business noticed is a tough road to travel. Keep in mind that your success in getting ink should not equate to your personal happiness. Getting press is important to increase exposure, but you want to be thoughtful when it comes to who you're pitching, how you're pitching them, and why. Also keep in mind:

+ Don't get discouraged if your story is part of a longer feature. It may take time to get an entire profile piece on you or your company.
+ Think outside the box in terms of what makes your story compelling.
+ Don't be lazy when reaching out to the press. Do your homework and try to make a journalist's life easier by providing important information upfront.
+ If you choose to spend time on a book proposal, remind yourself this may not be the project that pays for your new boat.
+ If you're hoping your book elevates your brand, helps you sell more products, or raises the bar for your speaking tour, pay attention to what's already on bookshelves and reaching your demographic. Don't write for the trends.
+ Whether you're working with a publisher or planning to print your book on your own, have a solid platform in place so you can sell as many books as possible.

Unfiltered

It's important to note that most things in life take time. While you're trying to make magic happen, be sure to surround yourself with solid people. If you find you don't know who your real friends are anymore, I hope the next chapter helps you regroup.

Part Five

Happiness Is Not a Pie

Chapter 12

Navigating the Friendshift

You're at brunch with your friends and pull out your phone because you remembered it's a colleague's birthday and you want to post something nice. As you open Facebook, you see picture after picture from an old friend's wedding. You had no idea she was getting married because you haven't talked to her in years. For some reason, you feel sad and have the waitress take a picture of you and your new crew. #squadgoals

Unfiltered

To make sure you're surrounding yourself with people who lift you up instead of bring you down, remember that friends are supposed to fight for you, respect you, encourage you, and support you. If you have one person who does all the above, you're lucky. If you have several people like that, you've hit the jackpot. These relationships are so important that I want you to jot down their names here and make sure you are checking the same boxes for them. Stay on top of what they're going through, what they need, and how you can be in their corner. In fact, feel free to put down this book and reach out to them right now just to let them know you're thinking about them and tell them how much you appreciate their friendship.

Keep a list handy of your go-to people so you can refer back to it when you're feeling lost or lonely. Like this:

I'm so grateful for:

1. Name: _____

2. Name: _____

3. Name: _____

4. Name: _____

5. Name: _____

Making this list can also help you take note of those friends who might have fallen off your radar. It happens. We all change, and life can take us in different directions. And that's OK. Think of your friendships like tectonic plates: They can overlap and shift over time. If you're currently distanced from a friend, or an entire friend group, you may be experiencing what I call the *friendshift*. This is different from a falling out, where you make up and move on. Friendshifts can happen throughout different chapters of our lives for various reasons.

SOME COMMON CAUSES FOR FRIENDSHIFTS

One friendshift I hear about frequently is the kind that comes with a really powerful experience in one environment but fizzles in another. Most people have gone on a business retreat, to a conference, or on a regular work trip and closely bonded with a member of their team only to get back to the office and return to being mere acquaintances. Other people have shared what it has felt like to outgrow friends who played an important role in their lives for many years.

For example, when I was in college, one girl in my group of friends made it her personal goal to gossip about me all the time. I tried to fly under her radar and not rock the boat as much as I could, but after we graduated, things got worse. I asked myself, "Why would I want to spend two seconds with this person? And why do my other friends tolerate her behavior?"

Everyone else in this group got married and had kids years before I did. During the years I was making $25,000 per year at my job, I spent money on bridesmaids' dresses, bachelorette weekends, bridal showers, and wedding gifts—not to mention flights and hotel rooms. Then I started to spend money on baby gifts. Of the seven women in the group, do you know how many of them in turn made a donation to any of the charity events I organized? Two. While any amount would've been appreciated, what I really wanted was their support.

In addition to chairing fundraising events, I was trying to build a career and working a lot of overtime so I could make more than $25,000 a year. I spent less time on catching up with them because in my limited spare time, I was dating nonstop and going to synagogue more. They were settled in their careers and relationships and I was unsettled in both departments. It took everything I had to go to my college reunion and see them with their significant others while I was still single and trying to make ends meet. From their actions and the things they said to my face, I knew some of those friendships hadn't just shifted; they were over.

Did this experience hurt? More than I can express. Does that mean I didn't wish them well? Of course not. Life is too short to carry around negative feelings. As you'll see from the following stories, friendships can change for all kinds of reasons. Unless you have done damage and need to seek forgiveness to repair a strained relationship, here are some lessons to keep in mind:

+ Sometimes you're just the odd one out—and it hurts.

+ Sometimes you experience a life change your friends can't understand.
+ Sometimes your environment changes.
+ Sometimes it's circumstantial.
+ Sometimes you have to date your career.

The funny thing about friendships is they can come back into your life. People mature and sometimes enough time passes, someone apologizes, or a life event brings people back together. If you're going through a friendshift now, that may be hard to fathom. Here's some life advice from people who faced different obstacles within their social circles.

HOW TO RALLY WHEN YOU'RE THE ODD ONE OUT

When Gabrielle Segev was in her late twenties, she owned a beauty salon in Australia. All her friends were engaged, married, pregnant, or had kids. "None of the girls in my group were sensitive to the fact that I was the only single one," she says. "I would be preparing everyone for their wedding and all of their bridesmaids. While I appreciated the business, at one point I went into the bathroom and just sobbed. I was going on dates all the time. My clients were setting me up with people. My business was the love of my life because it filled a void."

Gabrielle avoided things like engagement parties and decided to leave Sydney because she felt so alone. "I worked my ass off for ten years, and my plan was to go to LA for six months," she says. While in Los Angeles, a friend invited her to visit New York City. While in New York, she heard a cute guy talking and said, "Are you speaking Hebrew? Shabbat Shalom!" (Hebrew for "Good Sabbath"). Today, the two are married with two kids and Gabrielle is busy running a beauty salon in Los Angeles.

When you're the odd duck, Gabrielle reminds you:

+ Know you will be found.
+ Everything is timing. If I had gotten married sooner, I would have brought unresolved issues into my relationship.
+ Be patient and don't hesitate to spice things up. Change the coffee shop you go to. Change your gym. And don't focus on what people post on social media.

Unfiltered

SOMETIMES YOU EXPERIENCE A LIFE CHANGE YOUR FRIENDS CAN'T UNDERSTAND

Sometimes, a friendshift occurs not because of a falling out but because of a failure to relate. We're all experiencing different challenges at different times, so we can't always understand what someone is going through because we haven't experienced it ourselves.

When Jill's son was 2 years old and her daughter was 12 weeks old, her dad died of cancer. While friends were well-intentioned, she says it was hard to grieve while helping people around her navigate her newfound reality.

"At the funeral, someone said to my brother, 'Well, you're one-half an orphan!'" she says. "At Shiva, someone told me about his cancer scare and said, 'Thank God it was just a scare!' I mean, my dad just passed from cancer. Texts with the question 'How are you?' and 'Let me know what I can do to help' became more offensive than comforting. It is so nice that people reach out, but how was I supposed to remember who was available to help me? Plus, it's awkward to tell people what you need. I couldn't say, 'I need someone to watch my kids so I can have a nervous breakdown.' People would say, 'Let me know what you need'—but I didn't even know what I needed! One of my friends sent me a $100 gift card to Seamless (www.seamless.com). That was so helpful because all I had to do was order in dinner. She didn't say, 'Let me know if I can help.' She did something she knew would take something else off my plate. Your life doesn't stop. Your kids still have to wake up; they still need to eat."

A year after Jill's dad passed away, her mom was diagnosed with cancer, and Jill became her main caregiver, helping to go through her dad's stuff and dealing with the lawyers while raising her kids with her husband. "You seek out people who understand you," she says. "It's not that you're not friends with your other friends, but you become close with the people who have been in your shoes."

Clearly, Jill has seen her fair share of heartache, and she knows it can affect relationships on a cellular level. Here is what she recommends to get through such a friendshift:

+ *Jill's advice if you lose a loved one.* "You have different friends to call for different reasons. One day you may need to call a friend who will help you clean out a house. That may not be the person you break down the cancer with to discuss possible treatments."

+ *Jill's advice if you're supporting a friend who lost a loved one.* "Don't ask, just do. A friend called me and said, 'Jill, I'm taking my kid to the museum this afternoon. Can I take your son with us?' That was so much better than her calling me and asking what she could do for me."

She also suggests letting someone know you're thinking about them. "My friend is Catholic and I'm Jewish. Every time she goes to church, she lights a candle for me and sends me a picture. It's so meaningful."

If you haven't done anything to acknowledge someone's loss because you fear too much time has passed, Jill says, "too much time has *not* passed because the grief never goes away. We got a letter from one of my dad's co-workers who none of us knew, saying what an influence my dad had on him. It was so thoughtful that two years later, this man did something. You always want the person you lost to be remembered. It's very comforting to know that person made an impact and won't be forgotten."

+ *Jill's advice for everyone.* "They say when someone passes, the real work begins. I've spent months with my mom going through everything. I didn't know where the deed to the house was. We've done a lot of that work now. Everything is in a folder. I was given the gift of time with her, which is the best of the worst. We've written on the back of every picture we found so I know who is in the albums."

Jill also says to brace yourself when it comes to handling your loved one's belongings. "I live in my apartment. I was overwhelmed by all of my dad's stuff I was going through, not sure what I was supposed to keep. At first, you're not in the emotional place to go through everything. The more you can get rid of things while your loved ones are alive, the easier it may be for you to focus on your grief when the time comes."

Unfiltered

MANAGING A LONG-DISTANCE FRIENDSHIFT

Life takes you to new places, literally. And when that happens, you usually can't take your friends with you. While we can stay connected via social media when we're far away from friends and family, it's different from being able to grab coffee, meet up for dinner, or share celebrations IRL. So what do you do when the distance creates a friendshift?

Lindsay Tuchman knows the drill of long-distance friendshifts. She chose her career path long before she started college. She knew once she graduated that she would be moving to a small town. "I wanted to be a news reporter and anchor, and that meant starting in a small market," she says. "When that time came, I was sad to leave my friends but very accepting that it was part of my plan." All of Lindsay's friends moved to the same city and continued their fun college life together. "Meanwhile I was alone building my career," she says. "There were really tough times, feeling lonely a lot, but it showed me how important good friends are, vs. being with the group. My true friends were the ones that visited me, and I visited them back."

As Lindsay got older, she started to realize that even those relationships became difficult from time to time because their paths were just so different from hers. Her friends didn't understand the loneliness or the stress of her job, which led to odd hours and working weekends. She found herself feeling hurt when her friends didn't sympathize with her or didn't think to text her after a hard day at work. "That disconnect led me to start finding more comfort in making friends in the journalism field, who understood the trials and tribulations," she says. "There's something about a news career that is similar to an artist or actor; it's a deep passion, and not everyone understands that drive. My best friends remained my best friends, but I started to get more comfortable with the fact that there would be a piece of me that was separate from them—that would make us different."

Lindsay's Advice

Lindsay spoke very candidly with me about her experience following her professional dreams at the expense of some of her personal relationships. Below, she shares some advice on how to navigate the treacherous terrain of a distance-related friendshift. She says:

+ I admit I still get jealous when I see pictures of my old group of friends together and think of them all living in their nice apartment talking late at night about the dates they went on; meanwhile I'm at work at 11 P.M. on a Saturday. But whenever I visit, I'm always ready to go home, back to my reality, and back to my fantastic colleagues who really get me through and through. Make sure you don't lose sight of the amazing friendships you do have.

+ I had a big group of sorority friends who still get together as a group, but I still feel like the odd one out when that happens since they've all hung out more recently and I'm always the one who needs to catch up. I realize though, when I'm with them, that even though they all live amazing lives, it never would have been my path to happiness. Keep in mind, you're following your path for a reason.

+ I love having best friends across the country, and best friends in my office, and know that any of them would drop everything if I needed them. Social media makes FOMO (fear of missing out) a real thing sometimes, but my dreams and passions separated me from them, and I can't deny that. So remember, you may be riding different waves, but you can still meet at the shore.

In the end, realize that everyone comes into your life for a reason, and friends do shift over time.

SOMETIMES IT'S CIRCUMSTANTIAL

Sometimes friendships change because our circumstances do. Frankly, this theme came up the most while I was working on this book.

For example, one friend shared that when he sold his company for millions of dollars, his group of childhood friends started to treat him differently. "They made rude comments about me whenever I was with

Sometimes You Have to Date Your Career

When Melissa Ben-Ishay got fired from her advertising job, her brother told her to start baking and they would make a plan. Melissa had always loved to bake, and on that day, she made 250 cupcakes. Her brother said he would go into business with her, and that's how Baked by Melissa (www.bakedbymelissa.com) was born. While trying to fulfill orders and build her business, Melissa says she had to date her career and didn't have as much time to see friends. "All I did was work," she says. "I baked 17 hours a day, seven days a week, for a very long period of time. I had these two very close friends, who are still my best friends today, who would come to the kitchen, turn over an egg crate, and just talk to the back of my head while I baked." Melissa says that drive and dedication, and friends who understood her life, helped her get to where she is today. "It's so important to surround yourself with people who love you and support you and build you up when you're not feeling your best self because everyone has those days," she adds. While Melissa admits those people are few and far between, she says those are the people you need to keep in your life. When you're working 24/7, they won't ever make you feel bad for following your dreams. They'll be the ones who want you to succeed and be part of your cheering section. And if you just got fired, Melissa wants you to know "you are amazing and you can do anything you set your mind to."

To watch the interview I did with Melissa, go here:

entm.ag/bakedbymelissa

them and clearly weren't happy for me—even though they saw how hard I worked for so many years," he says.

Weddings seem to be another big reason why some friendships shift. Unless you've planned a wedding, it might be hard to understand how stressful making the guest list can be for a couple. In my case, I got married at 36 and have been lucky to make many amazing friends throughout my three-plus decades of life. But when it came to my wedding, I was juggling my parents' list, my in-laws' list, my husband's list, and my list. I have a large family, too, so that played another role in the number of people I could invite. I ended up losing some friends because they were hurt they weren't invited. But not inviting someone to my wedding wasn't a reflection of how much I liked the person. If I was throwing a fancy birthday party for myself, it would have been a different story.

If you've lost friends for the same reason, hopefully they will understand your situation once they're in it themselves. If you've lost friendships because your friends couldn't be happy for you or were envious of your success, you're probably better off without that negativity in your life.

REFLECTIONS

Friendships can change due to different variables. Whatever you do, don't bad-mouth one friend to the rest of your group. Resolve your issues only with the person you have a problem with. This way, when things blow over, you don't have to backpedal and apologize for things you said in the heat of the moment. Think about:

+ What is a relationship you want to repair?
+ What is a friendship you need to forgo?
+ Who has been there for you?
+ Who have you been meaning to reach out to or reconnect with?
+ How will you be a better friend?

Friends can make bad days tolerable and good days even better. And yes, it's totally fine to have friends play different roles in your life or have different dynamics with each one. For example, you may have someone in your life like my friend Tracey, who is your voice of reason about anything and everything. Or someone like Amy who will talk through every detail of a story with you and help you analyze every part of it, however long that process takes. Then there are friends you've had since childhood like Jill, who know years' worth of stuff about you and will leave you the most loving, supportive messages even if it's your turn to call them. You may have a friend who is in a totally different stage of life like Emily, who never drops the ball on your friendship or leaves you out of anything just because you're not living parallel lives (yet). You also may have a friend you've met through work like Frank who has become an honorary member of your family and will cry happy or sad tears with you. Perhaps you have new friends like Melanie and Tova who you met later in life and now can't imagine your life without them. You may have a partner-in-crime friend like Lindsay who you knew back in college and reconnected with years later and learned you had more in common than you ever realized. Among the different kinds of friendships you collect in life, there are also couples like Stefan and Lori, who you met through an ex and managed to keep in your life after the breakup.

There's also the group of people who become a big part of your life when you start a new chapter. Moving to Los Angeles was a big one for me because I loved my life in New York and never thought I'd leave. Friends like Mari and Lauren checked in on me every step of the way. Julie made introductions. Amy and Katie became friends I could call for anything.

So if you have one true friend, you're lucky. If you have a handful of loyal friends, you're truly blessed. Be a good friend to those in your circle and let them know how much they mean to you. As you will read in the next chapter, dating can bring on the tears, but a healthy perspective and good friends can help you find the sun on those cold and cloudy days when you feel alone.

Chapter 13

Being Single Is Not a Life Sentence

Just the thought of going to your relative's Super Bowl party puts you in a panic. You know everyone there is going to question you about your love life and tell you why you're still single. No one will believe dating is a beast because everyone else in your family got married before dating sites and apps. You post your status: "Sunday Funday with the Fam!" When you really want to post: #SMH

Unfiltered

Most of us go to college and study a few different subjects before picking a major. Many of us have had different internships to show us what careers we liked and which ones we didn't. Well, sometimes dating requires the same kind of time, effort, and research. If you're frustrated because people around you are making you feel crazy that you want a relationship *and* a career, take a break from dating to focus on you, your goals, or your business plan. There's nothing wrong with that.

If you just broke up with someone or someone broke up with you, and the thought of reading this chapter makes you want to cry, I'm so sorry. I know this feeling, and it stings. (If your ex was toxic, then I'm happy you are out of that relationship and proud of you for getting out!) I do know from lots of experience what it feels like when you have to start over. Sometimes dating, or even just the thought of it, is super painful. I wish I could press fast-forward for you, but I promise it will get better. One day, you will look back and be able to laugh about the times your IRL dating life looked nothing like what everyone else was posting on social media. In this chapter, we'll talk about life on the front lines of dating and share some truly hilarious stories from the trenches.

IMAGE STARTS WITH "I"

Before we get into what you should look for in a partner and how to live a life you love until you find it, we have to start with *you*. How do you see yourself? Do you love your body or loathe it? Do you like being by yourself, or do you need to be with people all the time? Are you competitive with the people you date? Always looking for an argument or someone to worship you? Or are you seeking someone to take care of you the way you take care of everyone else?

Knowing who you are is incredibly sexy. If you are aware of your gifts and your needs, that will help you understand where you are strong and where you may be able to lean on someone else's strengths. Being the CEO of your business, or your dating life, doesn't mean you're perfect in every possible way. It means you play up what makes you *you* and you surround yourself with people who can help you be a better person. When it comes to dating, being with a person who loves, supports, accepts, and appreciates you is everything. I want to make sure that's what you're putting out in the universe the next time you swipe right.

#ACTIVITY: Describe Your Partner

This is not the time to go into detail about your ideal partner's looks. I want you to spend some time thinking about this person in terms of how he or she will make you *feel*. Read through the following five questions and write your answers down.

1. Imagine you are going to your favorite place, whether it's a vacation spot, hiking trail, coffee shop, or relative's house. When you arrive with your person, how do you feel?

2. When you receive the best news and call your person, how does he or she respond?

3. How does that make you feel?

4. When you imagine holding this person's hand or exchanging a meaningful kiss, how does that make you feel?

5. When you are having a bad day and confide in this person, how does this person make you feel?

As we go through these sections, keep this person and these feelings in mind. If you're currently dating someone who doesn't make you feel like this person you just envisioned, you need to take another look at why you're in this relationship.

WHAT WILL YOU CONTRIBUTE?

Relationships work best when both people think about what they can do for the other person. If you wake up thinking about one nice thing you can do for your partner and your partner wakes up with the same thought about you, imagine how kind, loving, and supportive your relationship will be. So often people have expectations of what their partner will contribute or criticize every mistake they make, but relationships require both people to invest themselves. Sometimes one person gives more than the other due to circumstances. If you're the one being supported at the moment, make sure you have an attitude of gratitude and that you show your partner your appreciation.

My wish for you is that you find someone like my husband. We are best friends, but, equally important, we are each other's biggest champion. I never have to apologize for being me and vice versa. We never have to tone down our excitement or ambition because we're proud of each other's accomplishments. What makes our relationship so strong is that we both make an effort to make the other person's life better.

As I mentioned in the introduction, while I was writing this book (sometimes for 12 to 16 hours a day), I was pregnant and making the move from New York City to Los Angeles. Brett is the reason I got through that time. Whether it was helping me pack and unpack, going grocery shopping or cooking, or helping me get around when I was in a ton of pain, Brett did whatever he could to make my life easier. He bought a car seat, crib, stroller, and everything else a baby needs without ever making me feel bad. He still loved me on the days I didn't leave the apartment or even shower so I could write and write and write.

But relationships require two people to pitch in and show gratitude for the little things as well as the big. Since we got married, I've been able to help Brett recover from shoulder surgery and stand by him as he builds his new law firm. While I've needed a ton of support, I know, and Brett knows, I am here to return the love. Sometimes you need a Brett. Other times you *are* the Brett. So if you're dating, hold out for someone who will be a true partner.

IF YOU ARE NEW TO DATING

It's normal to feel nervous. And if you haven't dated for quite some time, it's important to know that some of the rules have changed. For example, you may never talk to your date on the phone prior to meeting.

Unfiltered

You may only exchange texts or communicate through a dating app. There may not be a follow-up call but rather a text that says, "I had a nice time, but I don't think we're a match. Best of luck." There may not be a text at all. So much has changed even in the past five or so years.

Take the end of the date. Who pays? A very sweet 22-year-old woman approached me after a speech and told me she wanted to date, but it gave her major anxiety—especially the last five minutes. "Who pays? What do I say when the check comes?" she asked.

I always offered to pay, or started to reach for my wallet when it was time to pay because I never wanted a date to feel obligated to pay for me or that I walked into the date expecting that he would. Some people disagree with me and believe the person who initiated the date should pick up the tab and the person who accepted should never offer. There is no defined rule here.

If your date takes you to a restaurant you cannot afford or orders the most expensive item on the menu and runs up a hefty drinks tab, compared to your $20 entrée and iced tea, you can reach for your wallet and offer to pay your share of the bill. Most likely your date will say, "It's on me." It's always smart for both parties to have cash on hand in addition to a credit card, just in case. If the other person pays, be sure to say thank you.

The young woman then asked me, "If I offer and he makes me pay, should I still go out with him again?" People are different and their circumstances are different, so it's hard to know why they may or may not pick up the tab. My feeling is if you really like someone, don't run for the hills if they have you split a meal. Finding someone nice and sharing a connection is not easy. I know very generous people with frugal partners who still have a happy relationship. So I would say go out again. If you learn the person is cheap about everything and that bothers you, or you somehow end up paying every time and you feel like that person is just going out with you for a free meal, then yes, by all means, *run*.

If you have more dating etiquette questions, reach out to your network

WATCH IT!

www.youtube.com/user/
matboggs

Unfiltered

(at least, the people with whom you feel most comfortable) and ask. You can also check out dating coach Mathew Boggs' YouTube channel.

Other Newbie Tips

Being in the right state of mind can make meeting new people a lot more pleasant. When you are in dating mode, however, it's easy to get caught up in a Hollywood romance. Sometimes it really *is* love at first sight. Other times, not so much. Take these lessons to heart to help you keep your head on straight:

+ *Go with your instincts and interests.* If writing out an online profile is scary, sit down with a friend or family member who knows you well and have them help you. If online dating isn't your thing, try joining a group. Whether it's a running club, a nonprofit committee, a cooking class—do something you enjoy and who knows? Maybe you will meet someone who enjoys it, too. If you sign up for an event and choose to go with a friend, make a rule that you can't leave until you both meet two new people. Even if you don't feel a spark with anyone, you will gain the confidence to walk into a room and own it.

+ *Don't send out a save the date before your first date.* If you have just been set up with someone or connected online, try not to get engaged to this person before showing up to your first date. It's great you think they're attractive and smart and you have some real chemistry. It's normal to be excited before a first date, but try not to walk in with the names of your future children already picked out.

+ *Take turns talking.* While on the date, make sure you are listening *and* talking—not just one or the other. Dating requires both people to put in an effort.

+ *To go out again or not to go out again?* After the date, if you know in your heart you didn't have a good time and really don't want to go out with this person again, don't. I forced myself to go out on so many second and third dates because I thought maybe something would be there down the road that wasn't there on day one. If you are on the fence, then of course say yes to a second date. But if the first date was tough to sit through, you have my permission to politely decline another one.

+ *Unless your name is Casper, don't be a ghost!* A 30-something asked me if it's OK to ghost when he's not interested in going on a second date with someone he met once. (Ghosting = blowing the person off with no closure.) The answer is NO. This person you met could have done anything with their time and chose to meet you. They got ready and had to take the subway, bus, Uber, or drive to get to you. They spent time getting to know you and sharing their own stories. If they weren't rude or an awful human, a simple text that says, "It was really nice meeting you. I don't think we had a love connection, but I wish you all the best," is nice and appropriate. This text is especially suitable if you have gone out with someone several times or were set up by mutual friends.

The only time I think it is OK to ghost is if you need to cut ties with someone who makes you uncomfortable for whatever reason.

FOR THOSE DATING ONLINE

If you are looking to hook up, ignore this section. I don't have advice for you because that's not why I entered the world of online dating. If you're serious about finding a partner online, there is a lot you can do to make the experience positive and productive. Try these tips:

+ *Capture the real you.* When you create your online profile, make sure your pictures are recent. No one should have a profile picture that is blurry, from a million years ago, or taken on top of a mountain 100 miles away. I'm not saying you shouldn't show your active lifestyle. I'm saying don't have your main picture be one where no one can tell if you're in it. I would also avoid your first picture being a photo of just your pet. Also, don't *just* have cartoons, pictures of you in costumes that include masks, or random body parts. People who are checking you out want to see your face.

Unfiltered

+ *It's raining men.* Guys, please don't post a selfie in the bathroom, even if you do have a six-pack. I'm sure you have one friend who is willing to take a nice picture of you. Bathroom selfies are so lame—not to mention if you don't turn off the flash, a ball of white will appear in the mirror and often hide your face.

+ *Skip the dick pics.* I can't tell you how many times I've been out with both male and female friends who said, "I'm so disgusted. I went out with a great guy last night, and this morning I woke up to a dick pic. Wanna see it?" Um, no. Unless you know the recipient is comfortable with that sort of thing, don't do it!

+ *All the single ladies.* Don't post a picture of you barely dressed. You're dealing with the internet and have no control over where those pictures may end up. Also, you can't expect a potential mate to treat you like the goddess you are if you're just promoting your sex appeal.

+ *If you're in a committed relationship . . .* Get off these sites and apps! OMG. Seriously. I can't tell you how many times someone's picture popped up on a dating app that was taken from his social media feed—and it was of the guy and his *wife.* Not ex-wife. Not deceased wife. But *wife* wife. Not OK.

+ *It's a match!* If you've matched with someone online, it's hard to know out of the gate if this person is serious about learning more about you or if they were bored and just happened to swipe right without really paying much attention to your profile. To avoid wasting your energy, invest some time into having a meaninful communcation right away. Instead of sending someone a message that says "hello" and nothing else, say hi and ask a thoughtful question. Such as, "Hey, Rocco. How is your week going? I noticed you like to travel. I just got back from Spain. Have you been there?" Or say something that actually breaks the ice such as, "What's up, Nina? Hope you're enjoying this amazing weather we're having. Are you doing anything fun this weekend?" You'll be able to get a

Unfiltered

sense if this person is interested in chatting much faster this way.

* *Safety first.* If you're meeting people online, please do your due diligence. You should be able to find something about the person you're meeting, whether it's a LinkedIn profile, Facebook page, or company bio. It's possible this person is not on social media at all, but you should be able to at least confirm they exist. Make sure whatever you find out about this person matches up with what they told you. If you have friends in common, don't be afraid to reach out to your mutual acquaintances to get some intel. There's no need to learn every detail about this person's life—you just want to make sure they're legit. I've met way too many people who discovered their mystery dates were in a relationship or lied about where they work, their age, or where they went to school.

It's always best to meet in a public place and let a friend, roommate, or family member know where you're going. Self-defense expert Jennifer Cassetta, whom you met in Chapter 10, recommends using the app Kitestring (https://www.kitestring.io/), which will alert your loved ones if you are somewhere and feel unsafe.

To help you get out of an uncomfortable situation, tell a family member or friend to call or text you at a certain time to check in, and be prepared to say something to the effect that they need you ASAP. With that said, you are not beholden to anyone, so if you ever feel uncomfortable you don't have to wait for your emergency call/text to come through. Either come up with an excuse for why you need to end the date or flat out say you have to leave.

If you're having a wonderful time, it's up to you whether to offer to walk your date home—just like it's up to you to accept or decline the offer. The key to safe dating is to trust your gut and take things slowly. Don't rush getting to know this new person—there will be plenty of time for movie nights if the relationship progresses.

Unfiltered

Last but not least, many people find it easier to get to know someone over drinks. Whether you're talking at a party, meeting at happy hour, having dinner at a restaurant, or at someone's apartment, watch how much you consume and keep an eye on your drink at all times to make sure no one slips you anything harmful.

DATING STORIES FROM THE "STRANGER THAN FICTION" DEPARTMENT

I spent hundreds of hours with clients of all ages while working on this book. Whenever someone told me a relationship story, I tried to share what I went through to help them remember the sun always rises—and laughter really *is* the best medicine. Here are some of the stories I lived through, and some stories from friends of mine, that I hope will make you smile, too, and realize that we all have dating experiences that sometimes go beyond the pale.

Bathroom Boy

The guy picked a Sunday night for us to meet and suggested a bar on the Upper West Side of Manhattan at 8:00. When I came in, he was sitting at the bar watching a baseball game. I walked up to him to say hello and asked if he wanted me to get a table or if he wanted to stay at the bar. Without skipping a beat, he said, "No, I want to stay here and watch the Yankees and Mets game." Now, I'm not a huge baseball fan, but I thought I would be nice and go with the flow.

The guy paid 80 percent of his attention to the game and 20 percent to me—and then, out of nowhere, he jumped up and said, "Oh my God, I have to go to the bathroom!" And ran for it.

A few minutes later, he texted me from the toilet: "Really good Mexican food has its downside. Gonna be a few minutes. :)"

He came back 20 minutes later. I asked him if he was OK, and he slapped the bar and said, "You know, I've been ebbing and flowing since the second I got here and I could feel it leaking and had to dump it out. You know that feeling when your stomach is rumbling and you feel like it's going to explode? That's what it was like."

Unfiltered

The waitress came over and asked if he wanted another beer, and he said, "Oh! Yes! I want another beer! I just got rid of what I needed to get rid of so I could make room for another one!"

I asked her what I owed for my Diet Coke, left cash on the bar (he never said he'd take care of it!), and said I would tell our mutual friend that we met. He said, "Yeah, you get up really early. If you need to leave, feel free."

I thanked him for being so understanding and laughed the whole way home. Talk about a crappy experience.

The Ghost

I took a guy to a party and couldn't find him at the end of the night. When I finally spotted him, he was making out with a friend of mine in the stairwell of the venue. Good times.

Pajama Boy

One Sunday, I met a guy who I met online for brunch. When he showed up, he was wearing pajamas. He said, "I only wear dry-clean-only shirts on second dates because dry cleaning is so expensive in New York. I figured, why waste a good shirt until I know whether I like the girl?" He ordered water (again, this was supposed to be brunch) and said, "If this works out, I can cross an item off my bucket list." I asked him what item that would be and he said, "I've always wanted to sleep with a news anchor." He then proceeded to tell me every fact he knew about every female news anchor. #socreepy

The Liar

This was a guy I met while I was interning in New York City during college. He lied about his name, family, and where he went to school because he was more religious than I was and thought if his family found out about me he would be disowned. We dated for two months and broke up at the end of the summer. I thought we broke up because I was going back to Northwestern and he was starting law school. A few months later, I ran into someone who had dated the same guy, and she told me the truth about him and his family. I was so hurt. I liked him enough as a person that had he told me the truth, I would have been happy to be friends.

The Catfish

This guy stole someone else's identity to create his online profile. We spoke on the phone several times, and he told me about the hospital he worked at and how he went into medicine because his mom died of cancer. We talked about the foundation he started in her memory, too. The night we were supposed to meet, he texted me to say he was running late in the ER. That was the last I heard from him. Luckily, I was with friends at a charity event and did not leave to go to the location where he told me to meet him. I later learned no one by that name worked at the hospital. The foundation in memory of his mom did not exist. I have no idea who was on the other end of those conversations, but the guy later catfished a friend of mine with the same profile. You can't make this stuff up!

The Dancer

Another guy I met online planned the most creative date—tango lessons! But let me tell you: If you've just met someone, and you're not feeling a connection, being pressed up against them for an hour—literally nose to nose, chest to chest, holding hands, is incredibly awkward. I do give him a lot of credit for being creative; I just think learning to tango is a better second date than a first. #thankgoodnessIshowered

One-Word Guy

This guy only responded to questions with one-word answers.

> *Me*: "So how was your week?"
> *One-Word Guy*: "Good."
> *Me*: "Oh, you mentioned your dad was in town. What did you do while he was here?"
> *One-Word Guy*: "Ate."

Unfiltered

Me: "Nice. Where did you go?"
One-Word Guy: "Restaurants."

After we managed to sit there for an hour and a half (89 minutes too long), he got up to use the restroom. I checked my phone and saw an email from the newsroom I had to answer about Fashion Week. I explained to my date I needed to take care of work, and we got the check. After we said goodbye, he started sending me crazy texts:

"That was the shortest date of my life."
"I think you were lying and did not really have to deal with work."
"I hate being bullshitted."

For one, I did have to deal with work. Second, those were more words than he said to me during our date! Cray. Cray.

The Hand Eater

I went on a date with someone who seemed so nice and normal. We went to brunch for our second date and decided we were having so much fun we would go to the movies. He took my hand during the movie, which was sweet. Within seconds he put my hand in his mouth and started sucking on it. I couldn't really shout, "WTF?!" because we were in a theater. I was so weirded out I just took my hand back politely and folded my arms. #FML

Steve Harvey

I went on Steve Harvey's talk show and let him set me up on a date on national TV. The episode was about how men in real estate are the best to date. The guy I picked at the end of the show turned to me and said, "That was fun! Thanks for picking me. I hope they bring me back again so I can sell another house."

My Health Coach

I'm not a size 2 and have never been a size 2. Well, that's not entirely true—I'm sure at some point when I was a toddler, I wore a 2T. In any event, I went out with a guy I knew through mutual friends and liked a lot as a person. I was surprised he even asked me out because I knew dating a skinny person was really important to him. I thought he was trying to be less shallow, but every date we went on he asked me what I ate that day and questioned me about every meal and how much I worked out. It was #bananas!

Gum Does Not Belong Under . . .

The answer is anything, including tables. I was on a first date in a very nice restaurant when the guy sat down, took out his gum, and stuck it under the table. I was so appalled by that, and by how he treated the waiter. I was out of there in 44 minutes. Ugh.

I Have Never Told This to Anyone

I was the queen of coming home with bad date stories that started with me being told, "I have never shared this with anyone, but . . ." Being arrested, stealing chickens, hating a parent, loathing life—I came home from more first dates where the guy cried, overshared, or thought I was his therapist than I would like to relive. I was always happy to help these men with resources for their anger, sadness, and pain; but when people gave me a hard time for being too picky, I had to explain again and again that it wasn't always me.

The Guy Who Brought a Friend

I showed up at a bar to meet a guy I had met on an app. When we found each other, he introduced me to the friend he had brought with him. Who brings a friend on a date? I tried to make the most of it. As the three of us chatted, it turned out the friend and I had a lot of mutual friends, which made the whole thing even funnier. I left to let them enjoy their date night and laughed my way out of the place.

More Tales from the Trenches

SUSIE: I went on a date with a funeral director, and he picked me up in a hearse.

Unfiltered

AMANDA: I was dating a guy, and we planned to have movie night at his house. We talked our way through a whole movie, and at some point he said, "I think I know you well enough that I could show you something?" Oh God, I thought! This is where he chops me up and puts me in his walls. Nope, instead he shows me to a man cave, and there's a stripper pole built into the ceiling! He said, "What are you gonna do about it?" I turned around and left.

BRAD: I went on a date with a girl who met me at a nice restaurant. When she walked in, she was wearing hardly any clothing. I asked her to put her jacket around her waist because she wasn't wearing underwear, which was evident for everyone to see. Her bare style made me uncomfortable, but I didn't want to be rude. We had one drink and went our separate ways.

JILL: I had a date with a guy I met online. He was a sports agent and ran late because he hurt his ankle. He came in and asked me for $20 for the taxi because the ATM wouldn't take his card and promised he'd pick up the tab. At the end of the night, he called his "driver" and sent me out to get the car while he paid. The "car" was a yellow taxi driven by this guy Jerome. Right after I got in, he popped into the cab. The waitress stopped the car door from slamming, saying he didn't pay. He shouted, "I totally did! Jerome, *drive*!" Jerome took off, and I asked if he paid the $100 bill. He said, "Yeah, I threw $150 on the table." So then I said, "If you had $150 cash, you just stole the $20 from me at the beginning of the night." I told Jerome to stop, jumped out, and slammed the door.

BRETT: I was meeting a woman who was driving an hour to meet me. She mentioned she would beat traffic and come to my area a little early and get her nails done while I was still at work. I told her since she was driving so far, I would be happy to take care of her appointment. When I went to pick up my credit card, the total came out to be $220. I have no idea what else she did there!

Now that we've all had a good laugh, let's get serious for a bit. Dating is *hard*—especially in our social media-saturated world, where every date can be scrutinized or chronicled for the world to see. If you are out there trying, we all give you a big high-five. Dating isn't always bad, though. I set up lots of friends with men I met who were NMH (not my husband). I got countless story ideas, made new friends, and even had a bunch of guys I met for a date join committees I was chairing for different causes. I want to help you enjoy this process and feel good about finding your person. So don't worry; we all have our stories.

IF YOU ARE THE ONLY PERSON IN YOUR GROUP WHO IS SINGLE

Many young adults have asked me if there is something wrong with them because they have not had a serious relationship. If you have asked yourself the same question, I am sure you are a wonderful person with so much to offer. If you have not had the opportunity to date or be in a serious relationship due to parental or religious reasons, that's valid. If you've been focusing on family issues or busy with your career, that makes sense, too.

If you are older and have never had a serious relationship, consider getting involved in your community, and don't be afraid to ask your friends to set you up. Many of my clients used to tell me they were ready to meet someone special but were overwhelmed by the thought of putting themselves out there and hated the idea of online dating. Other people said they wanted a relationship more than anything, but when I tried to set them up, they were married to their checklist. The girl had to be X number of pounds. The guy had to make X number of dollars. It was crazy! Don't be so married to your checklist that no one is good enough for you to marry. Be open to what the world has to offer. Just like in business, we don't always know what will be the true recipe for success until we go through the motions.

IF YOU DON'T FEEL LIKE DATING

A close friend asked me if I would speak to a young woman she met at a wedding. This 20-something had given an incredible maid of honor toast and wanted to be a motivational speaker. When I talked on the phone with Sydney, she told me she wanted to focus on her career. She was unhappy at her job and needed to make a change. To the dismay of people around her, she told me dating was not on her radar. I was so impressed with her. It was refreshing to hear someone know what she needed and not apologize for it. If you are happy being single with no need for a relationship, or you just need a break from dating, kudos to you for being your own boss. It is not up to other people to tell you what you need to do and when. If you have taken a break from dating for ten years but ultimately want to be in a relationship, you may want to consider why you still need a break. But if you are giving yourself time to be all about you, that is 100 percent OK. I have no doubt this investment in your personal growth will elevate the kind of partners you will attract in love and in business.

IF PEOPLE MAKE YOU FEEL BAD ABOUT BEING SINGLE

When I first wrote a version of this book, I was 35 and single. If you had asked me when I was younger where I would be at 35, I would have said, "Married with two kids and working at NBC." Instead, I was dating, running my own company, on a speaking tour, and freelancing at NY1. My life did not look one bit like I had pictured it, but that was not necessarily a bad thing.

For the most part, I was very happy with my life while I was dating. The times I would get upset about being single stemmed from two things:

1. Being on a horrible date that made me wish I had stayed home working on my company.
2. Going to a party or singles event where I would run into the same people I knew were hooking up with everyone in the group at every opportunity. The women often thought they would be the one to win so-and-so over until that guy moved on and hooked up with another woman at the next party. The women were friends who spoke badly about each other. It was nauseating, and I hated going to events surrounded by people who really had no

intention of being in a real relationship. They were in a relationship with the entire clique, and I found that so sad.

To make matters worse, I knew some people looked at me and thought I was not as successful, or happy, as other people my age because I was not married with kids. Let's call them "sillies." I wanted to say to these "sillies," "I know people who are married with kids and they are miserable, so I'm not sure why you think someone can only be happy and successful once they get married and have kids." It was infuriating!

"Sillies" were the same people who asked me lots of questions as if they were going to solve the "This is why you are single" puzzle. Without taking into consideration how much time I spent dating, people would launch into an interrogation:

- "Jessica, are you too picky?"
- "Are you too busy?"
- "Are you too career oriented?"
- "Do you hate men?"
- "Are you still in love with an ex?"
- "Do you think you intimidate men? Maybe you should play down what you do when you're on a first date."

This was my favorite game to play because it made me realize how disconnected some people are from what it is like to be single. It also taught me that sometimes people like to project their own issues onto other people—or they just really like to hear themselves talk.

The truth was, the answer to every one of those questions was no. I got set up with dates all the time. I had been on several dating sites and apps countless times. I had matchmakers set me up, and as you know, I even went on Steve Harvey's show to let *him* set me up! I was, without question, doing my part. I wasn't with the men I had dated because I knew they weren't right for me—or they didn't think I was right for them.

We often know when we are miserable in a class or a job. In college, chances are we switched courses. In the workplace, we may have asked to be reassigned or resigned from that job. In relationships, it can be so hard to trust your gut, and that is such a shame. You are smarter than you think, and to be in control of your dating life, you have to trust yourself.

IF YOU ARE TOO BUSY TO DATE

What makes the dating jungle even harder when you're an ambitious person is finding a partner who can understand and support that your passion is a colossal part of who you are. It's hard to hustle during the day and then go on what feels like job interview after job interview, over coffee, drinks, or dinner, trying to find a mate. The main difference with dating is that you are playing two roles: You are filling the open position of Mr./Mrs. Right in your life *and* trying to fill that role for someone else.

It is normal to go through periods of time where you need to be completely focused. Whether you are studying for an exam, about to pitch a new client, preparing for a performance, or about to launch a company, you may need to put all of you into that project for a bit. We addressed this with Melissa Ben-Ishay of Baked by Melissa in Chapter 12.

If your busy life has become a crutch so you don't have to put yourself in dating mode, ask yourself if you even want to be in a relationship. If you spend some time thinking about the positive aspects that a relationship may bring into your life (companionship, support, intimacy, laughter), it may make going on dates again feel less daunting. We all need to feel good walking into a job interview. We also need to remember that when we show up to that interview, the hiring manager wants us to be the one as much as we want the job. No hiring manager wants to face an open position day in and day out.

Similarly, while there are some people who are serial daters, the majority of people show up to a date hoping it is their last first date. So while dating your career is 100 percent OK at times, don't get so comfortable being busy that it hinders your relationships. Keep making time outside your busy life to meet people. Dates are a great time to try a new restaurant, learn something new about the city you live in, or even order your coffee a different way. Dating doesn't have to be the bane of your existence.

Unfiltered

I hope that after reading this chapter you feel better about dating. I hope you don't have to go through as many bad dates as I did, but the next time you go on a date with someone and know that person isn't the one, remember a lot of us have bad date stories, too.

As you date, make sure you're investing your time in someone who is looking for the same commitment that you are. It's sort of like the alphabet. The letter H has two lines and joined in the middle—it's almost as if the two lines are facing each other and holding hands. The letter V shares a point, but both lines are going in separate directions. It's a vortex, but that small point no matter how strong it is will never bring those lines together. Think back to your past relationship—were you heading in the same direction? Did you want the same things? If you didn't, you just did the bravest thing and I hope you start feeling better soon.

Also remember:

+ Think about the kind of partner you want so you can put that out into the world.
+ Be sure to think about what you want to bring to a relationship as well.
+ Whether you're new to dating or a pro, never compromise your values or safety.
+ When you do find love, don't lose yourself.
+ Don't feel pressure to be out there dating if you need some time off.

If you've been on a break from dating and it's time to get back out there but you're having a hard time taking the first step, check out the next chapter, where I'll talk about how to let go of your past.

Chapter 14

Mastering the Skill of Letting Go

You should be at the gym. After all, you're dressed and holding your heart-rate monitor in your hand. But your curiosity has gotten the better of you, and you want to check if your ex has posted anything (since you last checked at lunch). One site isn't enough, so you scroll through all their sites to see if you've been replaced yet. Before you know it, you've missed your boot-camp class and decide to order in dinner and binge watch *Game of Thrones*. #netflixnight

Unfiltered

If you are pining for someone you know isn't good for you and can't let them go, ask yourself: *If a friend came to me and described the person I am upset about, would I let my friend stay stuck on this ex?* I'm sure you'll agree your answer would be: *Never!* This is a good time to revisit the list of how you want to feel with a partner. Did your ex make you feel this way? If the answer is no, it may help you move on.

Often we get caught up in old memories, wanting to be in a relationship and worried we will be single forever, so we make do with what we have. What's important to keep in mind is that a relationship takes two people who want to be in it. It's not enough for one person to do all the work and all the compromising. If you are dating someone who is living his life and you are just an add-on, you're not in a balanced relationship. At some point, your partner will decide you're not the right accessory, or you will decide you need to be with someone who is as invested in you, your life, and your happiness as you are in his. I get that all this may be easier said than done. I learned this lesson by living it, and once I understood it, my dating life finally went forward, not backward.

#MYSTORY: Wrestling With "What If?"

One Sunday morning, I woke up and, out of the blue, thought, "Oh my goodness, Jake is going to get engaged any second." I had not seen him in years or heard his name in months. From that morning on, I felt like my heart was lying on the floor. We had broken up three years earlier and I had had another significant relationship since then. For the entire month of April, I felt like Jake and I had just broken up all over again, and I had no idea why. I hadn't thought of him (or missed him) in a long time. It was bizarre.

A few weeks later, my grandfather passed away. His funeral was on Jake's birthday. It was a hard day as it was, and that extra component didn't make it any easier. That same week, Jake got engaged. Surprisingly, when my friend called to tell me, I was not upset, but it did make me do some soul-searching.

For several days, I asked myself:

Unfiltered

- If he could find someone and get engaged, was I the reason we didn't work out?

- Was I right for ending it since he found someone else? That must mean I was right and we weren't right for each other. Right?

- Had I done things differently, could that have been us?

- Am I relieved it wasn't me because I wanted more out of a partner?

- Was it wrong of me to want more out of a partner?

- Should I have just gone with the flow so I wouldn't be single now?

- Was it really possible he loves someone more than he loved me?

But finally I took a step back and realized that even if I could switch places with this new girl, I wouldn't do it. Because when I was in that moment, in that relationship, I did what felt right. My heart loved him, but my gut said, "no: This isn't enough."

The friend who called to tell me Jake got engaged also told me about his fiancée. Hearing about her made me appreciate how different she and I were, and that made me feel better, too. In time, I realized I wasn't sad I was no longer with Jake; I was just sad about not having that special relationship in my life. I think he ended up with someone who is perfect for him, which is wonderful.

LET GO OF X TO GET TO Y

So if you just found out your ex is further along in the love department than you are, it is totally normal to feel out of sorts. However, that person's new relationship doesn't mean much in the grand scheme of things. It just hurts today. It may even hurt tomorrow. But make sure you don't lose sight of all the good things in your life. If you need to write them down and read the list every day, do it.

Do *not* get caught up in asking yourself these tough questions:

- Why aren't I at that place?
- Why is this so hard for me?
- When will it be my turn?

Unfiltered

I wish I could write a book full of those answers, but I don't have them, and you may not have them for a while, either. Focus on what you learned about yourself from that relationship and remember those lessons when you feel like dating again.

If you just ran into your ex and their new partner, I am *so* sorry! That encounter would make anyone feel sad, so just honor your feelings in this moment and come up with a saying that turns this negative into a positive. Like "I let go of X, so I can feel Y."

For example: *I let go of my sadness so I can feel empowered by my decision to be in a healthier relationship.* Life is hard enough as it is. Do not give yourself or your power away, especially to someone who doesn't deserve it. Also don't just rewind that old relationship in your head and watch all the good parts. Remember the times that were hard and the moments that made you realize you were not with the right person. You will continue to lead the life you were meant to live. The fact that this experience is making you question your choices and remind you of your flaws is actually healthy. You will not only catch up to your ex one day, but you will also thank that person for bringing you to a better place and to someone who is a better fit for you in the end.

Love is a powerful emotion, but it is not enough to sustain a relationship. I have had very serious relationships, where I loved my boyfriend with everything I had. But that could not compensate for the fact that we were different people who wanted different things at different times in our lives. So accept your feelings. Cry. Have a dance party. Meet a friend. Go for a run. Take some time off to let your heart heal.

Breakups, especially when you dated someone for a long time, are an adjustment. If you were friends before you started dating, the transition will need some time to figure itself out. Be nice to yourself right now. The people around you may say the perfect thing one minute and the least helpful platitude the next. It's annoying even when they mean well. Just know the older you will thank you for this decision. Looking back on the most serious relationships of my life, I can tell you that I may not have found the right person until I was 35, but I always knew I wasn't with anyone who was preventing me from finding him.

IF YOU ARE IN A BAD RELATIONSHIP

You deserve better. If someone is hurting you physically or emotionally, that is not OK. If you are in school, *talk to someone you trust.* Perhaps that's a friend, relative, guidance counselor, social worker, or someone in the student health center. If you are out of school, *talk to someone you trust.* Whether you share what's going on with a friend or family member or choose to look for a professional or a support group, you should not have to go through what you are going through alone. No one has the right to harm you in any way. If you're in an unhealthy relationship because you think this is what you deserve, you do not deserve this. If you are in an unhealthy relationship that reflects other dynamics you have witnessed or experienced, it is time to break the cycle.

> **TIP**
>
> If you need help, call 911; the National Domestic Violence Hotline at (800) 799-SAFE (7233); or the Rape, Abuse & Incest National Network (RAINN) at (800) 656-HOPE (4673).

If you just ended an unhealthy relationship, I am so proud of you for being so brave. Ending a bad relationship is never easy, but you deserve to be safe, loved, and happy.

HAPPINESS IS NOT A PIE

Life does not always spread happiness around equally or at the same time. It's not like there are ten slices of happiness to go around, and if your friend is happy, there is less happiness available for you. Your good news is coming soon enough, and you are going to want as many people around as possible when it does. Remember happiness is not an "only if" scenario. You will not be happy ONLY IF you are married. You will not be happy ONLY IF you are promoted. You will not be happy ONLY IF (fill in the blank). Happiness is a choice. Going out and finding what makes you happy and being open enough to let those things find you—those are also choices.

Unfiltered

IF YOUR HAPPINESS SCORE COULD USE A BOOST . . .

It's not always easy to be happy for others when your heart is in a million pieces; however, it is really annoying to be around people who can never share in your happiness unless they are happy first. If you are one of those people, spend some time working on your own issues. Look at the happiness hacks in Chapter 3 to help you. But don't give up. Work on loving yourself and the people around you, and celebrate that you are loved. Everything you need to be happy is already inside you. Make sure you share that with someone who's really worth it. Here are some other ways to boost your happiness quotient:

+ *Don't believe everything you see online.* Just because your friends are in relationships doesn't make them happier or more successful than you. And if your friends who are in relationships are acting like they are better than you, I would really question their happiness, not yours. Happy people are too busy living their lives to post pictures to social media every two seconds to prove to everyone else how happy they are. People who live their lives looking for validation from others are not as happy as they appear. Your life should not be defined by how many people follow you or like you. It should be full of people who love, support, and respect you in real life.

+ *There's always more to the story.* Stop spending so much time stalking other people online. As we have talked about a lot in this book, you have no idea what is really going on in someone else's life. Before you measure your happiness against theirs, remember they don't know every detail about your life and you don't know every detail about theirs. If you feel yourself getting down in the dumps after scrolling through your feed, take a break from your phone and go read Chapter 1 again. Make your mantra: head up, phone down.

+ *Your age is just a number.* All throughout life, you will see people reach milestones at different times. Just because you are not celebrating the same chapter at the same time they are doesn't mean your story will not have a happy ending. It just means you haven't gotten to that point in your story yet.

+ *Your time is precious.* From this moment until you meet the next person you date/marry/whatever, you do not get this time back. Stop for a second and think about that. You do not get those days, weeks, or months deposited back into your life account. Please don't spend every second of every day being upset over the fact that you are not in a relationship. Live your life. Do things that make *you* happy, and make sure the person you pick is someone who can share your happiness with you.

REFLECTIONS

To take charge of your dating life and make room for the right kind of partner, you need to part ways with people who no longer serve a purpose in your life. It may be hard. It may be painful. It may feel scary and even sad. But if being in a serious relationship is something you care about, then you need to make being honest with yourself a priority. This will not only help you in your romantic relationships but will improve your business relationships as well. Consider this:

+ If you think there is more you could be doing in the honesty department, let's start today.
+ What could be the reasons you are in this place?
+ If you have been close-minded, can you reconsider that setup you've been dismissing?
+ If you have been burying your head in projects, can you say no to the next one and leave some room for you to socialize?
+ Are you addicted to the "spark"—you know, the feeling of going out with someone new each week?
+ What can you be doing to keep your own happiness intact?

If you are going through a tough time, in the next chapter you will meet some inspiring people who want to help you turn your pain into purpose.

Part Six

Finding Your Happy Place

Chapter 15

Turn Your Pain into Purpose

It's the anniversary of a death. A birthday. A holiday. Mother's Day. Father's Day. You've been dreading it (like you do every other such occasion) and log onto social media to share your feelings—only to be reminded of where you were "on this day" x number of years ago. You look at the memory of you and your loved one celebrating, and your grief knocks the wind out of you. #stayinginbedtoday

Unfiltered

I once gave a TEDx Talk about how similar we all are to bees (https://youtu.be/pZ525k9BvFQ). When you get stung, you have a choice to make. Are you going to turn around and sting someone else? Or are you going to go out in the world and make honey? We all have the ability to turn our angst and anger into action. Every day, we can choose to make a change in our own life or in someone else's. But this can seem impossible when we're in pain.

Whether you just came home early from work and found a stranger's clothing next to the bed you share with your partner, returned to your home after being evacuated from a fire or hurricane, or just heard a doctor deliver devastating news, there are setbacks that are strong enough to bring us to a standstill.

When faced with medical decisions, disaster cleanup, having to move out, or anything else that follows a crushing life experience, it can feel like we're stuck in quicksand. But in these moments, former pro soccer player, *Survivor: Africa* winner, and two-time cancer survivor Ethan Zohn believes it is important to never let a crisis go to waste because it's an opportunity to do some very important things. "We are all survivors on this earth for a very short time, and it's not how or when you leave this world, it's what you do to make the most of each day and each crisis while you are here," Ethan says. "Making happiness real for others is the greatest gift we can give to each other and to ourselves." Here is how Ethan has turned his pain into purpose during some of his darkest moments.

HOW YOU CAN PULL POWER OUT OF PAIN

For 18 years, Ethan has been appearing on magazine covers, hosting TV shows, and giving keynote speeches. While winning *Survivor: Africa* put Ethan and his passion for philanthropy on an international stage, his commitment to his community started much earlier in his life.

Ethan grew up in Lexington, Massachusetts, outside Boston. "When I was 14 years old, cancer came into my home and it took my father away from me, and then it tried to take me. It was my family, friends from college, my teammates, my teachers, and my community that pulled me through. The community reached out and embraced me," Ethan says. The people around him gave him strength and reinforced his values in a time when he felt like he was alone. "Little did I know, loneliness was going to play a large role in my life later on."

In 2001, Ethan was cast for the third season of the hit CBS reality show *Survivor*. "What the show is really all about is this: I was part of a sociological experiment that happened to air on national TV in front of millions of viewers," he says. "What I wasn't prepared for on *Survivor* was the loneliness and isolation of being stuck on the equator in the center of Kenya with no family, no friends, and no technology. All I had with me were the clothes on my back and my one luxury item of choice: a hacky sack, a toy my father had given to me before he died."

Once all his distractions were taken away, Ethan was left with nothing more than the essentials of who he was. "It was just me and my guts—because once you take away the food and water and you're tired and hungry, your true colors come into focus, and all that is left is your character, perseverance, and the will to survive, which is the very essence of the human spirit," he says.

Once Ethan became aware that this knowledge of self is all that one needs to survive and prosper, he gave away his hacky sack to a little Kenyan kid. "This was my most prized possession, filled with dump trucks full of pain and emotional baggage, and I just gave it away. While it was a tough decision, it was a real moment of personal truth," he says. "At that moment in time, I realized that this small gesture of giving it away made such a huge difference—a toy to me was a luxury to him. And you know what? I was able to turn my pain into purpose and make happiness real for someone else."

When he won the show's competition and found himself $1 million richer, Ethan had to make some decisions. He invested his winnings into something much bigger than himself, co-founding a charity called Grassroot Soccer (GRS). According to its website, GRS is "an adolescent health organization that leverages the power of soccer to educate, inspire, and mobilize at-risk youth in developing countries to overcome their greatest health challenges, live healthier, more productive lives, and be agents for change in their communities." They have a presence in 50 countries and have graduated more than 2.1 million kids from the program. One of the coolest awareness programs GRS offers is its 3v3 PickUP Tournaments (www.grassrootsoccer.org/3v3-pickup). Last year, they held 60 events on high school and college campuses nationwide.

Through GRS, Ethan could help people and give them hope. But life wasn't through presenting him with challenges. In the time that followed his reality show run, Ethan became the one who needed people to lift him up.

In April 2009, Ethan was diagnosed with a rare form of blood cancer, CD20+ Hodgkin lymphoma, and endured multiple rounds of chemo, 22 blasts of radiation, and an autologous stem cell transplant. The cancer returned just 20 months later. "My life depended on selfless strangers who raised money for cancer research to fund a drug called Adcetris that was part of the treatment regimen that saved my life," he says. The final step in this horrible process depended on his brother, Lee, who was a perfect genetic match and donated his stem cells, which were used to save Ethan's life. "I personally benefited from people who participated in charity events in my name to raise money for a cure and felt like I had to do something to support people going through their own battle," he adds.

Lights, Camera, Action!

While many people associate Stand Up To Cancer (SU2C) with the entertainment industry because of their star-studded telecasts that have raised millions of dollars for cancer research, you don't have to be a media personality like Ethan or a famous actor or actress to get involved. SU2C offers patients information about clinical trials and inspires everyone to play a leading role in helping patients get access to better treatments by supporting SU2C's awareness campaigns. For more information, visit: https://stand-uptocancer.org.

Unfiltered

Ethan talked to the media, recorded videos in the hospital about his treatment, and served as a national ambassador for Stand Up To Cancer (SU2C) and the Leukemia & Lymphoma Society. "Unlike the children I met in Africa and other cancer patients I've met over the years, I was able to make my story very public. I exposed details of my life in the hopes I would provide comfort and inspire others to keep fighting. The most powerful tool for the cancer/service community to create awareness is to share our story with others. We are creating a network that is showing the world what cancer is really like," Ethan says. "But you don't need to be on national TV to support someone who needs you. You just need to show up and be there on the days when fighting seems impossible."

Ethan's Advice for Patients and the People Who Love Them

When you have a health crisis or are diagnosed with a chronic disease, it may seem like all bets are off. If you have to abandon your goals and aspirations to deal with whatever is going on, that can be devastating, but Ethan says you still have choices. "My number-one piece of advice to anyone facing a life-changing setback is to take control back over the small things that you can control," he says. "Making the right choices can impact how well you respond to treatments and your overall prognosis. Talk to the experts about dietary choices and approved physical activity that can also improve your overall sense of well-being and your outlook. Eliminate all stress and the stressful toxic people from your life including all your 'friends' on social media. Be transparent with the ones you love and medical providers, and they will respond by taking into consideration your thoughts and feelings as you go through treatment and into survivorship. It's easy to be blinded by the enormity of a diagnosis, but don't forget to celebrate the small victories along the way and embrace the good days."

If you're wondering how to cope with the pain *you* have watching someone you love, or are following on social media, go through a health crisis, put yourself in the shoes of the patient who is relying on others to survive. "I've learned that nothing is more empowering than the truth," Ethan says. "In supporting a fighter, be truthful with them about your feelings and thoughts: fear, love, happiness, sadness, questions, perceptions, etc. Often the thoughts and feelings a supporter is experiencing are similar to those of the fighter. As a supporter, think of ways to help the fighter continue doing what they enjoy. Do whatever it takes to continue enjoying life, regardless of cancer's intrusion. Just think how cool it is that there are complete strangers in this world running races, baking cookies, climbing mountains, sailing in a regatta, and working hard on Capitol Hill all raising money to fund the development of a new drug that helped save your life. For better or for worse, these painful challenges are a double-edged sword that are

Supporting Players

If you or someone you know is looking for support, check out these amazing resources:

+ *Imerman Angels* (https://imermanangels.org). Through its free and unique matching process, Imerman Angels introduces patients to a "Mentor Angel." These men and women are cancer survivors or caregivers who have faced the same type of cancer as the patient.

+ *Movember Foundation* (https://us.movember.com). Here you can find support for health issues, such as prostate cancer, testicular cancer, mental health problems, and suicide prevention.

+ *Last Cut Project* (http://lastcutproject.com). As a young adult cancer survivor and BRCA1 "previvor," Samantha Paige is on a mission to share the story behind her mastectomy and generate a dialogue with others about their life-changing moments. To watch my interview with Samantha, go here:

 entm.ag/lastcut

simultaneously upheaving lives yet also fostering small miracles every single day. It is those small miracles, and the people who make them happen, that keep us moving forward, taking risks, making strides, standing up, and living strong."

Ethan hopes his story helps you overcome your hardest hurdles, and if your family is suffering through a major loss and you're wondering how to make it through each day, Fran Boller hopes you find comfort in hers.

LEARNING TO LIVE WITH LOSS

While Ethan addressed how to overcome medical obstacles and support those facing them, what do you do when you lose someone in your family? Grief has different layers, and Fran Boller hopes her story gives you strength.

When you meet Fran, you learn how quickly she can own the room. Fran has a presence. She's stunning, no-nonsense, and always dressed in an incredibly classy outfit. The day I first met her, I was pitching my "Open Up Wednesday" YouTube series to her company, hoping they would be a sponsor. At first, Fran listened to my presentation with very little emotion. As I went through my deck, she started asking me questions about every charity project on every slide. I began to wonder if she had a sick child because her questions were so specific.

As our meeting came to a close, Fran said she really liked what I was doing and would discuss it with her team to see if they would hire me to produce content for their company or sponsor content for my channel. As I started to close my laptop, I asked, "Do you have kids?" She glanced at her colleague Caitlin, and I wasn't sure what was going on. "That's a good question and a hard one to answer," she said. "I had a son named Jordan. He died in February, and today is my first day back in the office."

I had previously heard that a woman who worked at Haddad Brands lost a child and everyone was heartbroken. I just hadn't known it was Fran. We spent some time talking about Jordan, and I promised Fran

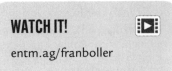

WATCH IT!

entm.ag/franboller

that I would do anything I could to help her spread the word about a foundation she and her family were creating in Jordan's memory. We started by doing this segment about The Jordan Krakauer Memorial Scholarship Fund for my channel.

HOW GIVING BACK CAN HELP YOU MANAGE GRIEF

If you follow Fran on social media, you will see pictures ranging from Jordan's baby photos and happy memories to quotes about heaven and losing a child. Fran is real with her grief, which inspires others to embrace theirs. While Fran says she's accepted she will live with a broken heart for the rest of her life, she knows keeping Jordan's legacy alive gives her strength. "Jordan was the kid who protected the bullied kids from the bullies. He stood up for the kids who had a hard time sticking up for themselves," Fran says.

Jordan died from a seizure on February 8, 2015. He was just 22 years old. He was passionate about sports and studied sports marketing and management, first at West Virginia University and then at William Paterson University. Fran and her family decided to start The Jordan Krakauer Memorial Scholarship Fund (http://www.jordanmemorialscholarship.com/) to celebrate everything Jordan represented and to help them heal. "I'm staying busy managing the fund and I'm helping someone else," she says. "That's what Jordan would have wanted. He was a very giving person, so we're turning our tragedy into good. It's bittersweet and horrible I have to do this, but this helps me from locking myself in the closet and crying every day. The pain will never go away, but this helps us deal with the pain . . . the grief will never, ever go away."

Unlike many scholarships, Fran says this award is not only for the scholar; it's also for the person who stands up for the underdog and helps those who are less privileged. The candidate must be majoring in sports marketing or management and must be enrolled full time at any college in the U.S.

I'll never forget when Fran called me to say they picked the first person to receive the $10,000 scholarship. "We picked a student named Will Bubenik. He's a student at Temple University's top-ranked sports and recreation management program," Fran told me. She said Will is originally from St. Louis and the youngest of four children. "His three siblings have disabilities and participated in the Special Olympics. That's what sparked his interest in sports." It sounded like they found the most special student to honor—someone Jordan would've loved. I asked Fran how Will found out about the scholarship. "He found your YouTube video!" she said.

WATCH IT!

In its first year, the Jordan Krakauer Memorial Scholarship raised more than $150,000. To learn more, you can watch the video we did with Fran here:

entm.ag/franboller2

If you're working through pain like Ethan did or coping with grief like Fran and her family, psychologist Tara Cousineau, whom you met in Chapter 7, says whether you're doing something to help others or help yourself, you may experience an upward spiral of positive emotions. People who use their grief to give back "are able to hold the part that is so distressing at the same time they're stepping outside it for some purpose greater than them," she says. "Shuffling between the 'me' stance vs. that 'we' stance is really empowering."

Fran was able to turn her pain into power because she embraced that sense of community that comes as a result of touching a place in people where they can still find hope. Community is powerful and can be amplified on social media as well as IRL. That sense of "we" doesn't just bring people together—it does so under the banner of a common cause. Focusing on the "we" is so powerful that psychologist Stephen Post has spent his entire career studying it.

TIP

If you're looking for a podcast that is "funny/sad/uncomfortable," check out this one that people rave about: *Terrible, Thanks for Asking* with Nora McInerny (www.apmpodcasts.org/ttfa).

WHY DOING GOOD MAKES US FEEL BETTER

As it turns out, gathering a community together for a common goal doesn't just feel good emotionally; it's also good for you physically. Stephen Post is the co-author with Jill Neimark of the bestselling book *Why Good Things Happen to Good People: How to Live a Longer, Healthier, Happier Life by the Simple Act of Giving* (Broadway Books, 2008). He has given speeches around the world, taught at several schools, and addressed Congress on volunteerism and public health. In his 2017 article "Rx It's Good to Be Good" (www.stephengpost.com/downloads/Rx%20Its%20Good%20to%20be%20Good%202017.pdf), published in the *American Journal of Health Promotion*, Post shares what he and his colleagues found through their research supporting why volunteering should be the universal prescription to live a good life.

Post believes we should consider volunteering the same way we advocate for a healthy diet and exercise to boost our well-being. In 2010, he consulted on a survey conducted by VolunteerMatch and United Healthcare (https://cdn.volunteermatch.org/www/about/UnitedHealthcare_VolunteerMatch_Do_Good_Live_Well_Study.pdf), which asked more than 4,500 American adults about their volunteerism over the course of 2009. The survey found people who volunteer for an average of 100 hours per year reported feeling less stressed and coped better with loss and disappointment. "The participants said volunteering helped them feel physically more robust, happier, and experience an increase in meaning, gratification, better friendships, and better sleep," Post told me during our interview.

"Some people thrive and do astonishing things while having endless energy and are radiant in the process. Other people aren't cut out that way," Post says. "You have to find your space and find what contributes to your flourishing. It doesn't have to be formal volunteering—doing things more casually, like helping your neighbor, also counts."

While there were many parts of the survey he found surprising, Post says this is what stood out the most for him:

+ Ninety-six percent of participants said volunteering makes them happier. This is important because we're living at a time when our Gross National Happiness (GNH) is not good. Americans are unhappy overall. People in parts of the world with much less material wealth than we have tend to be happier.

+ Sixty-eight percent of participants said volunteering makes them "feel physically healthier." It's easy to be sedentary. If you have a cell phone, you can get lost in a video or the internet while the hours fly by. Volunteering gets you up and gets you out. It also becomes easier to take care of your health when you're active in volunteering because you have a reason to be healthy that goes beyond yourself.

+ Seventy-three percent of volunteers reported lowered stress. Stress is very dangerous. If it's protracted, it's flat-out deadly over time. The mortality rates that have been published are astonishing. Stress can increase vascular disease and dementia and is known to slow wound healing. People are stressed because they're obsessing over some problem or under pressure to run from A to B. When you take enough time to get fully engaged in the flow of helping others, you get free. Stress can be a strong motivator to help us finish tasks, but knowing how to diminish chronic and everyday stress is vital to your well-being.

+ Seventy-eight percent reported volunteering helps with recovery from loss and disappointment. Volunteering can be a form of self-care. People who give back as a way to heal find more hope and resilience and are less likely to be trapped in a vicious cycle because they are drawing on the power of love to survive.

+ Twenty-five percent of participants said their connection to volunteerism came through the workplace. If employees get a chance to volunteer, they are much prouder of their corporation and more engaged with their peers and customers, and business tends to improve.

Post adds if you're a clinician, you may need a break from worrying about everyone else and benefit from spending more time focusing on self-care. Whether you're looking to boost your community's well-being or your own health, trying to network, or navigating the depths of loss and anguish, science proves we get a lot by giving—and it's not a tit-for-tat relationship. "The gains don't have to be reciprocal or reputational in order for you to benefit from a giver's glow," Post says.

Unfiltered

If you are going through a tough period in your life, it's OK to process everything at your own pace. If you need time for you, take it. You don't have to jump into helping others if you haven't figured out what you need for yourself first.

If you are ready to volunteer for a cause or start one of your own, be thoughtful about what you want to do and why. Be sure to account for the reality that there may be days that you can't touch whatever's on your plate. It's healthy to hold space for your pain.

If you haven't been personally affected by loss, tragedy, or trauma and don't know where you want to get involved, we will explore how you can find your passion in the next chapter.

Chapter 16

Find Your Passion

Your colleague and his wife are being honored for their commitment to a local foundation. Everyone on your team is going to the gala, and you even rented a tuxedo. At the cocktail reception, you run into someone you know and explain you're at the event because your company bought a table to support the honorees. Instead of being proud of your colleague, you feel totally inadequate because all you've done for charity this year is buy Thin Mints from your niece. Your assistant posts a picture of the two of you at the dessert table. #proudcoworkers

Unfiltered

Over the years, multiple people have told me that philanthropy makes them feel good and bad at the same time. They feel fulfilled whenever they know they're doing something to move humanity forward, but then they feel like crap that they're not doing enough. Tara Cousineau says, "We don't realize just how powerful each of us can be. We can ignite networks of generosity by intentionally inserting a positive idea, attitude, or behavior into a social network, whether that is online or offline."

Scientists Nicholas Christakis and James Fowler, who study the power of social connections, refer to the "three degrees of influence rule" in their book *Connected* (Back Bay Books, 2011). Cousineau says this shows that if you demonstrate a kindness, even when it comes at a cost to you, that generous behavior spreads to your friend (one degree), your friend's friend (two degrees), and your friend's friend's friend (three degrees), thus reaching people you don't even know. "Similarly, that third-degree friend you don't know can influence you, too, just by being in a network of shared social contacts," she says.

Actor and activist Alysia Reiner is a great example of how this rule works. She got inspired by another actor and activist and consequently became a social change agent empowering others to take action, too.

WHY ALYSIA REINER BECAME AN ACTOR AND AN ACTIVIST

You first met Alysia Reiner in Chapter 8 when she shared how she's involved in the Time's Up movement, but Alysia has seen the world through social entrepreneurial lenses since she was a kid. "I am so deeply grateful for my education at a progressive school," she says. "I remember learning what an ethical dilemma was in first grade! I went to Ethical Culture Fieldston School in New York City, and I learned not only ethics and to think for myself but that as a member of a community, of a society, it is your job to be active in that community, to be of service to that community, and to make that community better. And as corny as it sounds, it is your job to make the world a better place. I'll never forget when I was a kid—I was just starting to dream of being an actress—and I saw Meryl Streep advocating to have pesticides taken off apples because the chemicals were hurting children. Later, seeing her work in *Silkwood* that made audiences aware of so many injustices on a deep level, I was inspired beyond words. Her choices and activism helped make change. I remember thinking, 'You can be an actor *and* an activist—that is so cool!' I didn't think of an acting career in terms of the fame; I thought, 'Wow, you can make the world a better place. You have a voice.'"

That social conscience is still what drives her to this day. "I always recognized our criminal justice system as deeply skewed, as so unjust in terms of who gets incarcerated," she says. "But I thought, 'Who am I to make change about people in prison?' And then I got cast in *Orange Is the New Black,* and I felt like I was kind of being called to it—now *I* had a voice. So I became very involved in the Women's Prison Association, and when it came time to launch LIVARI, a zero-waste, ethical clothing company I started with Claudine DeSola and Tabitha St. Bernard-Jacobs, I asked, 'How can we hire formerly incarcerated women?'" So LIVARI entered a collaboration with a company called Road Twenty-Two.

Alysia knows no one can do everything, but she looks for ways she can do her part. "Let's be honest; it's a bit of a dark time in the world. And for me, waking up every day and saying, 'What action can I take to heal the world?' really helps me. Even a small action like just calling my congressperson about an issue that is important to me brings me a sense of peace and clarity about my purpose," she says.

If you want to be an activist, Alysia says the amazing thing about volunteering is that you can volunteer anywhere, starting tomorrow. "You don't have to have any particular skills and you don't need money; you just can give your time and hard work. Find what your passion is, find your voice, and find what you think needs the most love, service, and change. Whether it's around sexual harassment, the environment, women's rights, you name it—there are so many ways to volunteer."

If you are trying to figure out what you're passionate about and how you can do something to help, we will spend the rest of this chapter covering the basics.

HOW TO FIND YOUR PASSION

You have the ability to change lives and save lives. The first thing I want you to do before you go down the changemaker path is think about what makes you happy. Is it painting? Cooking? Playing sports? We often get so busy with our to-do lists that we forget what brings us joy. So take some time to think about what makes you feel alive and jot it down here:

When I am at my happiest, I am spending time_____

_____

If someone told you that tomorrow you have the day off and all your responsibilities are covered, how would you fill your free day? If you know what you would do to fill your time, organize those thoughts now. Please leave out errands and obligatory events. This day is for you!

My Free Day Rundown:

_____

_____

_____

If the thought is too overwhelming, take it section by section as I have broken it down in Figure 16.1 on page 243.

Now look at your list. Is there something you love to do that you can start incorporating into your daily or weekly routine? If so, what is it? Did mapping out a free day make you realize you really miss doing an activity you used to love? What do you need to do to bring back that old activity? Who can support you with this?

Talking to people connected to your interests and educating yourself on where there may be an opportunity for you to get involved is key. Maybe that person is willing to be your mentor or accountability partner (for more on mentorship, see Chapter 4). Perhaps that person will invite you to shadow them for a few hours or sit in on a meeting so you can be back in that world for a day. Put those people down here:

Unfiltered

_____

_____

_____

Now think about one of these activities and ask yourself if there are causes attached to them. Check out some examples in the "Map Your Cause" list in Figure 16.2 on page 244.

FIGURE 16.1: **My Free Day Breakdown**

What Do You Do upon Waking Up?
Do you meditate? Work out? Pray? Read the newspaper? Watch TV? Pick up your phone and scroll through your social media feeds? Play with your pet? Your kids? Take a long shower?

What's Next for Your Morning?
Do you work on that screenplay you've talked about writing? Reorganize your home? Spend time outside?

What's for Lunch?
Do you make lunch at home? Order in? Splurge on a fancy meal or choose a casual spot? Are you eating lunch inside or outside? Do you skip lunch? If yes, why?

What's after Lunch?
Do you nap? Go for a walk? Make some calls? Read a book? Go shopping? Clean up your home? Cook dinner? Volunteer? Play a sport? Go for a spa treatment? Spend time in nature? Make something crafty?

What's for Dinner?
Do you make dinner at home? Order in? Eat leftovers? Splurge on a fancy meal or choose a casual spot? Are you eating dinner inside or outside?

What's after Dinner?
A long bath? A nice stroll? TV or movie? Journal?

What Do You Do before Bed?
Reading? Meditating? Catching up on letter writing?

FIGURE 16.2: **Map Your Cause**

If you love to cook, can you volunteer at a soup kitchen?

If you love sports, can you volunteer with a running organization and help them with their next race? Can you be a volunteer coach?

If you are tech savvy, can you do design work pro bono for your alma mater or a local charity that needs a makeover?

If you love interacting with people, is there a nursing home, hospital, Meals on Wheels program, Candlelighters chapter, or Ronald McDonald House that is looking for volunteers to spend time with clients, patients, or their family members?

If you are connected to a religious institution or spiritual organization, they often have lists of places looking for more support.

If you love kids, can you read to a classroom? Can you look into the Make-a-Wish Foundation or be a Big Brother or Big Sister?

If you have a lot of experience in a certain industry, can you guest lecture for a local school (perhaps where you attended), a community event, or a religious group?

If you are creative and have time to spare, is there a gala or upcoming charity event that needs committee members? Can you help find the venue, pick the menu, decorate the room, or design the invitation? Can you help set up or break down the event? Can you help sell tickets or recruit guests to attend?

If you are close to someone who is sick or someone who is a caregiver, can you organize meals or help with daily tasks?

REFLECTIONS

In this chapter, we covered the benefits of being a social change agent and how to figure out what you're passionate about. The next time you want to take action but feel like you're standing in quicksand, you can revisit these questions:

+ What keeps you up at night?
+ If you had a free day, what would you do with your time? (What do you love to do and miss doing?)
+ What are some activities or causes tied to those interests?
+ Do you know anyone currently doing this activity you can talk to?
+ Can you shadow that person for a day? Attend their committee or board meeting?
+ Once you find what you are looking for, do not be afraid to ask someone in charge to find a place for you!

Now that you know what you want to take on, I want to break down how to take your activism to the next level.

Chapter 17

Amplify Your Activism

You're watching the news and can feel your heart beating faster and faster. The anchors go from a mass shooting to a wrongful conviction case to a reporter covering an emergency school meeting after a teacher hit a student. You don't know where your poster board or markers are or who would join your march down the street. After all, it's 11 P.M. and you're in your pajamas. You decide to forgo your, but you're upset about SO. MANY. THINGS. Instead, you start searching for quotes from Martin Luther King, Jr. and Nelson Mandela

and post your favorites. #changemakers

We all have a million things we could be doing at any given moment, from personal and professional responsibilities to making time to enjoy life. That's why when we watch the news and think about how we can make a difference, we can feel overwhelmed. In this chapter, I want to break down how you can figure out where and when to get involved. If you are an active volunteer or aspire to be a lay leader, I will share the steps I take to produce my events. There is a lot of information packed into this chapter to help you amplify your activism.

TWO QUESTIONS TO ASK YOURSELF BEFORE TAKING ON TOO MUCH

Before we launch into the nuts and bolts of changemaking, fundraising, and event planning, there are two questions every leader should ask themselves before getting in too deep.

1. Why am I leading?
2. Is this a good time for me to take this on?

You may have the best intentions to solve the world's problems, but before you throw on your superhero cape, if you're signing up to carry the flag for a cause for the wrong reasons—or you don't have the time to add one more thing to your plate—you may regret heading down this path. To avoid spinning your wheels and wasting other people's time, let's take these questions one by one.

Why Am I Leading?

If you are leading because you like attention, you like getting credit, or you're looking for validation or even a distraction, that's OK.

Unfiltered

Maybe your child just started school and you're looking for a way to interact with adults again. Perhaps, like we talked about in the previous chapters, you need something to feed your soul. All those reasons make sense. You may be thinking, "*What?* Isn't being a changemaker only about creating change?" The truth is, everyone chooses to be a social change agent for different reasons. What matters more is how you plan to go about creating that change and how you treat other people along the way.

If you are using the experience to give yourself a sense of power and authority so you can boss people around—that's not OK. But if you're doing a project to get school credit or to put the event on your resume, I do not judge you. I only take issue when people put an event on their resume or their name on the invitation but don't do any of the work.

The first secret to being a successful leader is if you want someone to join your cause, you have to be clear as to why that decision will have a good ROI for them. Being a leader is not about you being in the spotlight. It is about shedding light on something that needs your help—and everyone else's help, too.

The second secret is that great minds think *un*alike. It's good to have people around you who can challenge you in a constructive way. Not only will that help you cover your bases, but you also will have the opportunity to learn. Often we socialize with people who look like us, live and work near us, etc. Expanding your mission and vision to include different people will make you a more educated and more effective person.

If you are reading this and the thought of being on a committee is too much for you, don't worry about creating your own social justice platform today. Start by attending events. Later, if you choose to get more involved, let the people in charge know where you feel comfortable. Often, people don't get involved with their office, child's school, or community groups because they are shy. I want you to know you do not need to be the loudest person in the room to make a difference. There are a plethora of jobs that are behind the scenes and do not require you to be front and center. If you are shy, be sure to let your special gifts be known so you can stay in your comfort zone and contribute to the cause in a way that is meaningful and comfortable for you.

#MYSTORY: Check Your Leadership Ego

During my college campus speaking tour, I met two college students who told me the president of a leadership council they served on was a bully and bossed everyone around. This is *not* the way to lead. This is how you get people to want to leave your council.

Then, at a college conference, a student raised his hand after my keynote and shared that he loses his patience quickly and finds himself snapping at people on his committee and bossing them around. I asked him why he wanted the leadership role in the first place. "This is the only place I feel like people hear me," he said.

My heart sank. I asked him to list qualities he was proud of and whether he was implementing any of those qualities in his leadership style. He said he wasn't—he was too busy shouting at people, and as a result, he forgot he is creative, a good connector, and has great organizational skills.

When I started my YouTube channel, I launched a class of Ambassadors whom I mentored. One night, one of them called me very upset. He said no one was listening to him during his after-school meetings and that people who committed to doing different tasks never followed through. I listened to his frustration and simply asked: "Why are you in this role?" He replied, "I want to leave a legacy at my school and be remembered as a leader."

It wasn't a bad answer. At least it was honest. But here's the deal: If your committee members see a leader who is leading *solely* to be heard or to leave a legacy, that is pretty uninspiring. I asked my Ambassador, "Have you asked each committee member why they signed up for this group in the first place? Have you asked everyone what it is about the

group that they enjoy or one thing about the group they would change?"
He said no.

I asked him if he would feel comfortable meeting with everyone one-on-one
and ask how HE could support each person in their respective role in the
club. He said he would and he did. A few weeks later, he sent me an email
that things were getting better after he changed his approach to leading.
Not only were people following through, but he also found the experience to
be much more rewarding.

KNOW YOUR WHY

While these stories come from young adults, I have had countless
conversations with nonprofit professionals and lay leaders who struggle
with similar issues. Here is advice that applies to everyone:

+ *If you want to be seen, take a minute to see your talent first.* Try to help
  the people you are leading identify *their* talent if they aren't sure
  what they have to offer.
+ *If you want to be heard, make sure you listen to the people you are leading.*
  Go someplace quiet and try to hear your own thoughts, dreams,
  and fears. Make sure you are using those things to lift those
  around you and not projecting them onto your team. That will
  only weigh everyone down!
+ *If you want to be remembered, make sure the people around you know
  that you see them, hear them, and support them.* Your committee
  members won't remember every detail from every meeting, but
  they will always remember how you made them feel.
+ *If you want to create change, recognize there is power in numbers and let
  people share their thoughts and ideas.*

If you are afraid of failing, welcome to being a leader. If you are
afraid people will think you are a bad leader or that your idea won't
work, yelling at your team won't disguise the fact that you feel insecure.
Instead, think about all the things that could go wrong and build a
team with a point person on each issue. You may also be short with your

committee if you're overextended. Before you say, "Of course!" to the cause, make sure you're up to the task.

IS THIS A GOOD TIME TO TAKE THIS ON?

It is 100 percent OK to pass on a volunteer project whether you're burned out or you just don't want to. Give yourself permission to politely decline. You need you, too.

One reason it's important to assess if you have time to give, and how much, is because some commitments will need more of your time than others. For example, volunteering to help set up an event is a lot different from joining a board.

Scott Shay, the chairman of the board and cofounder of Signature Bank, says once you've established what kind of window you're dealing with, there are a series of other questions to ask yourself before joining a board. "With a not-for-profit board, you also have to decide, 'Am I willing to write a check?" he says. "Am I willing to be involved financially?' Of course, for-profit boards, it's for pay, but in either case, unless you have a serious interest in what the organization is doing, and unless that board service speaks to you, don't do it. Wait for a better opportunity. Wait for something that speaks to you or, even better, seek out a board that speaks to you."

If you are in the position of chairing a board, Scott says you have to look at who is on your team. "What is the best way for each of your directors to contribute to the business? Board members have different skill sets," he says. "It's a matter of matching those skill sets where we need the help. We encourage board members to speak up when they disagree because that's the way you fight against groupthink. The way you overcome making a bad decision is by having someone say, 'Well, have you thought of this? Have you thought of that? Have you looked at it from an angle that you would have never considered before?'"

TIP

If you are a senior-level executive woman looking to join a corporate board, check out the Women in the Boardroom website (http:// womenintheboardroom. com) for inspiration, helpful tools, and board openings.

Unfiltered

You may want to join a board at some point, but for now you may have more interest in turning your mission into a movement. If that's the case, let's go over how you can do that.

HOW TO TURN YOUR MISSION INTO A MOVEMENT

If you are starting something new, sitting on a committee, or getting ready to organize an event, here are some lessons I have learned over the years. These tidbits also apply to leadership beyond the nonprofit world and can change the way you do business and lead your team in the office.

Share your idea with as many people as possible, and start recruiting people to join your committee. If you're doing something around a news headline everyone is following, you'll probably find it's easy to get people onboard. When I organized an event to help victims of the 2004 Indian Ocean tsunami, I was not personally affected by the natural disaster, but I knew I could get people together to help the survivors in Thailand. I had no idea where to start but told everyone in my path about my idea to throw a party and raise money for the Chabad of Thailand, which I knew was helping people on the ground. One friend told me he knew the rabbi there, so he put us in touch. I asked 12 friends who were interested if they would be willing to be on my committee. We charged people $36 in advance and $54 at the door and ended up raising $20,000, which paid for a water purification system in a village outside Phuket.

If you're trying to support a cause people don't know much about, be prepared to educate them before you ask for their time or money. When I wanted to organize a black-tie event for a 2-year-old boy named Dylan Rabinovich, I couldn't just send out an email blast or invite and simply expect people to pay for a ticket and show up in a tuxedo or gown. Dylan was born with a rare chromosomal disorder called Emanuel syndrome, so every time I wanted to share the details of our event, the first thing I did was share Dylan's story. Then I explained why we were raising money and awareness to help other children and their families through Chromosome 22 Central (www.c22c.org). Once people understood how rare Dylan's condition is, they asked what they could do to help. I explained we were raising money to create brochures for doctor's offices and to help fund a biannual conference that brings families together from all over the world so they can share information and support one another. That's why people were willing to buy a ticket or make a donation. They wanted to be part of something that made someone else's life better. We didn't sell out the event simply by posting something to Facebook and calling it a day.

Crowdfunding sites and friends donating their birthdays to causes have made it easier than ever for people to hit the donate button; however, we're all bombarded with opportunities to give. To get people to support your mission, you have to make your message meaningful. In other words, to get people's attention, you have to get them to care.

Personalizing Your Ask

When my friend Rachel Cohen Gerrol celebrated her 40th birthday, she didn't just post something to social media. She emailed her network explaining a cause close to her heart, which made her "ask" to us much more personal. Here is what she wrote:

> Dear Friends,
>
> TODAY IS A VERY BIG BIRTHDAY FOR ME!!!! There is no better way to honor all the gifts that life has given me than by giving back, and I hope you will help me by doing the same. . . .
>
> A few years ago, I founded **The Survivor Initiative** after learning about the **nearly 25,000 Holocaust survivors living below the poverty line in greater New York City.**
>
> These survivors get by from month to month on meager assistance that **does not fully cover the cost of food, rent, heat, doctor visits, and medications.**
>
> They may go to bed cold, hungry, and feeling forgotten. Together we can help assure they feel remembered, honored, and cared for!

The Survivor Initiative raises funds to **strengthen the capacity of local agencies** that care for poor, frail, and **vulnerable Holocaust survivors** with complex bio-psycho-social needs. I hope you will join me in helping provide much-needed support survivors need to live their lives with the comfort and dignity they deserve.

A donation of any amount truly makes a difference:

https://ubackforgood.com/donor/#!/app/nonprofit/20814

With deep appreciation,

Rachel

To learn more about The Survivor Initiative, visit: www.survivorinitiative.org.

Remembering Ayelet

When my friends Hindy Poupko and Seth Galena found out their 1-year-old daughter, Ayelet, had a rare bone marrow failure disorder, they organized bone marrow recruitment drives around the country to try and find her a bone marrow match. They raised more than $330,000 for the Gift of Life Marrow Registry (GOL) to pay for swab kits to be sent to the lab and added to the international bone marrow registry—hoping their daughter's donor would be one of them.

In January 2012, we all woke up to the news we never wanted: Ayelet had passed away. Knowing her match could have been sitting in a room waiting to be processed was incredibly painful.

Remembering Ayelet, continued

During Shiva, the seven-day period where Jewish people mourn, I happened to be there the day Jay Feinberg, the founder of GOL, flew in from Florida. I told him I wanted to do something to help people like Seth and Hindy. It costs $60 to clear a kit, and they're constantly sent to the lab as donations come in. A few months later, I attended the organization's annual gala. Seeing bone marrow recipients meet their donors for the first time is one of the most emotional, heartwarming moments a human being can experience. That night, I got swabbed, paid to have my kit added to the registry, and told Jay and his team I wanted my next NYC gala to benefit the Gift of Life.

I built a committee of 150 people by scheduling coffee dates, lunch dates, and dinner dates with my friends, mentors, and colleagues. I even recruited some of the guys I'd met through JDate. Every time I asked anyone to get involved, I made it clear—I did not need them to come to meetings or require a lot of their time. I just needed their support and for them to identify one way they wanted to participate.

+ Some people sent out an email blast.

+ Others wrote a check.

+ I produced a celebrity music video with my friend Uri Westrich and asked Kelly Rutherford from *Gossip Girl* if she would host our event, called the Marrow Match Gala. Even though she was slammed with work, she said yes, and she got swabbed!

+ Some people used their contacts to get a celebrity to appear in the video or helped get one item for the silent auction.

Remembering Ayelet, continued

You can see the Marrow Match Gala music video here:

▶ https://youtu.be/f7vLfA7N_dg

We brought in close to $300,000 in donations, which was used to clear thousands of swab kits. To this day, I still send out emails and post to social media every time we make another match or facilitate a transplant. We have made 35 matches and facilitated eight transplants so far.

While more than 600 people attended the star-studded event, there were many all-nighters and stressful scenarios. It took a village to make it happen. Every single person who was involved helped make it successful. So make sure you follow those two secrets to being a successful leader I shared at the beginning of this chapter. When you're clear about what you're doing and why and make room for everyone, people will want to support your efforts.

HOW TO RUN YOUR OWN EVENT

Think you've got what it takes? Awesome. Let's get started. Here is the action plan I like to follow. I am giving you all this information to arm you, not alarm you. On the first read, it may seem overwhelming. Whenever I start a new project, I always feel so overwhelmed because it seems like there is so much to do and not enough time to do it. The good news is, once you make your list and start to cross off tasks it will get easier. And once you see your first event through, it will not be as scary the second time. You will start to see what you are good at and where you need help, and you'll learn from your mistakes.

Step 1: Know What You Want to Change and Why You Want to Change It

Before I asked anyone to get involved in the Marrow Match Gala, I established my goal: I wanted to clear all the swab kits Gift of Life had waiting to be added to the international bone marrow registry. While it was a lofty goal, we could still say we succeeded even if we did not reach it because clearing some kits was better than none.

Note that sometimes wanting to do something nice for someone else will rub people the wrong way. I know it sounds crazy because you would think everyone would help people in need, but you have to be prepared to face people who may not understand what you are trying to change or why you feel the need to change anything in the first place. These people are comfortable with things staying just the way they are, and they have no interest in getting involved.

Some people will question your motives. Some will think you are running from your issues and that's why you feel the need to be the solution to every problem. Some will resent you simply because there is something out there that motivates you. Those people will be annoyed by your enthusiasm and try to break you. Try your best not to let those people get the better of you. Lean on the people who support you instead. Trust me. As a leader, you will have a long to-do list. You will not have time for people who are trying to stand in your way for no reason.

Step 2: Ask Yourself: Who Can Help Me Make this Happen?

You can explain what you want to change and why. Awesome! Now ask yourself: Who can help me make this happen? If your answer is "no one," stop right there. Please don't go down this path all by yourself. If you are Type A, I get it. It's tempting to do it all. But you can do so much more as a leader if you have the right people supporting you.

I like to start with picking up the phone and recruiting people one by one. Yes, this takes longer than sending an email or a text. And yes, you could do a blast on social media asking who wants to be involved, but that's not the same as calling someone or meeting them in person and saying, "I want to do X and I would love for you to be involved." They may join you and/or recommend other people you have never heard of before. Send those people an email, set up a call, and *then* turn to social media to announce what ALL of you are doing together.

If you don't have any friends who can help you, look at what exists around you. If you have an idea that another organization is already working on, reach out to the president and/or the supervisor and ask to set up a meeting. Maybe they will like your idea so much they will help you get it off the ground. Perhaps they can point you in the right direction about how to promote it if you choose to do your own thing. Start going to that group's events. Make friends there. Volunteer. Once you get your idea off the ground, you can reach out to the people you helped and ask if they can help you this time around.

If you have one friend, ask him to help. Now the two of you can brainstorm and share the to-do list. Plus, when you're both in your respective classes, dorm rooms, or offices, you are around other people. You never know who you will meet next. It could be someone who can take your committee from two to three.

Step 3: Build an Executive Committee

Assuming you have reached out to people, had coffee dates, and are ready to get to work, I like to build an executive committee and subcommittees. The executive committee should be for the people who want to take on more responsibility for the event, attend meetings, and be involved in the overall planning and invested in the growth of the project. You cannot raise money, run the event, stuff hundreds of gift bags, and send email blasts by yourself. So assign each of your executive members a role. You should have one person as the chair or two people as co-chairs responsible for overseeing fundraising, PR, recruitment, design, logistics, volunteers, the silent auction, and swag bags. The members on your executive committee should serve as "leaders" for each subcommittee. So if you have ten friends who said they would be involved but don't have any time between now and the event, they will be great on the volunteer subcommittee. If you have a friend who loves designing stuff, you will need posters, an invite, and maybe a logo, and they will feel very fulfilled helping out on that team.

Some Tips to Help You Break Down Your Teams

Here is how I have broken down my teams in the past to help me produce large events:

* *Event chair.* This person oversees everyone and all timelines.
* *Fundraising chair.* The fundraising chair helps the event chair create a budget for the event and works with the executive committee to establish the fundraising goal. Some of the tasks that fall under this role are: leading the fundraising committee, meeting with donors, and organizing phone-a-thons. Sometimes the fundraising chair manages all sponsors and brand partners. If you're able to have a chairperson dedicated to soliciting sponsors and brand partners, that's ideal.
* *PR chair.* The public relations chair writes the press release, contacts the media to get coverage of the event, and writes

the suggested social media posts for all event chairs and committee members to use. This ensures every person involved in the event shares the correct language and information about the event with their personal networks.

+ *Recruitment chair.* The person in charge of recruitment should create a Facebook page for the event and organize happy hours or small gatherings leading up to the big day to educate people about the cause. The recruitment chair works with the host committee to make sure hosts are sending out invites to their networks about the event and posting them on social media.

+ *Design chair.* The design chair is the creative on your team who will set the tone for everything. This person works with the event chair to create the look, feel, and wording for all event materials. It's a good idea to have your executive committee and/or PR team involved in these discussions, too.

+ *Swag chair.* Swag is the stuff you give away at the end of an event. It may be products from your event sponsors and brand partners or something from the organization you're supporting, like a book. The swag chair is in charge of working with their committee to figure out what will go in the gift bags and where the gift bags themselves will be coming from (Will they be ordered? Donated? Are they reusable totes or paper party bags you throw away?).

+ *Silent auction chair.* The silent auction chair is responsible for collecting items for the silent auction, which is a fundraiser where people bid on the items throughout the event. The person with the highest bid at the end of the evening wins. Silent auctions can take a lot of planning, and if no one bids, they're not worth the effort. Make sure you know your crowd. The silent auction chair works with the silent auction team to collect the items and package them—some items may fetch more if they are paired with another item. The team should make signs explaining the item, any restrictions (such as an expiration date or blackout dates), and its valuation.

Swag Solutions

Rachael Honowitz Cosgrove is the founder of Gift Bags by Rachael (http://giftbagsbyrachael.com). For more than 15 years, Rachael has provided gift bags for events like the Screen Actors Guild Awards, the Grammy Awards, the Sundance Film Festival, the Emmy Awards, New York Fashion Week, the Academy of Country Music Awards, and the White House Correspondents' Weekend. Whether you're doing an event for your child's school, an awards show, or a fundraiser for your favorite cause, Rachael says, "Everyone loves free stuff!" If you and your committee have decided to create gift bags for your guests, Rachael suggests that the best bags take into account a combination of the event, the audience, and popular trends. To ensure your gift bags are a successful component of your event, Rachael advises:

+ Start working on your gift bags two to three months before your event.

+ Reach out to a lot of brands. For every 20 brands you contact, maybe two or three will actually donate to your event.

+ Have a fun mix of items in the bags. Everyone loves to try new things before they buy them, whether it's a new chocolate bar, skin cream, cell phone case, or piece of jewelry. You don't have to include the most expensive new headphones out there. And a few gift cards are OK but not too many. People like the instant gratification of touching and trying new things. If someone doesn't like something or it's not right for them, they can always regift it.

Swag Solutions, continued

+ Five to ten items is plenty. Everyone loves free stuff, but you don't have to go overboard.

+ Depending on your event, you might want to divide the bags into general admission bags and VIP bags. It might be easier to get a few higher-end things donated for your VIP bags if you are asking for a smaller number of items.

+ Depending on how many gift bags you are assembling, consider hiring a fulfillment center to stuff them for you and deliver them to your event. This will save you hours of agony.

+ Always offer something to your brands in return, like a social media post or guaranteed press mention. They will be giving you hundreds or thousands of dollars' worth of stuff, so the least you can do in return is give them a nice shout-out. If a celebrity or high-profile guest posts about one of the items in the gift bag on Twitter or Instagram, that's extremely valuable to the brand.

+ Include a printed acknowledgment card with the event logo and hashtag, thanking all the brands that contributed to the gift bag. Include their social media handles as well, which should encourage guests to post about their favorite items in the bag.

+ Save a few extra bags, just in case. It's always nice to have some bags on hand to send out as a thank-you to vendors, a VIP who couldn't make it to the event, etc.

+ *Logistics chair.* On the day of the event, you will need a lot of help. You will need to check in your guests, handle payment if you are selling tickets at the door, hand out gift bags, answer lots of questions, put out fires, set up, and break down. The list goes on and on. The logistics chair is responsible for working with the volunteers chair to make sure everyone is clear about their roles and shifts.

+ *Volunteers chair.* Often, as the event chair, I have also been in charge of logistics and volunteers. Take my advice: Put someone else in charge. People who love organizing work best in this role because mapping out all the volunteers for an event is one big puzzle. The volunteer chair will need to make a schedule with shift times and roles and have people sign up accordingly. If someone misses their shift, the chair will have to figure out how to fill it either by covering it personally or by having standby volunteers ready to jump in when needed. The chair must also make sure volunteers get a chance to take a break. Everyone needs to eat, and they should have time to enjoy the event. If someone would rather work the entire time, of course, that's fine, too.

+ *Host committee chair.* The people on the host committee like your idea and want to be involved but have no time to spare at the moment. Hosts are typically required to buy a ticket and invite people. They are crucial to any event because they are your buzz team. Again, you cannot reach everyone on your own—and even if you could, that would be so lonely! The host committee chair keeps track of all of the hosts and sends out the copy everyone can use in an email or social media post to spread the word about the event.

Once you have put your team together, figure out how you will keep them updated throughout the process.

Step 4: Determine How You Will Communicate with Your Team

Once you have a team in place, how will you keep them informed? Will you have meetings? Will you send weekly emails? Schedule a Google

Hangout? Get a sense of what your team prefers—and be prepared to do two updates (one in email form and one in person or via Skype for the people who are more involved, like your executive committee and subcommittee chairs). I held small meetings at our venue and sent color-coded emails once a month for the Marrow Match Gala.

Be prepared. If you go the email route, there will always be someone (or several someones) who will reply to your well-thought-out update with questions you have already answered. You will want to call that person and say, "Did you read the email I just sent you? All the answers are already there!" Try not to get frustrated. Remember these people are volunteering to help you and are doing the best they can. If the problem persists and someone is making your life harder than it should be, you may want to schedule a time to speak to her to see if she is still interested in being involved.

Running an activity, an event, or a club can be stressful and super isolating! Be sure to make time for you so you can enjoy the process.

Step 5: Figure Out How You Can Give Yourself Time Off and How Often

Are you feeling overwhelmed just reading through these steps? You need your strength to be a changemaker. No matter what you are trying to change or create, there will be ups and downs. It takes a lot of rejection sometimes before you get a yes, raise one dollar, revise a policy, or see the change take shape. Don't let an uphill battle crush your spirit. To prevent burning out, you need to give yourself time off. Make time to get together with your family and friends. Meditate. Listen to music. Do whatever you love that lets you turn off your brain. It is so important to give yourself downtime.

Creating a movement takes endurance; that is why I always say life is like a marathon, and I constantly feel like I am at mile 13. What does that mean? It means you cannot always be so focused on the miles you have left to go that you forget to look back on all the miles you have run. Take the time to be good to yourself, and you will be an even better leader for those around you (and you won't live on cough drops because you won't lose your voice before every event you stage).

Step 6: Identify Your Go-To People to Call on When Things Go Wrong

All leaders come up against moments when they think: *Is this going to work? Will we succeed?* On those days, turn to the people who love you and believe in you. Who is your voice of reason? Who can make you laugh? Who is your cheerleader? Who is going through something similar who can relate to how you are feeling? And who is so far removed from what you are experiencing that when you call they won't even know what you're up to? These are some of the most important calls I can make when I reach my limit.

I hit rock bottom with the Marrow Match Gala while covering Hurricane Sandy in 2012. I spent nine days in Jamaica, Queens, seeing firsthand how devastating that storm was for so many people. Our event was scheduled to take place on November 18. The hurricane hit at the end of October, and I felt torn over whether to postpone the event. Should we really have a black-tie gala when there were people in New York who were still living without electricity and with trees on top of their homes? On the other hand, should we cancel a fundraiser when there were potentially lifesaving swab kits that needed to be processed as soon as possible? What would you have done? We ended up holding the event but asked people to bring an item for Sandy victims. We collected bags and bags of cleaning supplies for people in need on Staten Island and were able to help them get their homes back in order.

Step 7: Be Flexible

Being a changemaker means you have a blueprint, but the best leaders try to anticipate every possible problem and can put out fires quickly. I always like to sit with my committee weeks before our event and make a list of everything that can go wrong. We start outside the venue door, head to registration the way a guest would, and walk through the entire space as though we are attendees ourselves. That's a great way to see where certain items may have fallen through the cracks. But while you do everything in your power to plan for hiccups, you have to be ready for things you never could have predicted.

Unfiltered

On the night of the Marrow Match Gala, I showed up hours in advance, and during my final walkthrough, I could not find the vodka our sponsor had delivered to the event—thousands of dollars' worth. We had plenty of beer because my dear friend Alyson Reeves had donated boxes upon boxes we had unloaded ourselves into the venue the day before. It turned out that the vodka had never been delivered! We had 600 people about to walk through the door expecting an open bar, sponsored by the vodka company, and I had to think fast. I asked the venue if we could use their vodka during our event, and they could bill me at the end. The venue agreed and ended up donating the vodka because they knew how hard we had worked on the event and wanted to help us reach our goal.

Step 8: Say Thank You

We had 200 people signed up for the Marrow Match Gala a week before the event. We had more than 600 the night of, which was stressful because I needed to make sure we could cover our costs, have enough food, and get all my thank-you notes done in time. Note to self: do not write a thank-you note by hand to everyone after an event with 600 people. (I ended up staying awake for 24 hours and wrote 180 in one shot the day before the gala.) But do make sure you invest time in your team and that you're the kind of leader others want to follow. Be the kind of leader that says, "We are so happy to see you!" when someone walks in the room, instead of, "Look who decided to show up!" You never know what it took for someone to get to your meeting. They may be late (again), which is really annoying. But at least they showed up. Try to be sensitive while respecting your standards. At all times, don't point a finger—extend a hand.

REFLECTIONS

If you don't feel like there is a problem you *have* to solve or a community you *have* to serve, you may run out of steam. Being a changemaker takes endurance, grit, and a sense of, "I JUST HAVE TO DO THIS OR I WILL

BURST." I hope these questions help you figure out what that cause is for you:

- What do you want to change or create? Why?
- Who can help you make this happen? Who do you want to have on your executive committee? Do you need subcommittees? If so, what are they?
- How will you communicate with your team?
- What will you do to give yourself time off? How often?
- Who will be your go-to people when everything is a hot mess?
- How will you be flexible?
- How will you say thank you?

The same way you will have to sign contracts with your venue, caterer, entertainment, and vendors, I want you to sign an agreement with yourself to keep you accountable to your goals. In the final chapter of this book, I've provided a template for you.

Chapter 18

Ready, Set, Goal!

Well, here we are. The last chapter. I hope you have enjoyed reading this book and feel like you've gained some tools to help you live your most authentic, unfiltered life. Let's review what we have covered so you know how to course correct the next time you feel like you're slipping into old habits or someone turns to you for help. I like to think of these takeaways as my "whenever" statements.

WHEN IN DOUBT, REMEMBER THE WHENEVERS

Whenever you log onto social media and feel crappy, thanks to the compare and despair trap, identify what is really bothering you about your own life. Go back to Chapter 2 to see if there are actionable steps you can take to get out of your rut. File a complaint. Find ways to step out of your situation, whether it's

Unfiltered

through spending less time on your phone, becoming more mindful, volunteering, or another outlet you discovered in this book.

Whenever you feel lost, remember this is temporary. Seek out a mentor or accountability partner to help you achieve your goals.

Whenever you make a mistake, allow yourself to be upset, but don't let this setback consume you for too long. Take ownership of what happened, recover what you can, and learn as much as possible from the experience. Keep in mind, not getting a job today may be steering you toward a bigger and better opportunity tomorrow. Getting fired may be directing you toward a profession that's your true passion. Realizing you're on the wrong career track is a powerful invitation to switch gears. Take a deep breath. Sometimes you're where you're meant to be.

Whenever someone posts about their awesome office view, team, project, or product, remember you can have that sense of work pride, too. Be strategic about where you are and where you want to go as well as how you want to treat yourself, and others, along the way. Being nice may be your superpower, but that doesn't mean you need to tolerate intolerance or toxic people. Know your rights. Know how to protect yourself. Be an upstander to bullies, and don't ever feel like you need to suffer through workplace harassment or discrimination in silence. Be the kind of leader who makes other people want to lead, and don't forget to take care of yourself along the road to success. Being in business isn't just about making money. It's also about living your message and living a life you love.

Whenever you find yourself in a different place from your friends, whether that's emotional or geographical, remind yourself that outgrowing certain dynamics is part of growing up and life is not a race. It doesn't feel good to feel on the outside of the circle whether it's because you're the only one going through something or because you don't fit into the group mold as well as you once did. Nourish the relationships that help you flourish, and make sure you're being the friend your friends need you to be.

Whenever you're on the verge of breaking up with dating and everyone around you is getting engaged, married, and having kids, stay in your lane. You don't know what's happening behind someone's smile, and there's no point in wasting your energy on being envious of someone else's life. Spend some time thinking about the partner you want to attract and what you want to contribute to a relationship. Trust your gut, don't be afraid to let go of your past, and believe that the best is yet to come.

Whenever life crushes you with bad news or a new reality, honor your feelings. Some days, you may be up for the fight. Other days, you may just want to stay home in bed and cry. Whether you're dealing with a bad diagnosis or grief, you are not alone. Seek support. Research activities you can do or organizations you can get involved in to help others and help yourself.

Whenever you see someone doing something inspiring, don't make fun of them because you haven't found your cause or calling. Think about what keeps you up at night and look into what you can do around that issue. Affluence is not a requirement for influence, and you don't need to be the loudest person in the room to make a difference. Once you get involved, remember donor fatigue is a real thing, and saying no doesn't make you selfish—it makes you self-preserving. Celebrate your accomplishments along the way, and always remember to thank the people who helped make your mission and vision a reality.

YOUR #UNFILTERED TERMS AND CONDITIONS

As you have seen throughout these chapters, I have gone through so many ups and downs to get to where I am today. And you know what? My life story fits into this book. If I made a tiny dot with my pen for each day I've been alive, I could fit them all on one piece of paper. Do you think I remember what happened on every one of those dots? I don't. Do you think I remember all the people who hurt me? I only remember some of them. I remember most of the goals I have achieved and the people who changed my life, but I'm sure I'm forgetting things here and there. So what we choose to hold on to is really up to us.

For me, it all comes down to my purpose in life, which, I believe, is to live my best life possible and help other people do the same. I encourage you to make your own life guide. After all, you didn't come this far only to get this far. As you move forward with living your life more authentically with #nofilter, make some promises to yourself to keep on track. Think of these as your own personal terms and conditions—but only sign on to what makes sense for you. Figure 18.1 contain some I recommend.

FIGURE 18.1: **Your #Unfiltered Contract**

+ I, _____, acknowledge I am doing the best I can with what I know and with what I have today.

+ I will not apologize for being ambitious.

+ I will not break others to fix myself and will not be afraid to ask for help when I need it.

+ I will not let negative thoughts get the best of me. I will, however, let them inspire me to do a personal reorganization if needed.

+ I will not let any setback define me or my value.

+ I will believe in myself more and regret less.

+ I will clear clutter that does not serve me. I will cut toxic ties by identifying the people in my life who bring me down.

+ I will use the time between today and whenever I meet my significant other to live out my dreams.

+ I will do the best I can to love the skin I am in and be grateful for everything my body does for me.

+ I will be kind to myself.

+ I will try to leave this world a little better than when I found it.

+ I will say "I love you," "I am sorry," and "No" when necessary.

+ I will try to keep my head up and phone down so I can enjoy more of what's in front of me.

+ I will remember life is amazing and so am I.

Signed _____

Date _____

Unfiltered

My wish for you is that you hold fast to your own personal terms and conditions, that you embrace your authentic life (both the highlights and the things you would never post), and that you live a life that is truly as happy and real as it looks on social media. You can't ask for more than that.

May you live #unfiltered.

Thank You

I would not be where I am today without my family. Mom and Dad, you have been through every up and every down with me. Thank you for your unconditional love; for believing in my dreams and for teaching me what it means to put family first. I am so lucky to be your daughter and I share this accomplishment with you. Alyssa, we are sisters by chance and best friends by choice. Thank you for seeing me through all of these stories and for always being there to celebrate good news or to share my pain. Big D, whether we talk about life or laugh about parenthood, our heart-to-hearts mean the world to me. Peanut and Munchkin, you are my sunshine! Aunt Sylvia, thank you for our epic phone dates and for always having my back. Uncle Randy, I'm your biggest fan. Matthew, Jordana, Eric and Chris, you're the best. Thanks for the countless brainstorming sessions we had about this book. Glynis and Mervyn, thank you for welcoming me into your family and for all your support while I transitioned to life in LA. Debs, thank you for all your TLC especially on the days I really need it and for being my guru. Brandon, I cherish our candid conversations about everything. Thank you for the many hours we spent talking about this project. Raph and Duckie, thank you for your cuddles and boom pows. I love you ALL!

Micah and Uri, thank you for your friendship and for all of the beautiful videos we've done together.

To everyone at Entrepreneur, especially Bill, Jason, Dan, Linda, Steph, Jenna, and Conrad, thank you for your unwavering support. Deepa, you make magic happen. Thank you for being my rock.

Jennifer and Vanessa at Entrepreneur Press, we did it! Can you believe how far we have come since our first coffee date? Thank you for having faith in me, and this book, from day one. It was an absolute privilege to work with you. Karen and Danielle, thank you for your attention to detail and creativity.

I wrote this book while moving across the country, making a human being and creating a fashion line for New York Fashion Week. Thank you to my East Coast and West Coast tribes for getting me through these labors of love. A special shout out to: my cousin Carl, Gilah and Team Andrusier, Rabbi T and Binie, Martina and Bebé PT, Dr. Cousineau, Dr. Bess, Carlene, David, Ian, Lori, Geoffrey, JSW, Ellen, Fran, and the *Elle* team.

To the man who loves me for me . . .

Brett, I waited my whole life to meet you. Thank you for making me laugh through every ache and pain of pregnancy and for encouraging me as I wrote this book morning, noon and night. You read these pages too many times to count and helped me make every deadline once we became parents. Thank you for everything. I love you more!

To our daughter, Alexa Maxx, you are the light of our lives. Thank you for choosing me to be your mom. I love you more than words can express and can't wait to read this book with you some day. Now back to the wheels on the bus! #BH

About the Author

Jessica Abo believes life is about more than *likes*—and no matter where we are in our careers, relationships, or communities, we are all a work in progress. A sought-after keynote speaker, Jessica has appeared at events around the country at companies including Facebook, Microsoft, and Delta Airlines, TEDx, as well as the United Nations and hundreds of conferences, nonprofits, universities, schools, and events.

A multi-award-winning television journalist, Jessica started her own production company in 2013, and her videos appear weekly on Entrepreneur.com. Her YouTube channel profiles athletes, celebrities, CEOs, and entrepreneurs who have turned their own struggles into strengths. Jessica is expanding her company with a fashion line debuting at New York Fashion Week in September 2018.

Unfiltered

In her spare time, Jessica is a passionate philanthropist, having raised more than a million dollars for several causes by organizing her own galas. Jessica sits on several boards and committees and contributes to their recruiting and fundraising efforts. A proud graduate of Northwestern University's Medill School of Journalism Jessica has been cast as herself in several shows and movies including: *House of Cards, Gossip Girl, Nurse Jackie, Girl Most Likely, Delivery Man,* and *The Amazing Spider-Man 2*. A New Yorker at heart, Jessica lives in Los Angeles with her husband and their daughter.

www.jessicaabo.com

Index